D1576723

1918–2018

The 100th anniversary of the formation of the Royal Air Force is an outstanding opportunity to commemorate, celebrate and inspire: to commemorate with pride 100 years of remarkable success, courage and sacrifice; to celebrate the achievements of today's RAF; and to inspire future generations to realise their ambitions and potential.

Our centenary is not just about telling people what we do. It is also about letting everyone know who we are as an organisation – open to all, interested only in a person's merit, with a world-class reputation for training and development, always aiming for excellence.

The RAF is currently busier than we have been for at least a generation, from defending the skies of the UK, to fighting Da'esh in Iraq and Syria, from operations with NATO in Europe and in Afghanistan, to disaster relief in the Caribbean following Hurricane Irma. We have an outstanding record of responding quickly, successfully and in force to emerging crises, deploying and sustaining aircraft and supporting capabilities at considerable range, in a way that can only be delivered by our air and space power.

The RAF100 Appeal is a vital part of our overall campaign and draws together our principal charities – the RAF Association, the RAF Benevolent Fund, the RAF Charitable Trust and the RAF Museum – in a wide range of national and regional fundraising events and activities, to ensure that we can both support the RAF100 aim of reaching out to future generations, while also looking after the needs of the whole RAF Family, serving and veteran.

The most important aspect of RAF100 will be the legacy we leave beyond 2018 and into the RAF's second century. The foundations of that legacy already exist in the heritage and ethos of our first hundred years. It is a legacy built upon daily by our outstanding men and women as they demonstrate their excellence in air and space power. And it is a legacy we will secure for our second hundred years by using RAF100 to help inspire young people from across the nation.

Air Chief Marshal Sir Stephen Hillier
KCB CBE DFC ADC MA RAF

CONTENTS

COMMEMORATE

C1114

ORIGINS AND EARLY YEARS

Born in a time of conflict, the RAF quickly proved its considerable worth, both in war and in peace

On 29 November 1917, an Act of Parliament establishing an Air Force and an Air Council received royal assent. Just over four months later, on 1 April 1918, the Royal Air Force came into existence.

It was the culmination of many years of effort. Heavier-than-air flight was a relatively new invention at this stage, less than 15 years old, but Britain's armed forces had actually been experimenting with military flight for many decades. Since their development in the 1780s, hot air balloons had been used for military observation – as far back as the French Revolutionary War – and the British military had even set up a Balloon School in Woolwich in 1878. Four years later, the Royal Engineers established a "Balloon Factory" and training school in Chatham, Kent, which was later moved to Farnborough, Hampshire (the UK's oldest military airfield).

The first army airship – a dirigible balloon – was not put into service, however, until 1907 – by which time the airship was quickly becoming supplanted by heavier-than-air flight. Not long after Orville and Wilbur Wright's historic first manned flight in North Carolina in 1903, some elements in the British military were asking the Wright brothers to continue their experiments in the UK, but His Majesty's Treasury refused to finance these proposals. At the same time, another American – a showman and horse-seller called Samuel Franklin Cody – was experimenting at the Balloon Factory and ended up making the first powered flight in the UK on 16 October 1908 in a biplane called the British Army Aeroplane No.1.

Eventually, by 1911, the War Office had agreed that aircraft had some potential to perform a military role, and the old Balloon Section in Farnborough was expanded into an Air Battalion, with an Aeroplane Company based at Larkhill on Salisbury Plain. However, by the end of

Previous pages
RAF personnel of 1 Squadron at Clairmarais aerodrome in France, 1918

Opposite, clockwise from top left
Jan Christian Smuts; "Father of the Royal Air Force" Hugh Montague Trenchard; the observer of an Airco DH4 is handed a magazine of photographic plates before the start of another sortie

the year, there were still only 11 flying men in the British Army and only eight in the Royal Navy.

Prime Minister Herbert Asquith asked the Committee of Imperial Defence to examine the question of military aviation and it was decided that Britain needed some kind of efficient air force, and some means of training pilots. On 13 March 1912, the Royal Flying Corps was set up, with military and naval wings (the latter became the Royal Naval Air Service in 1914). Two months later, the Central Flying School (CFS) was formed in Upavon in Wiltshire, tasked with training the UK's first military pilots. By the outbreak of war in 1914, the British Expeditionary Force was backed by 63 aircraft, while the CFS was expanded to train more personnel.

Even by the outbreak of war, the military top brass remained sceptical of air power, according to the statement that is usually attributed to General Douglas Haig. "I hope that none of you gentlemen is so foolish as to think that aeroplanes will be usefully employed for reconnaissance purposes in war," he is reported to have told officers in July 1914. "There is only one way for commanders to get information by reconnaissance, and that is by cavalry."

Ironically, the cavalry would become one of first victims of the Great War. Not only was the maintenance, mobilisation and feeding of vast numbers of horses becoming a logistical nightmare on the Western Front, but increased firepower meant that they were being slaughtered by the hundred. In contrast, the reconnaissance value of the aeroplane was becoming clear to the military at an early stage.

"I wish particularly to bring to your lordships' notice the admirable work done by the Royal Flying Corps," said the Commander of the BEF, Sir John French, in his first official dispatch, dated 7 September 1914. "They have furnished me with the most complete and accurate information, which has been of incalculable value in the conduct of operations. Fired at constantly by both friend and foe, and not hesitating to fly in every kind of weather, they have remained undaunted throughout." It was soon realised that preventing the enemy from obtaining information was just as important as obtaining it, and fighter aircraft were developed to destroy reconnaissance aircraft.

FATHER OF THE ROYAL AIR FORCE

Major General Hugh Trenchard was appointed Commander of the RFC in France in August 1915. He is now considered "the Father of the Royal Air Force", although Trenchard personally credited his predecessor Lieutenant General Sir David Henderson as the true founder of the air service. Henderson was a Sandhurst-trained infantry officer who trained at the Bristol Flying School at Brooklands in 1911 and later developed some of the central roles that would be carried out by the RAF – aerial reconnaissance, fighter interception and tactical support.

Not long after his appointment, Trenchard was fighting battles with the War Office to ensure that the RFC was supplied with new types of aircraft. Even General Haig now saw that he had a case, and by 1916 he was requesting 20 more air squadrons to be deployed to the Western Front.

One problem remained: during a time of war, how was the service to supply and train pilots, observers and engineers, particularly when the CFS in Wiltshire quickly reached capacity? Additional training squadrons were

LIFT HERE

Left
Aircrew of 27 Squadron examine a 230 lb bomb

formed in England, and then in 1916 in Egypt, but the demand for replacements was insatiable and in 1917 further training units were established in Canada. When the perils of the Canadian winter became apparent later that year, the RFC started to use three airfields in Fort Worth, Texas, in a deal that would see cross-nation training and flying tactics shared, with British personnel also training American pilots for the US Air Service. One of these sites is still in use, a century on, and is currently home to 30 RAF personnel receiving Lightning II Joint Strike Fighter technical training.

As the war dragged on, the threat from German Zeppelin or Schütte-Lanz airships was creating localised fear and national anger in Britain, and calls for retribution. Between January 1915 and the end of the war, the Germans had conducted more than 50 bombing raids on the UK, killing 557 people and injuring another 1,358. The *Daily Mail* described these raids as the country's greatest humiliation since the Dutch navy sailed up the Thames in 1667. One response was to attack German airship sheds, with bombing raids carried out by the Royal Naval Air Service.

AN EXPANDING ROLE

The RFC was not just active on the Western Front. In November 1914 the first RFC detachment arrived in Egypt, and airfields were constructed along the Suez Canal and the Nile Delta. From here, air support was provided to land campaigns in the Sinai, Transjordan, Palestine and Syria. In Mesopotamia (modern-day Iraq), the RFC provided reconnaissance to the Indian Army Expeditionary Force and even attempted, unsuccessfully, to resupply by air the besieged garrison at Kut-Al-Amara. The RNAS was involved in the Gallipoli campaign and in Macedonia against the Bulgarians, and was also active in the Western Approaches and the North Sea.

"By the end of the war, the RAF was the most powerful air force in the world"

Aid was given to the Italians with attacks on the coasts of Austria, Italy, Montenegro and Albania, while air force action was also seen in the North-West Frontier of India, Gibraltar, Malta, Aden and the Red Sea.

Improved defences had made the Zeppelin attacks increasingly perilous, but in the summer of 1917 a new and even greater danger materialised in the skies over Britain. Formations of German twin-engined Gotha bombers flew over London dropping bombs and were largely untroubled by the defences. The sight of German aircraft apparently parading unhindered over the capital created something of a political storm. Competition between the RNAS and RFC for engines, aircraft and resources had already encouraged some military and political figures to call for unification between the two services.

Prime Minister David Lloyd George turned to the South African soldier-statesman Jan Christian Smuts, who was in London and had been attending the War Cabinet as the South African representative. Lloyd George formed a Cabinet Committee consisting of Smuts and himself to consider not only the air defence of London but the organisation of the air services. Smuts in essence did all the work and, having consulted Sir David Henderson and others, quickly recommended the amalgamation of the RFC and the RNAS: his report was just as quickly accepted by the British Government and the process of forming the Royal Air Force began.

Trenchard was initially sceptical of the need for the unified force, thinking it a distraction during wartime, although he soon accepted that Smuts and Henderson were right to press for the creation of the RAF. He did, however, continue to clash with the Air Minister Lord Rothermere, even tendering his resignation in March 1918 but delaying the announcement until the unified Royal Air Force was finally born on 1 April 1918. Rothermere was replaced by Sir William Weir, who offered Trenchard complete command of the air forces, based in Nancy in north-eastern France.

Within six weeks, Trenchard had put together an RAF "Independent Force", tasked with conducting a strategic bombing campaign against Germany. For the last five months of the war, this Independent Force bombed chemical factories, aeroplane factories, blast furnaces and railways in a number of German cities including Frankfurt, Cologne and Mannheim. There was some loss of production in German factories. This was not sufficient to affect the war effort significantly, but large numbers of German forces were diverted into air defence units at a time when the German war effort was under its severest strain.

By the end of the war on 11 November 1918, the RAF had complete air superiority over the Western Front and was the most powerful air force in the world, with over 295,000 personnel and 22,847 aircraft on charge. The amalgamation had worked well, and the RAF even had surplus aircraft to supply American squadrons. Also formed at this time was the Women's Royal Air Force (WRAF), which employed thousands of women as clerks, fitters, drivers, cooks and storekeepers.

AFTER THE GREAT WAR

The end of hostilities and subsequent demobilisation saw the RAF reduced radically; within 18 months it was down to just 20,000 people. Initially, it looked as though the RAF could be wound down after "the war to end all wars" – Prime Minister Lloyd George did not want to maintain it as a separate department – but Trenchard managed to

The Royal Air Force and Women's Royal Air Force were both formed on 1 April 1918

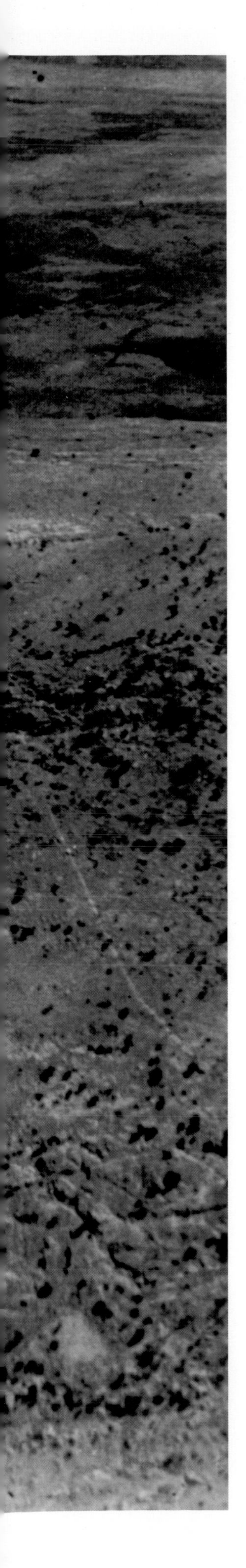

Left
De Havilland DH9A aircraft of 30 Squadron in flight over Iraq, 1924

convince the new Secretary of State for War and Air Winston Churchill that a separate air force was necessary to develop airmanship and engender "air spirit". A memorandum was issued on 11 December 1919, officially titled "Permanent Organisation of the Royal Air Force".

Not long after the Armistice in 1918, the RAF was embroiled in a related conflict – this time with Britain's former ally, Russia. Two revolutions in 1917 had seen the formation of the Soviet Union and the end of Russian involvement as a wartime ally of Britain and France. The RAF's first post-war act was to go to Russia in 1918 and train anti-Bolshevik fighters, as well as to carry out operational sorties against the Bolsheviks.

Churchill explained to Parliament in December 1919 that: "The first duty of the RAF is to garrison the British Empire." In this role, it had advantages over the other services, in that it could cover large and often undeveloped areas far more quickly than the army or navy, and could also police regions at an acceptable cost to governments that were conscious of post-war spending.

Two early operations, in Somaliland and Iraq, saw the RAF develop the operational theory of "air control". In Somaliland in 1920, a rebellious jihadist cleric called Mohammed Abdullah Al-Hassan, known colloquially as "the Mad Mullah", had frustrated attempts to bring law and order to the region. The army had estimated that it would need many divisions and several million pounds to subdue the unrest. The RAF offered to do the job using just one squadron of 12 de Havilland DH9s, along with elements from the 2nd (Nyasaland) Battalion and 6th (British Somalia) Battalion of the King's African Rifles, and an Indian battalion. Within weeks the force had bombed the Mad Mullah's forces and driven them from their positions, maintaining order. The operation cost less than £80,000, making it possibly the cheapest war in 20th-century history.

In 1922, another conflict emerged in northern Iraq, where Kurds were rebelling against their former rulers, Turkey. As a crisis developed, the RAF carried out the world's first air evacuation, lifting out some 70 British forces and civilians. The following year, another airlift was launched, but this time in reverse, with some 480 troops being taken to Kirkuk, in the Mosul region. The Turks were shocked that the British were able to reinforce their positions, despite appalling weather, and attack a Turkish cavalry incursion into Iraq. While the region continued to present a problem for the British, the Turkish element had been removed, and at a reasonable cost. "I cannot emphasise too much," said Trenchard to the commander of forces, "the value that your successful command in Iraq has been to us." These operations established the policy of air control as a method of policing isolated and inhospitable areas.

Other than these skirmishes, the inter-war years were relatively peaceful times for the RAF, with only minor actions occurring across the British Empire. During this period, the service sought to establish a reputation for long-distance, high-altitude, high-speed flight across the world. It developed new air routes to serve the empire, initially to Egypt and then on to India, Singapore and

Right
The Handley Page Hampden production line, Radlett, 1939

Australia. Flights were also made across Africa – pioneering journeys between Egypt, Sudan, Kenya and the Cape, later to be followed by civilian airlines. These long-distance flights culminated in 1938 when a Vickers Wellesley flew 7,000 miles non-stop from Ismailia in Egypt to Darwin in Australia.

PREPARING FOR WAR

Other developments would prove to be vital in the prelude to the Second World War. The Spitfire and the Hurricane had made their way from the drawing board to operation, with the first orders made in 1934, and prototypes flown in 1935 and 1936. A new defence minister, Sir Thomas Inskip, helped to change strategic thinking, changing the emphasis from bombers to fighters – the latter being quicker, cheaper and ultimately proving more useful in the defence of the nation during the Battle of Britain. 1936 saw a reorganisation of the RAF's command structure with the creation of Fighter Command, Bomber Command and Coastal Command. The Naval Air Branch was also de-merged and renamed the Fleet Air Arm under the control of the Royal Navy.

However, the service was still not ready for war. Had Prime Minister Neville Chamberlain's negotiations failed in 1938, the RAF would have been less than 40 per cent prepared, and that extra year was used to bolster air power. Nevertheless, when war broke out in 1939, the RAF was only at half the strength of the Luftwaffe, which only makes its subsequent achievements all the more remarkable.

THE SECOND WORLD WAR

The RAF's heroic exploits during the Second World War boosted the morale and captured the hearts of a nation

If the notion of "air power" was in its infancy for the duration of the First World War, it had truly come of age by the start of the Second World War. The Royal Air Force, which had been preparing for conflict since the mid-1930s, underwent rapid expansion following the outbreak of war in September 1939. This included the training of aircrew overseas under the British Commonwealth Air Training Plan, and the secondment of whole squadrons and tens of thousands of individual personnel from Commonwealth air forces. During the Battle of Britain, for instance, 20 per cent (595) of aircrew were from Commonwealth, Allied or neutral countries, including 145 Poles, 127 New Zealanders, 112 Canadians and 88 Czechs.

In the early stages of the war, the RAF played a crucial role in preventing Nazi Germany from invading. During the dark months after the Dunkirk evacuation of June 1940 and before the entry into the war of the Soviet Union (June 1941) and the United States (December 1941) – Britain stood alone and the RAF seemed to be single-handedly boosting the morale of the British people.

It was the Battle of Britain that was to become the defining period of the RAF's existence so far. Over the summer of 1940 the RAF held off the Luftwaffe in perhaps the most prolonged and complicated air campaign in history. The RAF's valiant defence of Britain's skies foiled Hitler's plans for an invasion of the British Isles and helped to turn the tide of the war.

"The Battle of Britain was not just a local, territorial success, but one of the most significant conflicts of the war"

THE BATTLE OF BRITAIN

The Luftwaffe, operating from bases in Norway, the Low Countries and France, ringed Britain with three massive air fleets. In all, the German air fleets numbered around 2,800 aircraft at the start of the battle. Fighter Command, by contrast, had 60 squadrons with only 700 operational aircraft. Of these, 400 were Hurricanes, 200 were Spitfires, and the rest were less effective Blenheims, Defiants and Gladiators, which were no match for the Luftwaffe's Messerchmitt Me 109s. The average age of an RAF fighter pilot was in the early 20s.

On the most active day of the entire battle, 15 August 1940, the Germans flew 1,786 sorties against 974 RAF sorties. The Luftwaffe lost 75 that day and the RAF 34. In one two-week period, 295 Hurricanes or Spitfires were lost, 171 badly damaged, and 231 pilots were killed or wounded. Just as Fighter Command was being put under great strain, the Germans made the strategic error of switching away from engaging Fighter Command to launching large-scale bombing raids on London – something that the RAF was better equipped to counter and that bought it time to repair its damaged airfields and keep its fighters close to the battle area. After losing around 2,600 Luftwaffe aircrew throughout the whole of the Battle of Britain, Hitler postponed his invasion plans.

The Battle of Britain was not just a local, territorial success over the south of England in the summer of 1940, but one of the most significant conflicts of the Second World War, and the only major, self-contained and absolutely decisive air battle in history. Not only was invasion prevented, but the Allies now had a base for the invasion of Normandy in 1944.

Five hundred and forty-four Fighter Command aircrew were killed in the Battle of Britain. Winston Churchill paid tribute to them in his House of Commons speech of 20 August 1940, just over three months after he had become Prime Minister. "Never in the field of human conflict was so much owed by so many to so few," he said. "All hearts go out to the fighter pilots, whose brilliant actions we see with our own eyes day after day, but we must never forget that all the time, night after night, month after month, our bomber squadrons travel far into Germany, find their targets in the darkness by the highest navigational skill, aim their attacks, often under the heaviest fire, often with serious loss, with deliberate, careful discrimination, and inflict shattering blows upon the whole of the technical and war-making structure of the Nazi power."

Churchill was, of course, referring to the largest RAF effort during the war – its strategic bombing campaign against Germany. After the loss of mainland Europe in 1940 and the Dunkirk evacuation, the only way to inflict damage on the enemy was through bombing raids. Initially, these were directed against key points in the German war machine, but the bombers – Wellingtons, Whitleys and Hampdens – could not survive German air defences by day and so night-time bombing was adopted. Accuracy was often poor, but it certainly

DW D
DW D

Previous pages, from top
Pilots rush to their aircraft during the Battle of Britain; Supermarine Spitfires of 610 Squadron, 1940

Left
Wing Commander Guy Gibson (centre) and crew board their Lancaster for the "Dam Busters" raid of May 1943

boosted British morale – and also showed the United States and Russia that Britain was more than capable of fighting back.

Lessons were also learned from these costly campaigns and would result in Bomber Command's attacks of 1942–45 under the leadership of Air Chief Marshal Sir Arthur "Bomber" Harris, who took over as Commander-in-Chief of Bomber Command in 1942. Harris believed that German morale could be destroyed by the destruction of the nation's industrial cities, and was responsible for the intensive bombing of cities such as Hamburg. "Berlin should be bombed until the heart of Nazi Germany ceases to beat," he once said. As the war progressed, Bomber Command developed the ability to launch more accurate raids, culminating in the major offensives of 1944.

In 1942, the RAF managed three 1,000-bomber raids – the average night raid for most of the year being around 300. The following May saw the celebrated "Dam Buster" attacks, when the "bouncing bombs" of Barnes Wallis were dropped from specially modified Lancasters of 617 Squadron to destroy two hydroelectric dams (the Mohne and the Eder) in the Ruhr valley and damage a third (the Sorpe). Some have questioned the wisdom of this bombing policy – not least because it resulted in floods that killed more than 1,000 Soviet POWs and around 700 German civilians – but there is little doubt that the attacks disrupted the German economy and forced the Nazis to take huge amounts of labour and resources away from the war effort to repair their hydroelectric

Opposite
Fighter aircraft provided air defence over the beachhead on D-Day

power supply. Wing Commander Guy Gibson, Officer Commanding 617 Squadron, was subsequently awarded the Victoria Cross for his part in leading the attack.

The thousand bomber raids of 1942, the Battles of the Ruhr and Hamburg in 1943 and the Battle of Berlin in 1943/44 caused enormous damage to many of the cities and industries of Germany and forced the enemy to devote increasing resources to home defence and damage repair. These bombing raids did much to turn the course of the war. "The air war opened a second front long before the invasion of Europe," wrote German armaments minister Albert Speer in 1959. "That front was the skies over Germany, every square metre of the territory that we controlled was a kind of front line. Defence against air attacks required the production of thousands of anti-aircraft guns, the stockpiling of tremendous quantities of ammunition all over the country, and holding in readiness hundreds of thousands of soldiers, who in addition had to stay in position by their guns, often totally inactive, for months at a time."

Air superiority was crucial when it came to the Normandy landings in June 1944. Allied air forces flew a total of 14,674 sorties during the first 24 hours of the operation. "You needn't worry about the air," said General Eisenhower to troops before D-Day. "If you see a plane it will be ours." Fighter cover for the invasion beaches was provided by six squadrons of Spitfires at any one time during the day, with other squadrons out to the flanks, while Typhoon and Mustang fighter-bombers of 2nd Tactical Air Force (TAF) flew armed reconnaissance missions further inland. Such was the Allied air supremacy that the Luftwaffe only flew 319 sorties in the same period.

Airborne forces were able to secure the flanks of the invading force and hold vital bridges (notably Pegasus Bridge, across the Caen canal). Bombing raids were regularly launched on railway centres in the ongoing "Transportation Plan", which crucially delayed the arrival of German reinforcements into Normandy. British forces had less success in securing vital bridges over rivers in the Netherlands, resulting in the failure of Operation Market Garden at Arnhem in September 1944. They learned from this failure and, in March 1945, Allied troops crossed the Rhine, with airborne divisions taken in one lift and supplies dropped the same evening.

BEYOND EUROPE

The RAF's role was not just confined to north-western Europe. In North Africa it played a vital role in supporting the British Army between 1940 and 1943. The RAF enjoyed success against the Italian Regia Aeronautica, which was equipped with much the same type of vintage fighters and bombers as the RAF. However, when Field Marshal Erwin Rommel's Afrika Korps and the Luftwaffe entered this theatre of war they proved a much tougher proposition, and the land battle between the Afrika Korps and the British Eighth Army

JF

An Avro Lancaster during a daylight bombing raid on German facilities in the French port of Le Havre

"You have shown the world the unity and strength of air power"

seesawed to and fro in the desert from 1941–43. By mid-1942, the Germans had control of most of the Mediterranean, with the exception of brave, embattled Malta, and the RAF's Desert Air Force (DAF) was often spread thinly, as campaigns in Greece, Crete and Syria also required resources.

However, even though the army was pushed back to Egypt by 1942, the RAF was able to achieve a degree of air superiority with attacks against enemy airfields. As German forces were repelled, the RAF attacked the stores and supplies of the German and Italian units. In the final battles in Tunisia, the Allied air forces destroyed the last attempt by the Germans to reinforce their ground forces by air from Sicily and, in turn, prevented a Dunkirk-style evacuation of those Axis forces. In three weeks in April 1943, 432 enemy transport aircraft were destroyed for the loss of 35 fighters. By May 1943, victory had been achieved in North Africa. "You have shown the world the unity and strength of air power," said Air Chief Marshal Tedder to air and ground crews.

With North Africa secured, the same strategy would be repeated in Italy, and the RAF played a key role in securing air superiority so that an airborne and amphibious assault could be launched on Sicily in July 1943. The invasion of mainland Italy in September was preceded by a bombing campaign and, following the Italian surrender on 8 September 1943, the RAF was able to occupy enemy airfields and use them as a base from which to attack Axis units in Albania, Bulgaria, Greece and Yugoslavia.

While doing all of this, the RAF also had a more routine task of defending Britain's coastline and shipping, as well as those of the British Empire in the North Atlantic, the Mediterranean and the Indian Ocean. One of the RAF's most important contributions was in the Battle of the Atlantic, which was at its height between mid-1940 and the end of 1943. During the First World War, Britain had come close to being starved into surrender because of the German U-boat campaign. This was even more of an issue by 1939, when British forces were unable to provide sufficient escorts for merchant shipping. Losses were high – by November 1942, 800,000 tons of cargo had been sunk – and the RAF used bases in the Azores and Iceland to help bridge the Atlantic.

It was the RAF's development of an air-to-service vessel radar (ASV) and the Leigh Light (LL) that proved crucial in the Atlantic. These made it possible to detect and attack German U-boats on the surface at night, denying them shelter and forcing the Nazis to withdraw their submarines to the Bay of Biscay. British shipping losses dropped dramatically by the end of 1943. The Battle of the Atlantic also prevented German ships from beating the blockade established by the Royal Navy in the English Channel and the North Sea, and meant that forces could assemble for D-Day without the threat of German U-boats.

Right
Manhandling a Spitfire of 607 Squadron through the monsoon mud at an advanced airfield on the Burma border, 1944

THE FAR EAST

Air power was also crucial to the campaign in the Far East. As in Europe, the RAF lacked resources at the start of the war, and its units in Malaya and Singapore were defeated within a few weeks, with those that survived retreating to India and Burma. Once it had recovered and replenished its resources, the RAF was able to launch attacks on the Japanese – something it did in coordination with the United States Army Air Force after December 1941. More importantly, the RAF was able to resupply some 300,000 soldiers, who would be able to reconquer Burma in the spring of 1945. Even when surrounded by Japanese forces, the RAF were able to move large numbers of troops into vital areas.

The air force's role carried on after the end of the war – supplies were dropped to former prisoners of war in camps, while others who needed urgent medical treatment were evacuated. In some places, including Java – where Allied POWs were held by Indonesian independence fighters even after the Japanese surrender – this process would not be complete until August 1946.

THE COLD WAR

The post-war era presented new challenges for the RAF as an "iron curtain" descended across Europe, dominating global affairs for decades to follow

Britain emerged victorious from the Second World War, but was left virtually bankrupt, and its depleted armed forces had several new international tasks to perform. First of all, the Royal Air Force needed to demobilise its huge force of more than a million. The slow process faced some unrest, including strikes by frustrated RAF personnel across the Far East, but, by April 1947, the RAF had been reduced to less than 300,000. It also needed to address urgent post-war recovery operations, the bringing home of troops and prisoners of war, and the transportation of food, clothing and medical care to sites across the world.

The RAF was also having to deal with a new world order: one in which the West's often shaky wartime alliance of convenience with the Soviet Union was beginning to deteriorate rapidly. As early as March 1946, Winston Churchill, now leader of the opposition, made a famous speech in Fulton, Missouri, stating that: "From Stettin in the Baltic to Trieste in the Adriatic, an iron curtain has descended across the Continent. Behind that line lie all the capitals of central and eastern Europe." A state of "Cold War" would soon engulf most of the world.

THE BERLIN AIRLIFT

The first manifestation of this conflict came in Germany in June 1948, when tensions between the Western Allies' plans for the areas of western Germany they controlled and the Soviets, who controlled all of eastern Germany except for the isolated Western-controlled zones of Berlin (those administered by US, the UK and France), led to a complete Soviet blockade of the Western Berlin enclave. The Western

Avro York C1s of Transport Command being unloaded at RAF Gatow during the Berlin Airlift

XH557
XH558

"It was an astonishing logistical enterprise, and one that proved the air force had an important peace-time function"

powers were faced with either surrendering control of West Berlin – a sign of weakness in this new Cold War – or keeping the two million Berliners in the Western part of the city supplied with food, fuel and clothes. From June 1948 until the Soviets ended the blockade in May 1949, the RAF delivered 394,509 tons and British civil aircraft 147,727 tons out of a grand total of 2,325,808.7 tons. It was an astonishing logistical enterprise, and one that proved the air force had an important peace-time function.

The RAF also reorganised, as technological advances in air warfare saw the arrival of jet fighters and bombers. After the development of a British atomic bomb in 1947, the RAF's V-bomber squadrons took sole responsibility for carrying Britain's nuclear deterrent until the deployment of the Royal Navy's Polaris submarines in 1968, following which the RAF's strategic nuclear role was reduced to a tactical nuclear one, using WE177 bombs. This tactical role was continued by the V-bombers into the 1980s and from 1982 by Tornado GR1s, until 1998 when Britain withdrew its tactical nuclear arsenal altogether.

THE END OF EMPIRE

As the sun started to set on the British Empire, its armed forces were tasked to ensure that the transition from colonial rule to independence was peaceful. However, many of the nationalist campaigns became linked to Cold War battles between the Soviet and Western blocs. In June 1948, Britain became involved in what became known as the Malayan Emergency when communist insurgents, most of them Chinese, started attacking rubber plantations and tin mines in an attempt to take over the British colony of Malaya. Britain's role in this counter-insurgency conflict between 1948 and 1960 became the nation's longest campaign since the Napoleonic Wars. Ground forces took the brunt of the task but the RAF played a crucial role, conducting air strikes, providing reconnaissance, dropping leaflets to persuade guerrillas to surrender, and moving troops and supplies in and out of the jungle. It provided a model for counter-insurgency and eventually brought peace, and independence, to Malaysia.

Commitments in Malaya meant that the RAF only had a limited role in the Korean War of 1950–53, providing Sunderland flying-boat patrols against sea-born incursions and helping to ferry troops to Korea. RAF pilots were seconded to fly combat missions with 77 Squadron Royal Australian Air Force and with the USAF squadrons. The RAF also deployed armed versions of the Harvard trainer, as well as Lincoln heavy bombers and photo reconnaissance aircraft in the counter-insurgency against the Mau Mau rebellion of 1952–56 in Kenya.

However, the Suez Crisis in 1956 saw the RAF assume a larger role, with aircraft mainly flying from Cyprus and Malta. The Egyptian leader, Colonel Nasser, nationalised the Suez Canal Zone in retaliation for the withdrawal of US and UK financial backing for the Aswan High Dam project. Britain and France, which both had considerable commercial interests in the region, built up their forces in Cyprus and Malta. They started to attack Egyptian airfields and attempted to prevent the Egyptian air force (using Soviet MiG-15 fighters) from attacking British and French troops. The RAF achieved this in two days, employing high-altitude precision bombing (using Canberras

Previous pages
Two Vulcans fly over RAF Fylingdales early warning site on the North Yorkshire Moors

Right
An English Electric Canberra B2 of 12 Squadron being prepared in Malta during the Suez Crisis, 1956

and Valiants), and also dropped paratroops to seize the Gamil airfield (using Hastings and Valettas). After seven days, the British had put the Egyptian air force out of action, and United Nations forces took over the Canal Zone. Despite overwhelming military success at minimal cost for the RAF, the British ended up withdrawing from the zone after diplomatic pressure and the unwillingness of the US to support the attack.

FROM CYPRUS TO ADEN

Cyprus, as well as being a base for the Suez crisis, became a centre of operations between 1956 and 1960, when the Greek Cypriot guerrillas of the EOKA (Ethniki Organosis Kyprion Agoniston) started terrorist operations with the aim of uniting Cyprus with Greece. Sycamore helicopters, provided by 284 Squadron, pioneered the techniques of night flying and landing troops by abseiling down ropes from a hovering helicopter. The squadron also dropped food, ammunition and stores, as well as evacuating 222 casualties from the hills and forest areas. According to Field Marshal Lord Harding, the Governor of Cyprus and a senior British Army officer, "the RAF contributed more to fighting terrorism on the island than any other single unit" between 1956 and 1958.

Cyprus was also the base for operations in 1961 when Iraq threatened to seize the oil-rich sheikhdom of Kuwait – a premonition of what would happen again under Saddam Hussain 30 years later. Ground-attack Hunters and Beverley transports from Aden were the first to arrive, but the major RAF task was to lift an entire parachute battalion from Cyprus to Bahrain and one complete Marine Commando from Aden to Kuwait. Within six days all British forces were in position and supplied. In total, nearly 10,000 men and 850 tons of freight were airlifted by the RAF, deterring Iraq from any further hostilities.

In 1963, the RAF were called back into Southeast Asia when the newly independent Malaysia came under threat from neighbouring Indonesia. Indonesia was angered by the creation of Malaysia, which united the Federation of Malaya (the peninsula now known as West Malaysia) with the British protectorates of North Borneo and Sarawak (formerly British Borneo, now East Malaysia). Known as the "Konfrontasi", it involved the RAF deploying air defence and reconnaissance of Malaya, Singapore and Borneo. Ground attack Hunters were deployed from Singapore, while helicopters (Whirlwind, Wessex and Belvedere) and short-range transports (Beverleys and Pioneers) worked alongside the tiny Malaysian Air Force to provide mobility for British, Commonwealth and Malaysian troops in the jungle. Canberras and V-bombers were sent to Singapore as a further deterrent. By 1966, due to a combination of deft diplomacy and selective ignoring of certain events by both sides, the confrontation had come to an end without escalating into a full-scale war.

WH951
H212
LD12

WT374
WJ783

"Two Avro Vulcan bombers set out on what was then the longest bombing mission ever"

Back in the Arabian Peninsula, the RAF was called upon in Aden (now known as Yemen) in 1964 when tribesmen from the Radfan mountains, supported by Yemeni forces, began an armed revolt. RAF Hunters were able to attack rebel targets, but the Radfan rebels gathered momentum and, by 1967, the RAF had to evacuate service families and British troops from Aden. Between May and November 1967, the air force evacuated 6,000 troops and 400 tons of equipment from RAF Khormaksar, ending a connection that had lasted since 1839.

A POST-WAR ROLE

With the decline of the British Empire, the RAF's global operations were scaled back and its primary role during the Cold War years was the defence of Europe against potential attack by the Soviet Union. By 1968, the British military had started a large-scale withdrawal from overseas and was instead concentrating its resources on Europe. The RAF had withdrawn from Malaysia, Singapore and the Persian Gulf by 1971. Residual forces were kept in Hong Kong (until 1999), Malta (until 1979) and Cyprus. Without a need for strategic airlifts on a large scale in Asia, the RAF transport force was reduced by half with the withdrawal of the Comets in 1975, the Britannias and Andovers in 1976, and the Belfasts in 1977.

The RAF's emphasis on emergency rescue and humanitarian interventions continued. Within the UK, this often meant deploying Search And Rescue (SAR) forces, Marine Craft Units and Mountain Rescue Teams. Internationally, the RAF was increasingly being called on to assist with humanitarian operations. In the aftermath of a 1961

Previous pages
Three English Electric Canberra B2s of 249 Squadron near Limassol, Cyprus, 1960

Opposite
Hawker Siddeley Harriers, Sea Harriers and a Sea King on the flight deck of HMS Hermes during the Falklands War, 1982

hurricane in British Honduras (now Belize), a 1970 cyclone in East Pakistan (now Bangladesh), a 1972 earthquake in Nicaragua, and 1973 famines in Mali and Nepal, the RAF was able to deliver food, shelter and medical equipment to stricken communities.

RETAKING THE FALKLANDS

It wasn't until the Falklands Conflict in 1982 that the RAF undertook another major action, as part of the task force that won back the islands from Argentine control. This feat was all the more remarkable considering the logistics involved, and for the RAF, the first consideration was a relatively simple one – range.

The RAF's large aircraft of the time were intended for use in Europe and over NATO waters, so air-to-air refuelling capability for these types was previously considered unnecessary. Suddenly Hercules, Nimrod, Victor and Vulcan aircraft were required to fly almost 4,000 miles, loiter on mission and then return, covering the same distance again. RAF engineers worked around the clock fitting probes and tank systems to a variety of types, testing the new fittings almost as the paint dried.

The practical result of this frenetic activity was that just before midnight on 30 April, two crews from 101 Squadron climbed into two Avro Vulcan bombers to set out on what was then the longest bombing mission ever attempted; the Black Buck raids. One aircraft was to act as airborne reserve and, in the event, a technical problem forced the primary Vulcan to turn back and the reserve aircraft actually flew the mission. The target for the bombing missions was the airfield at Stanley, the only hard runway on the islands and vital to the Argentinean forces for supplies and reinforcements.

The service played a number of vital roles during the conflict, with its Harrier GR3s flying from HMS *Hermes* (the first operational use of land-based RAF aircraft from an aircraft carrier since the Second World War), its Phantom F4s protecting Ascension Island, its maritime patrol aircraft scanning the South Atlantic, and its tanker and transport fleet helping in the enormous logistical effort required for the war. As a result, the Argentine force that had invaded on 2 April had been defeated by 14 June, and the RAF had shown that air power was an essential part of any successful military action.

In the decades that followed the Second World War, the RAF's role continued to evolve. It has managed to play a vital part in Britain's ability to project power without having to commit ground or naval forces. This way, political objectives could be achieved rapidly, but force could be withdrawn when this has been achieved. It's a role that would become even clearer in the 1990s and beyond, following the collapse of the Soviet Union and the end of the Cold War.

THE MODERN ERA

New challenges have emerged over recent years, but the RAF still holds by its tenets of courage, professionalism and dedication

A major change in government policy on 20 July 1989 finally saw female aircrew able to be employed in all specialisations in non-combat roles, although it wasn't until 1994 that all restrictions were lifted with the full merger of the WRAF and the RAF. Many more women joined the service subsequently as aircrew, and are now flying every type of aircraft in the RAF inventory.

This was not the only important change to happen in the RAF's recent history. The fall of the Berlin Wall in November 1989 and the ensuing collapse of the Soviet Union and the Warsaw Pact might have suggested at the time that the British Armed Forces and their NATO allies would be winding down activities. However, it became the start of one of the busiest three decades in the history of the RAF, as a politically unstable world threw up a series of fractious conflicts that seemed to defy the simple binary logic of the Cold War.

In August 1990, Saddam Hussein's Iraq invaded Kuwait. Iraq had long regarded its southern neighbour as its 19th province, and this invasion was an echo of an earlier attempt to annex Kuwait in 1961. It was, in part, a response to the economic problems faced by Iraq after its crippling eight-year war with Iran. Oil-rich Kuwait had angered Iraq by refusing to write off Iraqi debts after the Iran–Iraq war, and Saddam's troops quickly captured Kuwait City.

After Iraq refused to heed the United Nations demand for withdrawal, the UN passed Resolution 678, which authorised a military response. Britain joined a US-led coalition of 17 nations,

Opposite, from top
A Panavia Tornado GR1 takes on fuel, with a Jaguar waiting its turn, Operation Granby, 1990; a Panavia Tornado F3 flies over burning oil wells, Kuwait, 1991

primarily based in neighbouring Saudi Arabia. More than 100 RAF aircraft took part in Operation Granby – the code name given to the British military operations during the first Gulf War. The RAF deployed Tornado strike, fighter and reconnaissance variants and Jaguar ground attack aircraft, along with tanker, transport and maritime reconnaissance aircraft, as well as transport helicopters and airfield defence units. The RAF was also prominent in the airlifting of equipment and personnel: by March 1991, it had transported some 25,000 people to the Gulf and moved around 31,000 tonnes of freight.

Following the failure of diplomatic efforts to negotiate the withdrawal of Iraqi forces from Kuwait, on 17 January the coalition began offensive operations to eject them by force. RAF Tornadoes and Jaguars flew offensive sorties against Iraqi airfields, logistics bases, artillery and missile batteries and troop positions, as well as naval targets in the Gulf. Operation Granby was the first time the service used precision-guided munitions in significant numbers. RAF helicopters carried troops and supplies to the front. The air phase lasted six weeks and was followed by a ground invasion that took just 100 hours to force the Iraqi ground forces, which had been severely depleted and demoralised by the air attacks, to withdraw from Kuwait.

Following on from Saddam Hussein's defeat in Kuwait, Kurds in the north of Iraq attempted to establish a separate Kurdish area. This prompted a massive retaliation from the Iraqi military, which attacked Kurdish areas with chemical weapons. This prompted the UN Security Council to pass Resolution 688, demanding that Iraq respect the human rights of its population, including its Kurdish citizens. The US, the UK and France were among 13 volunteer nations who used the resolution to enforce a no-fly zone, with RAF forces based at Incirclik in Turkey. In the south, Iraqi forces singled out Marsh Arabs for reprisals, prompting the US and UK to enforce another no-fly zone in their defence.

Britain's involvement in the region continued after UN Resolution 687, which requested that Saddam Hussein hand over his weapons of mass destruction (WMDs). By November 1998, his refusal to cooperate with the UN Special Commission brought the British back into the area, and the RAF took part in coalition attacks around Baghdad, Tikrit and Basra as part of Operation Desert Fox. Of a total of 250 bombing missions, 12 Squadron's Tornado GR1s flew 32 medium-level sorties and dropped a combination of 61 UK Paveway 2 and Paveway 3 laser-guided bombs. One of their targets was a hangar

"Camp Bastion in Helmand province became the UK's fifth-largest airfield, with the capacity for 600 aircraft movements each day"

at Tallil containing the so-called "drones of death" – remotely piloted vehicle (RPV) aircraft capable of carrying chemical and biological weapons.

BALKAN CAMPAIGNS

The collapse of the Soviet Union after 1990 lifted the lid on long-suppressed nationalist tensions in some former communist countries of Eastern Europe and the Balkans, particularly Yugoslavia. Croatia and Slovenia had already broken away from the Yugoslav federation by 1991, and the Croat and Muslim population of Bosnia-Herzegovina supported a referendum calling for an independent, multinational republic. However, Bosnia's Serb population refused to secede and, in 1992–93, Bosnia-Herzegovina was torn apart by a bloody and bitter civil war.

The RAF was initially involved in humanitarian flights, bringing food and medical aid to the Bosnian capital Sarajevo. When Serbian President Slobodan Milosevic increased attacks on Muslims in Bosnia, ethnically cleansing them from areas claimed by Serbia, the UN intervened and the RAF helped to enforce a no-fly zone. Serb aggression continued, prompting NATO to bomb Serb targets. It was the first time that air power had been used offensively in Europe since 1945 – this time to contain aggression, save lives and force Serbia to accept the UN peace framework.

In 1999, the RAF was back in the Balkans with a deployment of Tornadoes, Harriers, tankers, helicopters and AWACS aircraft as the Serbian president was encouraging more ethnic cleansing against Albanian Muslims in Kosovo. As part of Operation Allied Force, NATO embarked upon a systematic bombing campaign against Serbian forces there and infrastructure targets in Serbia itself, aiming to force the withdrawal of Serbian troops from the province of Kosovo. Once again, the RAF flew missions from bases in Italy.

BACK IN THE MIDDLE EAST

The terrorist attacks of 11 September 2001 ultimately brought the RAF into more expeditionary action. The suicide missions on New York and Washington had been orchestrated by Osama Bin Laden and his Al-Qaida network, who were believed to be hiding in Afghanistan under the protection of the country's Taliban leadership. Britain joined the US-led coalition, including anti-Taliban forces in Afghanistan, to overthrow the Afghan government, and the RAF undertook reconnaissance action and air-to-air refuelling in Afghanistan as part of the campaign known as Operation Enduring Freedom. The coalition's overwhelming air power and cruise missiles destroyed Al-Qaida's bases and training camps, and the Afghan government soon fell.

However, the coalition forces were left with the problem of maintaining and extending control across the region. RAF Harriers and Tornados, based at Kandahar, supported US forces, and RAF helicopters supported ground troops, while the RAF Regiment also provided ground defence capacity. An air base was established at Camp Bastion, in Helmand province, which became the UK's fifth-

Previous pages
Royal Marines brace themselves against the downdraft from an incoming Chinook, Afghanistan

Right
A Merlin helicopter delivers supplies in Maysan Province, Iraq

largest airfield, with the capability for 600 aircraft and helicopter movements each day. Unfortunately, overthrowing the Taliban proved much easier than establishing a stable alternative, and Britain finally withdrew from Afghanistan in 2014.

At the same time as the Afghanistan campaign, the British military was also drawn into the invasion of Iraq. By November 2002, the ongoing issue of Iraq's WMDs resulted in the UN Security Council passing Resolution 1441, declaring that Iraq was in breach of previous resolutions. When Saddam refused to comply, the British joined a US-led coalition to remove him, starting military operations on 20 March 2003 under the name Operation Telic.

The RAF had played an important part in patrolling and enforcing the northern and southern no-fly zones over Iraq for more than a decade, and since 1991 it already had some 25 aircraft and 1,000 personnel in the Gulf. For Operation Telic, it drafted in a further 7,000 more personnel and 100 more aircraft. These included Tornado GR4s and Harrier GR7s in the offensive role, Tornado F3s for air defence, VC10s and Tristars for air-to-air refuelling, Nimrods and Canberras for

Munitions are unloaded from a Hercules C130 in Erbil, Iraq

"It is thanks to the dedication of those who serve in its ranks that the RAF is respected across the world"

reconnaissance, E3-D Sentries for advanced early warning and control, and Hercules and the new C-17s for air transport. Support helicopters were also provided – 20 Chinooks and seven Pumas.

Throughout Operation Telic, RAF aircraft flew 2,519 sorties, 1,399 of which were offensive strikes, and released 919 weapons, approximately 85 per cent of which were precision guided. Operation Telic also saw the first use of the Storm Shadow stand-off precision air-to-ground missile. The bulk of the mission ended in April 2009, but some British forces remained in-country with the aim of assisting the Iraqis to develop effective security forces to help re-build the country and support its democratically elected government.

A HUMANITARIAN ROLE

As well as these expeditionary campaigns, the RAF has been increasingly active in humanitarian work over the past 30 years. It has addressed natural disasters: mud slides in Chile in 1991, a 1992 earthquake in Turkey, hurricanes in the Caribbean in 1992, a horrific famine in Somalia in 1993, a 1995 volcanic eruption in Montserrat, forest fires in Cyprus in 1995 and 1998, and 2002 floods in Mozambique. In addition, RAF air transport was used in Guinea, Liberia and Sierra Leone during the Ebola outbreak of 2013–15. In 1994, the RAF delivered aid to Rwanda following a civil war; the following year brought humanitarian missions in Angola, and in 1996 an RAF Canberra PR9 flew reconnaissance missions to Zaire (now the Democratic Republic of Congo) to monitor a humanitarian crisis in neighbouring Rwanda. Closer to home, the RAF has assisted after floods in the Netherlands in 1995 and in the UK in 1998.

RAF air transport planes have also evacuated British nationals from Yemen (1994), Albania (1997), Central African Republic (1997–98), Eritrea (1998), and Sierra Leone (1998). A military operation in Sierra Leone in 2000 saw RAF Harriers operating from an aircraft carrier moored off the west coast, and four Chinooks, which made the astonishing 3,500-mile transit in 30 hours – the longest self-ferry by RAF helicopters. Later in the year, Chinooks and Hercules were involved in the rescue of six soldiers of the Royal Irish Regiment, who had been held hostage by the notorious West Side Boys, a gangster group that was a splinter of the Armed Forces Revolutionary Council.

Military aviation has changed a great deal since the RAF's formation as an independent air force a century ago, but one thing has remained constant – the unwavering courage, professionalism and dedication of the men and women who serve in its ranks. Its personnel are trained and ready to rise to any challenge. The technology behind the hardware may evolve, but that commitment remains and it is thanks to this dedication that the Royal Air Force is so widely respected across the world – an agile, adaptable and capable fighting force that is ready to meet each and every challenge that may lie ahead.

CELEBRATE

A FORCE FOR GOOD

The modern-day RAF continues to play a central role in the security and prosperity of the UK

Not only does the Royal Air Force play an essential role in the defence of the UK and its overseas territories, but it also contributes enormously to the nation's stability, prosperity and standing on the global stage. The RAF offers a broad range of capabilities in an increasingly uncertain world, providing a rapid, effective and scalable response to a crisis or threat anywhere across the globe. Its international reputation for professionalism, effectiveness and inter-operability, together with modern equipment, mean that the RAF can operate alongside its allies and partners if required.

The RAF has been at the forefront of technological innovation throughout its history and maintains its combat advantage through a combination of high-end technology and the quality, skill and innovation of its people. It has also led the way in its innovative solutions to aircraft support, improving performance and reducing costs for more than a decade.

As the service looks to the next 100 years, the challenge for the future is to ensure that the RAF continues to deliver decisive air power effect in an increasingly complex and contested environment. For the past century, the RAF has defended the skies of Britain and continues to project the nation's air and space power across the full range of global operations.

OPERATIONAL FOCUS

Beyond the immediate air defence of the UK, Operation Shader remains the primary defence commitment, with important progress having been made in the campaign to defeat Da'esh. RAF aircraft have flown extensive armed reconnaissance patrols across Iraq and Syria, identifying Da'esh positions and supporting Iraqi troops and the Syrian Democratic Forces in their respective ground operations.

Previous pages
The Red Arrows perform a display over the marina in Singapore

Right
A Tornado lands from a Shader mission, 2017

RAF aircraft have carried out more than 1,700 strikes against Da'esh in Iraq and Syria since 2014.

The work is intensive and demands the highest accuracy, achieved through a combination of careful targeting, close coordination between crews, the Combined Air Operations Centre and supported unit, and the employment of precision weapons. Reaper, Tornado and Typhoon continue to inflict telling damage on Da'esh throughout Iraq and Syria, with constant, critical tanker support from the Voyager and employing intelligence gathered by RAF and Coalition Information, Surveillance, Target Acquisition and Reconnaissance platforms. Less obvious to the immediate fight but no less significant, Atlas, C-17 and Hercules transport aircraft maintain vital supply chains to bases on Cyprus and in the Middle East.

RAF aircraft flew on operations against the terrorist group every day over the Christmas 2017 period, striking terrorist compounds, trucks, mortars and pockets of fighters engaged in close quarter, street fighting with Syrian Democratic Forces.

"The dangers we face are changing and are intensifying rapidly," said Defence Secretary Gavin Williamson. "Eliminating the threat from terrorism is critical to our security at home and abroad. Our brave Armed Forces are working tirelessly, day and night, to defeat Da'esh after helping to recover significant territory in Iraq."

Mosul may have fallen, but Da'esh remains a threat that the RAF is engaging with vigour across the region.

WHOLE FORCE SUCCESS

The RAF has a well-earned reputation for excellence in delivering air power and is at the heart of the Government's approach to conflict and crisis management, offering political choice, global agility and value for money to the UK Government.

The service manages risks and operates safely within an inherently risky environment, but it is also essentially "joint" and international in its outlook and the way in which it operates. The RAF's proud history of success is framed by innovation and its ability to exploit technology, all of which is underpinned by the enduring quality of the Whole Force. The successful delivery of air power depends on the RAF's highly talented and motivated men and women, who drive the service to distinction.

With the future operating environment presenting new challenges, fuelled by new technology and by the willingness of adversaries to fight in different ways, the RAF's challenge is to adapt and stay ahead of potential threats. Delivering planned growth and building a modern workforce are vital to achieving these ends. New opportunities must also be identified in order to improve efficiency and augment front-line capability.

Succeeding on operations, growing the RAF and building a workforce capable of overcoming the challenges it will face in the future operating environment will deliver the Next Generation RAF.

Such a force will need to fly and fight in an environment that will be more contested by agile and more capable enemies, prepared to fight ambiguous and "hybrid" warfare, and more able than we have seen for a generation to challenge its strengths and exploit its vulnerabilities.

Underpinning all elements of the Next Generation RAF will be its people. Having the right number of people with the right skills is important, but how they think is crucial to the tasks at hand. In the data-rich and complex future operating environment, the ability to think differently, challenge the status quo and innovate will be fundamental to success.

Control of the air and space remains essential to joint operational triumph. Adversaries will take advantage of

135

"Future conflicts will inevitably require closer collaboration with international partners"

new and rapidly evolving opportunities to degrade the ability to conduct operations against them. RAF aircraft and systems need to be able to operate in this increasingly contested environment and combat the enemy's information and command and control systems.

GLOBAL REACH

Future conflicts will inevitably require closer collaboration with the RAF's international partners, not only on operations, but on equipment development, training and exercising, to build strong, effective relationships and experience at all levels.

Twenty-first century partnership reached a milestone when Typhoons from 1(F) Squadron and II(AC) Squadron flew 20,000 miles in three separate back-to-back exercises in Malaysia, Japan and Korea in 2016. The biggest Red Arrows overseas tour in a decade was also seen by one billion people taking in 18 displays in 63 days across 17 countries, including China for the very first time.

The event was called Eastern Venture, a key overarching initiative for UK Defence Engagement in the Asia-Pacific and Middle East regions, where the RAF Aerobatic Team; Typhoon multi-role fighters; Voyager tankers; C130 Hercules, C17 Globemaster and Atlas (A400M) transport aircraft projected UK influence and British excellence across the globe. The exercise demonstrated the UK's strategic reach and wider interests, while contributing to the Government's GREAT campaign supporting UK business, trade and education, and promoting the best of British innovation, technology and creativity.

"Aviation is a truly global language," said Wing Commander Martin Higgins, Officer Commanding RAFAT, "and it is our hope that we have inspired the next generation of engineers, scientists and aviators."

Air Chief Marshal Sir Stephen Hillier, Chief of the Air Staff led the High Level International Engagement across the region in the Far East. In Japan, he met with Chief of the Japan Air Self-Defense Force,

Previous pages
Engineers at RAF Benson prepare a Puma for airlift out to the Caribbean

Right
A Puma on the beach at Cane Garden Bay in the British Virgin Islands, delivering essential aid to the locals

General Yoshiyuki Sugiyama and the Japanese Defence Minister Tomomi Inada with Tim Hitchens (then Her Majesty's Ambassador to Japan) in attendance. II(AC) Squadron hosted local dignitaries and high-ranking officers from the Japanese MOD and HQ JASDF. In the Republic of Korea, the Chief of the Air Staff met Chief of the Republic of Korea Operations Command, Lieutenant General Won In-Choul. And Commander of the US 7th Air Force, Lieutenant General Tom Bergeson visited II(AC) Squadron.

"By any measure this was an astonishing deployment that involved all elements of the service. Given the distance, the short duration and the number of nations involved, this was the most ambitious deployment by the Typhoon Force," said Wing Commander Roger Elliot, then OC II(AC) Squadron.

IN THE WAKE OF IRMA

Triggered in the immediate aftermath of Hurricane Irma, Operation Ruman saw a huge airlift mounted out of RAF Brize Norton, while Puma and Chinook helicopters joined Royal Navy Merlins and Wildcats over the British Virgin Islands.

After a state of emergency was declared by the British Virgin Islands, RAF Brize Norton was tasked with the delivery of aid and personnel to help with the recovery of areas devastated by Hurricane Irma. Under Operation Ruman, the station prepared to deliver an important element of its mission, to assist in time of crisis.

In the first week, 376,529 kg of freight left Brize Norton, along with 1,256 passengers and three RAF Puma helicopters. The first flight out was a 99 Squadron C-17 Globemaster bound for Barbados, carrying 52 passengers and 16,329 kg of freight, including pallets of shelters and other aid from the Department for International Development.

The Pumas provided essential lift throughout the region, while a pair of RAF Chinooks embarked HMS *Ocean* at Gibraltar and subsequently flew from the ship, moving people, freight and heavy equipment. In many cases only helicopters could navigate the devastated landscape, reaching those most in need.

The intense five-week period saw more than 2,000 UK military personnel involved, including members of 38 Expeditionary Air Wing (EAW). The unit enabled the delivery of 1,500 tonnes of freight and humanitarian aid. Having successfully completed its objective, 38 EAW returned to Brize Norton to be welcomed back by Station Commander, Group Captain Tim Jones.

Group Captain Jones remarked: "It's been an extraordinary five weeks. Within 24 hours of getting the call we had four aircraft out there and several hundred Royal Marines coming through Brize Norton. It's been RAF Brize Norton at its best, every single aspect of the station playing a really important role. I'm pleased for the team really, everyone has come together and done their bit and I'm very proud of everyone."

Foreign Secretary Boris Johnson flew into the area on board an RAF A400M Atlas. He said: "I've seen the response that our Armed Forces are getting on the streets here, and it's phenomenal. It's fantastically important for the Armed Forces to be here to deliver reassurance. The RAF is critical to that."

ROYAL
AIR FORCE

CAUSE FOR CELEBRATION

The RAF100 Appeal spans a broad range of elements, from supporting current and former personnel to nurturing the service of the future

The Royal Air Force has a wide global community, all rooted in excellence in aviation across 100 years of service to the UK, the Commonwealth and our allies. Conceived and proven through the need to protect these islands in the greatest conflicts of the 20th century, the RAF has since grown in scope, capability and mission, defending the values of democracy and the rule of law worldwide with integrity, determination and unparalleled skill.

In this centenary year, the RAF100 Appeal has a significant role to play. Maggie Appleton, who is Chief Executive of the RAF Museum and on the Appeal Board – is well placed to assess how 100 years of history inform the modern-day RAF. "The RAF100 Appeal is both a part of and a support to the RAF100 programme," she says. "The focus of this programme is to commemorate, celebrate and inspire. Those are three really important strands because, while it's important to give thanks for 100 years of achievement and sacrifice, it's a celebration of the professionalism of today's serving personnel and also – something that is so important to the RAF and Appeal partners – thinking about how we look to the future and how we inspire the generations to come."

A FORCE FOR CHARITY

The RAF100 Appeal brings together five partners: the RAF Benevolent Fund, RAF Association, RAF Charitable Trust, RAF Museum and the Royal Air Force itself. The Appeal Board comprises

Opposite, from top
The RAF Museum's Chief Executive Maggie Appleton; the Museum has undergone an impressive transformation

a trustee and the chief executive of the four key charities, two representatives from the RAF and two independent trustees. For Appleton, the process is underpinned by a spirit of collegiate cooperation. "We share the work together as a partnership and play to all our strengths," she says, "working with the governance of the charities, on the events and on the fundraising, publications and merchandising, keeping each other up to date and supported."

Maggie Appleton has been the RAF Museum's CEO since 2014, having started her career at the Royal Armouries and worked in community museums in Stevenage and Luton before becoming CEO of Luton Culture. She remembers visiting with her own (now grown-up) children and has always had an affinity with the RAF, with her father having served as an armourer on Lancasters for 57 Squadron during the Second World War.

Appleton shares the RAF's passion to inspire the next generation, and believes that the Appeal can have a lasting effect on the wider community. "Just before Christmas, we had a big STEM [Science, Technology, Engineering and Mathematics] launch at the Museum's Cosford site, to encourage work with schools and young people," she says. "We had a couple of hundred pupils from West Midlands schools, learning about different scientific principles and techniques – really hands-on fun examples for good practical engagement. It's our role to flick that switch on at primary school age and get children thinking, 'Yes, I am keen on science. And it's really exciting what I've learned. I could do this'."

INSPIRING YOUNG MINDS

Getting children engaged and retained in maths and science to A-level and beyond is a perennial problem for UK schools and, despite STEM initiatives raising numbers in recent years, a government Green Paper in 2017 cited research claiming 40 per cent of UK employers have problems recruiting staff with relevant STEM skills. This supports the anecdotal evidence that there is plenty of work still to be done.

"The lack of numbers coming through the workforce is a massive issue for our defence industry partners, as well as for the RAF," says Appleton. "There isn't just one silver bullet – it has to be on a number of levels." It's why, as part of the centenary, the RAF has launched the Trenchard Group, a wide-ranging platform of practical initiatives to attract and retain young people in STEM subjects and help them see the air force as a viable career option.

MountainTrike

"It's a chance to show off the best of the service, a great opportunity for people to interact with the RAF

That it should be named after the "Father of the Royal Air Force", Viscount Trenchard, is more than a mere nod to history. Innovation and technical expertise have been at the heart of the RAF's mission since 1918. When aeroplanes were first pressed into military service, they demanded the utmost bravery of pilots operating at the very edge of technology. The Battle of Britain was decided not just by skill and courage, but by marginal design and performance gains of the Spitfire and Hurricane over Germany's highly capable ME-109. And today's challenges range from cyber-attack and surveillance to the development of pioneering thermal paint to protect aircraft carriers from the extreme heat of a new generation of vertical-landing stealth fighters. In short, we need brains. "We absolutely need to support young people into these industries," says Appleton. "It's the only way to keep the RAF – and UK plc – ahead of the curve."

The Trenchard Group scheme aims to foster innovative thinking through its own three strands of development – ideas, scholarships and pathways – offering what it calls "a full spectrum of training, education and conceptual development for anyone to anywhere". This includes a new think tank on air power, academic placements, flying scholarships, and professional and leadership routes mapped out "from air cadet to air marshal".

None of this works, however, without awareness. And it's hoped that the RAF100 events and the associated Appeal will bring to a wider audience the importance of education, plus greater visibility for those current and former forces personnel who play such a vital role in our national story. "It's about using this landmark anniversary to start a national conversation about the RAF," says Appleton, "in terms of awareness and understanding about what it does, what it's achieved and how it's affected all of our lives."

A YEAR OF CELEBRATIONS

The centrepiece of the celebration takes place on 10 July, with a centenary service in Westminster Abbey, followed by a parade in The Mall and mass fly-past. The museum will be supporting the public display on Horse Guards Parade and the RAF100 national tour with the provision of aircraft such as the Sopwith Snipe and the Harrier GR3. "It's a chance to show off the best of the service," says Appleton, "whether that's through air shows or themed regional events. It's a great opportunity for people to interact with the RAF."

Alongside the RAF100 event programme, the RAF Museum is collecting oral histories that will be shared in new exhibitions and online. Interviews are with serving personnel, as well as veterans and the broader supporting RAF Family. This extraordinary community is supported by all the RAF100 Appeal charities: the RAF Association, Benevolent Fund, Charitable Trust and the Museum.

"It's important to think about how society has changed over the past hundred years and how our freedoms are, and have been, protected every day by our military personnel," says Appleton. "Much of the work that will be funded by the Appeal is thinking about families and veterans, and how we support people who have been in the RAF to flourish and lead interesting and fulfilling lives post-service. So it's a cradle-to-grave piece of thinking. For us at the

Previous pages
The RAF100 Appeal charities support service personnel past and present

Right
Last year's STEM launch at the Museum's Cosford site

Museum, much of our input is about telling the story of the broader RAF family, which has changed beyond recognition in the past 10 or 20 years. It's much broader than those who are directly employed, because there are civilians working for the RAF and industry partners in the supply chain, working together, many of them on RAF bases."

A LASTING LEGACY

This, for Appleton, is the key to legacy for the RAF100 Appeal – to ensure deeper, long-lasting relationships beyond 2018. She says key sponsors such as BAE Systems, Babcock and Fujitsu will no longer see themselves as working in parallel with the RAF but as part of a wider organisation. "A complex but exciting ecosystem," as she puts it. "One that benefits from shared expertise and pathways to unlock the skills of our youngsters."

Up to a certain level, funds raised by the Appeal will be shared equally between the five charity partners. Beyond that, there will be opportunities for grant applications to be made. It's a hugely complicated task to marshal the multiple facets of the RAF100 Appeal effectively, not least for Appleton as – when interviewed for this article – she was in the midst of a complete transformation of the Museum's London site for a June relaunch to coincide with the celebrations.

"We've got three new exhibitions and we've been transforming the landscape of the site, so it's really been all hands to the pump," she says. "We're proud of the work that's been put in over the past months and years, and we'll be full of exhilaration and exhaustion in equal measure, I should think. But we'll be ready to go!"

This level of commitment is being mirrored right across the RAF100 Appeal and thus promises to support the force's wider family, providing a practical legacy for an exciting and innovative new century of service.

WOMEN OF THE AIR FORCE

Over the past century, the responsibilities of women in the RAF have grown to the point where every role is now open to male and female personnel alike

Over the last hundred years, the role of women within society has changed radically. During wartime, vital support roles were undertaken so that men could be released for combat. Today, women are serving permanently in their own right.

During the First and Second World Wars, women serving with Britain's Armed Forces contributed greatly to the country's war effort and in doing so broke down social gender stereotypes. Given the opportunity and training they proved that women could successfully undertake male military roles under difficult circumstances.

The Women's Royal Air Force (WRAF) was created on 1 April, 1918 (the same day as the RAF) and disbanded in 1920. Princess Mary's Royal Air Force Nursing Service, was established as a permanent branch of the Royal Air Force in 1923. The Women's Auxiliary Air Force (WAAF), formed for war in 1939, was continued after the Second World War ended. It was re-formed as the WRAF, a permanent female peacetime force in 1949 and was fully integrated into the RAF in 1994.

One key figure in the history of women in the RAF is Dame Helen Gwynne-Vaughan. A formidable leader and inspirational speaker, she laid the foundations and set the standards for all women's air services. During the First World War, Gwynne-Vaughan was invited by the War Office, along with Mrs Chalmers Watson, to help form the Women's Army Auxiliary Corps (WAAC). As Chief Controller stationed in France, she was instrumental in creating a respected and disciplined force.

"Within the year, tens of thousands of women had volunteered to serve"

As a result of her success with the WAAC, Helen Gwynne-Vaughan was transferred to the Women's Royal Air Force (WRAF) in September 1918. Given the powers of a Brigadier, she began the task of reorganisation. In a short space of time, she revised the standing orders, overhauled the administrative system, opened and equipped Berridge House in Hampstead for the training of officers, authorised the new blue uniform and introduced military protocol. Her professionalism helped change male attitudes towards women in the air service.

In 1935, Helen Gwynne-Vaughan played a pivotal role in forming the Emergency Services, an organisation established to train female officers. In September 1938, with war once again on the horizon, the Auxiliary Territorial Service (ATS), the women's branch of the British Army was created. Helen Gwynne-Vaughan was appointed Director, the position which she held until her retirement from military service in 1941.

"By the end of the year the WRAF was the best disciplined and best turned-out women's organisation in the country," said Air Vice Marshal Sir William Sefton Brancker, a pioneering figure in British aviation. "This remarkable achievement was due to Dame Helen Gwynne-Vaughan."

THE WAAF

On 28 June 1939 King George VI established the Women's Auxiliary Air Force (WAAF) for duty with the RAF in time of war. Since 1938, RAF Companies had existed within the Auxiliary Territorial Service (ATS), the female force equivalent to the Territorial Army. These companies were affiliated to Royal Auxiliary Air Force squadrons but, by May 1939, the government decided that a separate women's air service was necessary.

The WAAF was not an independent organisation, nor was it completely integrated within the RAF. Rather, it was interlinked with its "parent" force for the purpose of substituting, where possible, women for RAF personnel. It was mobilised on 28 August 1939 and, within the year, tens of thousands of women had volunteered to serve.

In 1941, the WAAF became part of the Armed Forces of the Crown, subject to the Air Force Act. This was greeted with pride and enthusiasm by its members. With conscription for women introduced from December 1941, the ranks swelled further so that by July 1943 a peak strength of 182,000 had been reached. By 1945 a quarter of a million women had served in the WAAF in over 110 different trades, supporting operations around the world. They were an integral and vital part of the RAF's war effort.

With war coming to an end demobilisation began. By June 1946, over 100,000 had left the service. The Government was conscious of the contribution made by the WAAF. Proposals for retaining a permanent female peacetime force were discussed and, as a result, the Women's Royal Air Force was re-formed on 1 February 1949.

T C DUGDALE

R. A

Previous pages, clockwise from top left
Dame Helen Gwynne-Vaughan; Dame Felicity Hanbury – the WAAF's last director and the first director of its successor, the WRAF; women of the WRAF boarding light tenders, 1919

Left
Members of the WAAF assist with re-arming Lancaster bombers

More than a quarter of a million women served in the Women's Auxiliary Air Force (WAAF). No fewer than 183,317 were volunteers with a further 33,932 women called up from December 1941. The majority were aged between 18 and 40. They came from all walks of life and from around the world. By 1943, 48 nationalities were represented in the force including Irish, Caribbean and Polish women.

AN INTEGRAL ROLE

Despite organisational differences, which included a separate ranking system and pay, which was two thirds of their RAF colleagues, the women realised they were integral to the RAF. The initial scepticism and humour that greeted many WAAFs soon turned to respect and admiration as female personnel proved time and again their dedication and skill. Day in, day out, they diligently did their duty. Great strength of character was required by many WAAFs in continuing to work despite the loss of friends and loved ones.

Many WAAFs were decorated for their gallantry. Daphne Pearson, a medical corporal, rescued a pilot from his crashed aircraft at RAF Detling on 31 May 1940. As the aircraft and its bomb load exploded, Corporal Pearson threw herself on top of the pilot to protect him from the blast and splinters. As a result of her action, Corporal Pearson was awarded the George Cross.

"In 45 years, women had progressed from a temporary wartime support role to become full members of the world's oldest independent air force"

The women of the WAAF were a vital part of the RAF's war effort and through their example demonstrated the contribution that women could make to Britain's Armed Forces. The work undertaken by the Women's Auxiliary Air Force (WAAF) was wide ranging: from cooking and meteorology, to administrative duties and maintaining and repairing aircraft. Women replaced RAF personnel in those trades where there were shortages. There was an ebb and flow of requirements. The safety and physical well-being of the women were primary concerns. Except for nursing orderlies, aircrew duty was never approved. Women did fly aircraft in Britain during the Second World War, but they did so as civilian pilots of the Air Transport Auxiliary.

The success of the WAAF was due, in part to it being interlinked with the RAF, but difficulties did arise. WAAF officers were not able to command RAF personnel until after the WAAF became an element of the Armed Forces of the Crown in 1941. Once this took place, further roles became open to them. In 1944, for example, the first female station commander was appointed.

Officers and airwomen were selected by interview, but unlike during the First World War, training was provided. Some trades required several weeks' attendance at specialised schools before posting took place. Certain work, such as code and cipher duty, was restricted to officers. Particular trades needed suitable qualifications such as a relevant degree. Overseas service was available to officers from 1940, but only to airwomen from 1943 onwards. The practical work undertaken by the WAAF, combined with the intangible comfort and moral support they provided to their RAF colleagues, was essential in keeping the RAF flying.

RETURN OF THE WRAF

The Women's Royal Air Force was reborn on 1 February, 1949, offering women a full professional career in the air force for the first time. Although women had served alongside the RAF before, it had always been in a temporary wartime capacity. The passing of the Army and Air Force (Women's Service) Act in 1948 created the opportunity for a permanent peacetime role for women in the Armed Forces, in recognition of their invaluable wartime contribution.

From the outset, the WRAF was to be integrated as fully as possible with the RAF, a source of much pride for its members. All new entrants were commissioned or enlisted in the RAF, taking the same oath as the men, and subject to the same conditions of service and disciplinary code. The only restriction placed on their employment was that they should not undertake combatant duties. King's Regulations were rewritten to include the WRAF and, except in issues of women's welfare, WRAF personnel were in principle to be treated like their male counterparts.

Initially, female entrants underwent basic training separately, joining their male colleagues for professional training in their

W·A·A·F

TAKE THE
ROAD TO
VICTORY!
JOIN
THE WAAF

Princess
Mary's
ROYAL
AIR
FORCE
Nursing
Service
at home
and
overseas

WOMEN!
The Royal
Air Force
needs your
help!
SERVE YOUR
COUNTRY BY
JOINING THE
W·R·A·F
There is fit work for every
FIT WOMAN
WOMEN'S ROYAL
AIR FORCE

JULIE GIBSON

Previous pages
Recruitment posters for the WAAF, the WRAF and Princess Mary's Royal Air Force Nursing Service

Opposite
The RAF's first operational female pilot, Flight Lieutenant Julie Gibson

Right
Jean Lennox Bird – the first woman pilot to gain her RAF wings – in the cockpit of a de Havilland Chipmunk, 1952

chosen branch or trade. On completion of training, WRAF personnel were posted to RAF stations both at home and overseas, serving as far afield as Singapore, Burma and Iraq. Despite their non-combatant status, the WRAF found themselves at the heart of Britain's numerous post-war conflicts in places such as Malaya, Kenya and Cyprus where they performed vital support roles, often in dangerous situations.

From 1949, about 80 per cent of trades were open to women including driving, ground signalling, clerical work and catering. Opportunities to fly existed for members of the WRAF Volunteer Reserve, but regulars were not yet accepted as aircrew. In time, more technical trades became available such as mechanic and air traffic control. In 1959, the new trade of Air Quartermaster was opened to women. In 1962 these became the first females to be recognised as aircrew.

The WRAF and the RAF grew ever closer over the following years and, in 1968, female officers adopted the rank titles of their RAF counterparts. Training was also consolidated both at recruit and officer level and, in 1970, the first female entrants were admitted into the RAF College, Cranwell. Soon after, women began to be promoted to senior appointments and in 1975 Group Captain Joan Peck became Deputy Director of the Signals Branch, the first woman to hold such a position.

Despite such breakthroughs, the majority of women remained firmly on the ground. It would be over 10 years before the concept of operational female aircrew became a reality. In September 1989, the first female navigators commenced training at RAF Finningley, graduating in 1990 to take up posts in the Hercules fleet. Just five months later, Flight Lieutenant Julie Gibson became the RAF's first operational female pilot, flying Andovers and the multi-engine Hercules transport.

A UNIFIED SERVICE

In 1994, women served in all branches of the RAF with the exception of the RAF Regiment. Ninety-six per cent of RAF jobs were open to women – the highest proportion in any of the British Armed Forces. The majority of women were employed in administrative and technical ground trades, but an increasing number were involved in operations.

That year, Flight Lieutenant Jo Salter broke new ground by becoming the first operational fast jet pilot, flying Tornados with 617 Squadron. Since then, female pilots have flown operationally in various theatres, including Afghanistan and Iraq. The impact of their contribution was highlighted when, on 7 March 2008, Flight Lieutenant Michelle Goodman became the first woman to be awarded the Distinguished Flying Cross. In March 2009, Flight

Right
As of last year, the RAF opened up all roles to women, including those in the RAF Regiment

Lieutenant Kirsty Moore of 13 Squadron was appointed the first female pilot in the Red Arrows. Other firsts for women followed. In August 2013, Elaine West was appointed as Director of Projects and Programme Delivery at the Defence Infrastructure Organisation in the rank of Air-Vice Marshal (the first regular service AVM), and in December 2013 Sue Gray was appointed Director of Combat Air Defence, Defence Equipment and Support in the rank of Air-Vice Marshal.

From September 2017, in what was called a defining moment, the RAF became the first British military service to open up all roles to men and women. Women who want to join the RAF Regiment for "Ground Close Combat" roles are now entitled to apply, meaning that there are no longer any RAF roles that exclude women from participation.

"We want the best and most talented individuals to join the Air Force, regardless of their gender, race, or background," said Chief of the Air Staff, Air Chief Marshal Sir Stephen Hillier. "A diverse force is a more effective force, and we need the best people to deliver the important work we do, be it defeating Da'esh in Iraq and Syria, or protecting Britain's skies."

INSPIRE

THE CHALLENGE AHEAD

Air Chief Marshal Sir Stephen Hillier reflects on the origins of the service, and on its future role and objectives

We celebrate the 100th anniversary of the formation of the Royal Air Force, the world's oldest independent air arm. The formation of the RAF in 1918 was the culmination of rapidly growing wartime experience, and of a vision. That vision was based on the evidence, from the most terrible war the world had yet experienced, that a new form of warfare – war in the third dimension – had emerged, and that it would continue growing rapidly and become decisive in any future conflict.

It was a vision also based on the realisation that the ability to fight and win in the air was important in itself, with an existence that was beyond just providing direct support to navies and armies. And most importantly in relation to this anniversary, was the belief that success in air warfare, whether in 1918 or looking into the future, would most effectively and efficiently be achieved by a unified and independent air arm – what would become the RAF.

THE BIRTH OF THE RAF

The formation of the RAF was not simply a matter of improving military effectiveness at a time of immense courage and sacrifice on the Western Front. One hundred years ago, on the home front, formations of German Gotha bombers were dropping bombs, unopposed and in daylight, on London and other towns and cities in the south and east of the UK. Many civilians were being killed and the physical scars can still be seen today. But the psychological damage to a nation insulated for centuries against attack by geography and the Royal Navy was far greater. Air warfare had exposed a critical vulnerability; warfare was never going to be the same again and something had to be done.

Previous pages
Air Chief Marshal Sir Stephen Hillier, Chief of the Air Staff

Left
Members of the Air Defence Cadet Corps at Dunstable, 1939

Previous attempts to unite the efforts of the Admiralty and the War Office in improving and cohering air capabilities had proved ineffective. Prime Minister David Lloyd George therefore acted swiftly and appointed a Cabinet Committee to investigate not just the air defence of London, but how to organise the nation's air power. Within a month, the principal report had recommended that "we must create ... a new Ministry and Air Staff which can properly handle this new instrument of offence, and equip it with the best brains at our disposal for the purpose". The path to the formation of the RAF – an act also of bold, inspirational and visionary political leadership – was assured.

The Air Ministry was formed on 3 January 1918 and the RAF itself on 1 April 1918. The RAF rapidly became the world's most formidable air force, with 22,647 aircraft, 103 airships, 133 squadrons and 15 flights overseas. By the end of the First World War, the RAF had more than 300,000 men and women. By the peak in the Second World War, there were over one million in the RAF with 487 squadrons, engaged continuously with the enemy in every theatre of war, from the first day to the last. The vision of 1918 that air warfare would become decisive, and the efficiency and effectiveness of a unified air force, had been vindicated in the most emphatic terms possible, and has continued to be in every conflict since.

This is the history of the formation of the RAF, but of at least equal importance to the facts has been the spirit, ethos and character

"The willingness and ability to innovate, adapt and improve has always been an essential part of the RAF story"

of the service. From the very start it was conceived and regarded as different to the other services. The founding members of the RAF were pioneers, exploiting a new environment and at the cutting edge of innovation and the latest technology of the day.

The new service sought out talented, innovative and ambitious men and women who were either already highly skilled or had potential that could be unlocked. With so much talent at all levels, it was also a service with a less hierarchical, less deferential outlook on life – one where every individual was valued and judged on merit alone. The first Chief of the Air Staff, Lord Hugh Trenchard, said "We open ... widely and to all." It is a principle that continues to be our very essence as an organisation today.

100 YEARS AND COUNTING

Our RAF Centenary Programme, RAF100, embraces that egalitarian spirit. We commemorate the precious legacy of extraordinary success, achievement and sacrifice that is at the heart of the proud tradition and ethos of our service – something that continues to inspire everyone in the RAF today. We celebrate the skill, professionalism and achievement of the people in today's RAF, airborne every hour of every day, protecting the UK's interests at home and abroad. Perhaps most importantly of all, we will, as we have always done, aim through RAF100 to inspire the next generation. Our focus has always been on the future and the legacy of RAF100 as a launch pad into our second century. We aim to ignite young people's passion for air, space and cyber through science, technology, engineering, art and design, and mathematics programmes and institutions, reaching out to students from all backgrounds, demonstrating that we remain a dynamic engine of social mobility, where everyone can fulfil their true potential. We will also promote the importance of our aerospace and technological industries, whose support is as vital to our operational effectiveness today as it was in 1918, and who help us secure our technological cutting edge for the future. The final important part of our centenary will be the RAF100 Appeal, involving the RAF Benevolent Fund, RAF Association, RAF Charitable Trust and RAF Museum. Together, these charities help protect our precious heritage and look after every member of the RAF Family, serving and retired, families and dependants.

As the RAF heads into its second century, what lies ahead? The RAF has been extraordinarily busy and successful on operations across the world for the last three decades, but risks and threats are increasing again, and the character of the conflicts we can expect to fight is changing too. Our extensive operational experience has consistently confirmed the need for the full breadth of air-power capabilities: control of the air and space, precision strike, ISTAR (intelligence, surveillance, target acquisition and reconnaissance) and air mobility. It has also confirmed the need for those capabilities to be at high readiness, giving speed of response; to be sufficiently flexible and well-trained to be able to adapt quickly to rapidly evolving operational environments; and to be ready to deploy and operate worldwide, most likely with our key allies and partners.

VISITOR
RAF 100
ROYAL AIR FORCE

Previous pages, from top
The RAF100 Appeal will help to support former service personnel; and inspire a new generation

Left
The F-35B Lightning represents part of the RAF's future capability

DELIVERING THE FUTURE

We have outstanding platforms and capabilities that will allow us to do all of this, but we must develop further our understanding and ability to integrate those capabilities and gain maximum effect, especially in the information environment; and to fuse air, space and cyber capabilities within fast, agile, multi-domain command and control. This is an enormous challenge, but I know we will succeed. It will require constant change and transformation in the way we think and operate – but then the willingness and ability to innovate, adapt and improve has always been an essential part of the RAF story. And we continue to have outstanding people in the RAF, across every branch and trade – their extraordinary skills, motivation and commitment are what will deliver the Next Generation Air Force and secure our future.

In our 100th anniversary year, we cherish the rich heritage of the RAF. Our history has shown us that we need to be ready – today, tomorrow and every day – to meet the challenges that will confront us in the air, in space and in cyber. We have done so with enormous success throughout our first 100 years and we can be confident that we will continue to do so in the future, as we head with immense pride into our second century.

A BRIGHT FUTURE

The RAF's new training system will keep the air force and its next generation of pilots at the forefront of air power

It is rare for a military service to make a wholesale change in the way it does business. This is particularly true of an air force, where the challenges of introducing technologically advanced systems are particularly acute. Typically, a new platform might be introduced, building on the capabilities of a previous system, adding new weapons and an advanced sensor suite, but seldom does a service branch change all its platforms and supporting infrastructure, and design new methods for employing them.

Yet such is the RAF's Military Flying Training System, or MFTS. It began with the Hawk T2 and Royal Navy Avenger platforms and is now moving at pace to replace another five training aircraft types, install dramatic new synthetic technologies and recreate RAF Valley on the island of Anglesey as a training hub, alongside RAF Cranwell and RAF Shawbury.

Group Captain David Catlow, Assistant Director Plans, Directorate of Flying Training, 22 Group, is deeply immersed in the MFTS programme. He is a former Officer Commanding 45 Squadron, training multi-engine aircrew on the King Air at Cranwell.

"We've been careful to make sure MFTS doesn't mirror the current system exactly, but if you look at it on a larger scale it's quite familiar," he says. "We're partnered with Ascent, our commercial training service partner, with whom we've got a long-term relationship to transform the flying training system. Once we're up and running, a lot of the responsibilities we used to have, including courseware, continuous improvement and pipeline planning will be transferred to Ascent and some elements of these roles have already been taken on. In terms of

The Hawk T2 is helping produce fast jet pilots of outstanding quality

G-MFTS
G-MFTS

"We see real potential for expansion and for a step change in training philosophy"

the future system, it's still broadly recognisable from where we are now; we still have Elementary Flying Training, Basic Fast Jet Training and Advanced Fast Jet Training, for example, but there's a significant difference in course content. The next challenge is to see where we take it once we're up and running with the new platforms and systems."

However good the initial syllabus – and there's no reason to think it will be anything other than excellent – the first students passing all the way through the system, and their instructors, are almost certain to expose areas where it could be better. This means that they may be positioned to influence the way UK military flying training is delivered for decades to come.

PREFECT

While the Hawk T2 remains as the Advanced Fast Jet Training platform, there has otherwise been a clean sweep of new aircraft. As a result, the Grob 120TP Prefect is replacing the Grob G 115E Tutor, the Embraer Phenom 100 takes on the King Air's role and the Shorts Tucano makes way for the Beechcraft T-6C Texan II (to be known as the Texan T Mk1 in MFTS service). Rotary students will experience the Airbus Helicopters H135 Juno, which takes over from the Eurocopter Squirrel, and the H145 Jupiter, which replaces the Bell Griffin HT1.

With the exception of the Texan, by early November 2017 examples of all these platforms were on their operating stations and the Prefect was already flying from RAF Barkston Heath, adjacent to RAF Cranwell, with 57 Squadron. Developed from the Grob G 115, but with turboprop power and a glass cockpit, the Prefect is a very different aircraft indeed. So, how is it fitting into the Elementary Flying Training role?

"Our first course started recently and those students finished ground school and began flying early in the New Year," says Group Captain Catlow. "For the next 12 to 16 months we'll be in a transition phase between MFTS and legacy flying training, so we'll still have some Elementary Flying Training on the Tutor at RAF Wittering, for example. By mid-2019 we'll be completely on the MFTS system.

"In terms of its performance, we're incredibly excited about the Prefect, perhaps more so than any of the new fixed-wing platforms. A major change compared to Tutor is that we're bringing in simulation at the Elementary Flying Training stage. We haven't had that before; we see real potential for expansion and for a step change in training philosophy and capacity. Right now, although it's a little difficult to assess until we have students in it, the Qualified Flying Instructors working with the Prefect are telling us it's performing beyond expectations. They say it's an amazing platform and they can't wait to start working with students.

"We're introducing desktop training and flying training devices, or FTDs, alongside the Prefect. The FTD isn't a full motion simulator, but it's still very good and because it costs far less, we can have plenty of them. They're potentially brilliant devices for students to practise procedures in. We know we're going to get benefits from simulation at this early stage, we just don't know how big those benefits will be."

Previous pages
The Prefect bears some semblance to its predecessor, the Tutor, but is essentially a new aircraft

Opposite, from top
Equipped with a suite of modern avionics, the T-6C offers a swathe of additional capability; the Phenom is proving a highly effective multi-engine trainer

Considering just how good modern high-fidelity simulators are, it makes sense to introduce students to them at the outset of their training. The simulator may become as much a part of their flying career as the aircraft itself and exposure to instruction and practice in the sim will inculcate skills that need to remain sharp for years to come. An experienced multi-engine and Tucano instructor himself, Group Captain Catlow sees tremendous opportunity in simulation.

"Flying hours are an expensive resource," he says, "especially on the frontline, but the beauty of the simulator is that you can do the learning on the ground, rehearse manoeuvres and tactics, work at it until it's right or stop, reset and repeat. Once it's good enough, you carry on in the air and maximise those live hours. I think as instructors we get better at teaching through fully exploiting the synthetic environment. In the multi-engine world, I believe we'll also get better at observing two students operating together as a crew. We've not been able to maximise the opportunity to observe our students operating together until now and the new synthetics will be a real boost."

TEXAN T MK1

Basic Fast Jet Training is moving onto the Texan T Mk1, featuring a modern glass cockpit in keeping with the Prefect from which students will come, and the Hawk T2 onto which they'll progress. While all the new MFTS platforms bring with them their own unique infrastructure and syllabus, the Texan T Mk1 also means a change of station for Basic Fast Jet Training.

"MFTS is a four-base solution using Valley, Shawbury, Cranwell/Barkston Heath and Culdrose," says Group Captain Catlow. "It was always planned that Basic Fast Jet Training at the Tucano's RAF Linton-on-Ouse home base would cease, and rather than building supporting infrastructure and flying a new aeroplane from there, it made sense to put the Texan straight into Valley. Where Valley used to operate 60 or 70 Hawks, today it has a maximum of 28 Hawk T2s, so introducing the Texan will have no impact on safety or any other factors.

"Compared to the Hawk T1, the T2 also operates over a much wider area, employing its much-expanded capability, so although Valley will be busier, it's not going to be too busy. The Basic Fast Jet Training unit will remain as 72 Squadron, operating two aircraft types at different stations until the transition to Texan and Valley is completed."

PHENOM

Ascent and its subcontractors have sourced and are supporting the new fixed-wing elements of MFTS; they're supplying five Phenom 100 business jets to meet the RAF's requirement. Ascent is contracted to deliver MFTS, but under military supervision, and the Armed Forces' part of the deal is to supply instructors from the RAF, Army and Royal Navy.

An incredibly successful entry-level business jet, the diminutive Phenom 100 is also in service with the Emirates and Etihad flight-training academies. In keeping with the Prefect and Texan, it has an advanced glass cockpit featuring the latest navigation and situational awareness tools.

Compared to the King Air fleet currently flying in the multi-engine flying training role with 45 Squadron, five Phenoms seems a very small number; Catlow explains the provision. "Originally, we had 11 King Airs," he says, "but for the last four years only seven have

323
N2824B
323

PR-PHK

"The most important question is will it begin delivering crews in time to meet demand?"

been in use. Of those, four are B200 Classics and three B200GTs, with glass cockpits. If we'd had a fleet only of GTs, we'd have managed with less than seven, so with five Phenoms, combined with the excellent simulator we're commissioning and some FTDs, we're actually improving the training provision."

Multi-engine training is currently the preserve of the King Air and previously fell to the Jetstream – both twin turboprops. Did the choice of Phenom 100, an unusual twin-jet machine with straight wings, raise eyebrows among the RAF's flying training community?

"There was maybe a little bit of surprise," says Group Captain Catlow. "We've been training on turboprops for many years and perhaps we expected another. But the Phenom is very successful, it has a cutting-edge cockpit and exceptional availability rates, so we'll be able to fly it lots, and it can do everything we need it to."

The Phenom will replace the King Air on 45 Squadron's roster, but the squadron also has a large training commitment for rear crew going on to fixed-wing and rotary platforms. Simultaneous with the Phenom's introduction, much of this training provision is also changing.

"We used to train navigators, acousticians, electronic warfare operators and loadmasters, plus the start of the helicopter crewman phase on 55 Squadron," says Group Captain Catlow. "In 2010, with Nimrod's withdrawal and Tornado drawdown, much of the unit's training requirement disappeared. But we still needed loadmasters and helicopter crewmen, and their training is now contracted under MFTS. There's a brand-new rear crew training system at Cranwell. It's effectively the aft end of an A400M, computerised for a huge variety of instruction and simulation. For rotary-wing crewmen there are now synthetic devices at Shawbury, moving our training on with some aplomb."

Right
The Tutor will remain in service with the Air Experience Flights and University Air Squadrons

HAWK

It's an inescapable fact that by the time the Texan joins the Hawk T2 at Valley in 2019, the Hawk training system will have been operational for almost a decade. Does this mean it will have fallen behind the capabilities offered by the more recent MFTS aircraft?

"The T2 remains an amazing platform and we've upgraded the syllabus to cope with new tactics and procedures, adding items that the frontline wants," says Group Captain Catlow. "Right now we believe the T2 is completely suited to training our future Lightning and Typhoon pilots; upgrade, primarily through software, is a more distant likelihood."

ROTARY REVOLUTION

At RAF Shawbury in Shropshire, the Airbus Helicopters Helionix integrated avionics system of the Juno and Jupiter helicopters is already impressing instructors. "I'm hearing similar views from the fielding team at Shawbury as I am from the Prefect team at Barkston Heath," says Group Captain Catlow. "And although I'm not a helicopter pilot, from my experience looking at the station's new training system, I can say it's another step change in training capability. The aircraft are reportedly simple to fly, which is great from a safety point of view, while their common avionics enables students to move between cockpits with relatively little additional training. This means those precious airborne hours are not wasted learning systems that don't replicate the frontline, they just represent helicopters generically."

Historically, students have converted from the Squirrel onto the Griffin in order to gain experience and new skills in the larger type, which most are learning to fly only to be able to advance their helicopter learning. With Juno and Jupiter, the larger type's cockpit

05
G-CJIW
DEFENCE HELICOPTE
FLYING SCHOOL

Left
The Jupiter (right) and Juno arrive at their Shawbury base

and the skill set necessary to fly it are essentially the same as those of the smaller helicopter, minimising the conversion process.

"Over the years we've got much better at, say, using the Squirrel to train future Chinook pilots," says Group Captain Catlow. "We've become far less focussed on learning systems on training aircraft that aren't relevant to the frontline. With Juno and Jupiter we're taking that a step further. It's expressed in a number of clever details. They're both twin-engined, for example, adding a safety margin to the Juno compared to the Squirrel, and Gazelle before it, during engine failure training. On the older types the engine was powered down, but the problem can be simulated on the Juno using its engine failure mode, which doesn't fail it at all, but gives the pilot the impression that it has."

As expected, Shawbury also has a full set of synthetic training devices to complement its 29 Juno and three Jupiter helicopters. These include five high-fidelity Juno FTDs and two for the Jupiter, plus winch trainers and other systems.

As it does today, Valley also has a role in the rotary training programme, since the Jupiter is replacing the Griffin on the station's 202 Squadron, providing search and rescue and mountain flying training to UK military helicopter pilots. On the other hand, compared to Shawbury's incumbent Defence Helicopter Flying School, the new system will see some consolidation, with basic rotary wing training falling under an Army Lieutenant Colonel and the advanced component under a Royal Navy Commander.

"Under them we'll still have 60 and 202 Squadrons flying the Jupiter, while Army Air Corps and Fleet Air Arm squadrons will operate the Juno," says Group Captain Catlow.

Right
The Hawk's advanced emulation systems are employed in a range of training scenarios

JUST IN TIME?

With the RAF's Lightning Force gaining momentum and two new Typhoon squadrons on the horizon, perhaps the most important question of all for Group Captain Catlow and the entirety of MFTS is will it begin delivering *ab initio* crews in time to meet demand?

"We're going to be just in time," he says. "There's not so much growth in our rotary-wing requirements, but it's significant in fast jet and multi-engine. Part of the response to the demand is in how we use the new assets. Is there more we can do with Prefect? Can we use the Texan slightly differently to Tucano? How can we maximise the benefit of the synthetic assets? We won't know exactly how that works until we've evaluated what we have now and how well it delivers.

"Right now we're looking in detail at the new platforms and acknowledging what a big step-up MFTS is going to be from where we are. Looking at the Prefect compared to the Tutor, for example, it's amazing. Everyone who's flown it so far says what an incredible aeroplane it is. It potentially brings challenges at the beginning of the course, but might also realise opportunities at the far end, taking students further than previously possible."

Considering the Prefect's advanced glass cockpit, it's tempting to ask exactly where the challenges lie. Will the next generation of smart young Elementary Flying Training students actually take to it with ease, having grown up with touchscreens and graphical interfaces, rather than switches and dials?

"It's an interesting debate," he says. "I've been flying for 20 or more years and have been exposed to glass cockpits more recently. I considered the change from analogue to digital cockpit quite a challenge – perhaps it's my age or just what I'm used to? But when our digital-savvy students did the same transition midway through the King Air course, it proved a very straightforward process."

Catlow explains how the move to MFTS has been planned for many years. "We're confident of what we're getting," he says. "Ascent and its contractors have been in place on the stations for more than two years in some cases and the relationships are working well. But it's the recapitalisation of a complete system involving five new aircraft types, a bunch of infrastructure and a completely different methodology of how we're going to do training, and it would be naive to say there aren't teething problems. We're confident of what we're getting, though, although we won't know exactly how well it works for another 12 to 18 months.

"It's a holistic system designed to take the guys and girls who walk through the door at Cranwell for their Elementary Flying Training right through to the end of their advanced training. It's effectively a pipeline and only when the first students reach its conclusion will we know just how good it is. For now, I'm confident that we've created a world-class training system."

NO STEP

The Ballistic Missile Early Warning System has been operational since 1963

THE FINAL FRONTIER?

With significant fixtures at RAF Fylingdales and RAF High Wycombe, the Royal Air Force is employing space-age radar detection and satellite technology to ensure the defence of our nation

The story of RAF Fylingdales and the Ballistic Missile Early Warning System began on 4 October 1957. The nation awoke to hear an early-morning news bulletin featuring the "bleep! bleep! bleep!" of the Soviet Union's *Sputnik I* – the first man-made earth satellite to be put into orbit. It became clear that, from this point, the Soviets had the potential to make a missile attack on the West launched from within their own land mass.

Sputnik I showed that there were no current means of stopping an incoming missile. It's why the Ballistic Missile Early Warning System was conceived to allow retaliatory strikes to be launched. The ability to warn of an attack and to respond rapidly brought peace through deterrence.

The home of this system was RAF Fylingdales, a small unit on the North Yorkshire Moors. BMEWS III – a series of huge, circular, radar-detecting spheres known as "golf balls" – was first declared operational in October 1963 as one of three radar sites in the Ballistic Missile Early Warning System: the other two sites were built in Clear, Alaska and Thule in Greenland. These three locations gave the better radar coverage necessary to detect an intercontinental ballistic missile attack from Russia.

The three giant radars in the golf balls had a coverage of 270 degrees looking over to the north. The 84-ft diameter dishes were capable of detecting and tracking ballistic missiles and providing

Right
The view from inside one of the Ballistic Missile Early Warning System's "golf balls"

advanced warning of an impending nuclear strike from Russia. During this period of the Cold War, the station attracted opposition from peace protesters and other groups, who established a peace camp outside the gates and regularly protested at the militarisation of the moors. However, more recently, the protesting groups have come to acknowledge the base as a permanent feature and peace campaigners are regularly invited onto the unit to discuss the Royal Air Force's defence role.

In the mid-1980s the radar required modernising, so the UK and US governments announced their agreement to modernise the mechanical system. In October 1992, the Solid State Phased Array Radar (SSPAR) became operational. The SSPAR is a unique construction with three radars designed to have a 360-degree field of view. It uses changes in electrical phase to steer the radar beam and searches out to 3,000 nautical miles, continuously looking for missiles. While carrying out this role, it is also able to track some 800 separate objects simultaneously and, as a result, the space-surveillance capability has been greatly enhanced.

Following agreement from the Secretary of State for Defence in 2003, the US Department of Defense undertook to upgrade the SSPAR with the latest technologies to improve the radar's missile-tracking capabilities. This would allow the US Missile Defense Agency to utilise the information produced by the radar for US defence purposes. Testing and acceptance of the Upgraded Early Warning Radar – as it is now called – took place in mid-2007, and formal certification of capability to support the fourth mission of US Missile Defense is expected in the near future.

Today, the unit comprises 80 service personnel, 80 MoD policemen and policewomen, and a further 200 civilian staff and contractors. The site's independent power provides critical mission support, utilising 1.8 megawatts of power to send beams of energy into space, working 24/7 to provide an integral part of the operational output. The public services provider Serco has a strong link to the station. The first Serco management contract was RAF Fylingdales and the new SSPAR build. Since then, Serco has become one of the largest worldwide service companies with a global footprint.

RAF Fylingdales has also been involved in various space missions, including the first British astronaut to be part of the International Space Station mission. Tim Peake's Soyuz capsule was detected and tracked by the RAF radar on a number of occasions as it orbited the earth before docking. The tracking and monitoring of other space launches is a regular occurrence at the station and has attracted celebrity interest – from Brian Cox and Tony Robinson to Sir Ranulph Fiennes.

> *"The motto 'through adversity to the stars' has never been more appropriate than it is today"*

THE SPACE OPERATIONS CENTRE

The Space Operations Centre (SpOC), located at RAF High Wycombe, evolved from the former UK Missile Warning Centre in 2008 to reflect its adoption of much broader space operations tasks. The unit's mission is to deliver space control and space situational awareness capabilities in order to understand and exploit the space domain. The ultimate aim is to protect and secure access to critical space capabilities, defend national interests, and provide space support to military operations.

Space situational awareness includes gathering intelligence of satellite overflights; space object re-entries; the risk of collision between space objects (with space debris growing, access to space surveillance and tracking data is vital); space weather forecasts and their likely effects; and satellite communication outages.

SpOC supports air, land and maritime space-related education and training through briefs, hosting visits and involvement in a variety of joint exercises. The unit also executes tactical command of the Ballistic Missile Early Warning Radar at RAF Fylingdales.

The Government's contribution to space operations, most notably within the RAF, is about to embark upon a process of enhancement that will witness increased numbers of personnel. These will include reservists, regulars (including a first army post) and civilian contractors, plus a reconfigured infrastructure and a streamlining of mission-critical equipment – i.e. the "Whole Force" capability. Increases in the number of personnel have already begun and, by mid-2021, the numbers will have more than doubled. This will enable planning, training, analysis and dedicated intelligence support of operations, while facilitating further development of space missions.

A Whole Force approach to the space enterprise is already well underway with reservists at 7006 (VR) Intelligence – a squadron based in RAF Waddington in Lincolnshire – routinely supporting the SpOC. Their development of new working methods, coupled with a spectrum of intelligence products and services, has provided much-needed context and resulted in an enhanced level of understanding within the operations team.

Additionally, a Senior Operations Officer role (to be filled by a member of the army) and a UK Space Agency-funded Orbital Analyst will enhance the unit's output for both government and defence. The SpOC continues to work closely with the UK Space Agency

Previous pages and right
RAF Fylingdales' Solid State Phased Array Radar stands guard in the North Yorkshire Moors

in the development of national space situational awareness in line with the tenets of the National Space Security Policy. Moreover, reinforcing the UK's long-standing relationship with the US regarding space operations, the RAF makes a significant contribution to the five-eyes Combined Space Operations initiative, in which the UK joins partner nations the US, Canada, Australia and New Zealand. Closer to home, the SpOC is still fully engaged with the European Union space surveillance and tracking framework programme, a consortium comprising the UK, France, Germany, Italy and Spain. The SpOC plays its part through the delivery of space-derived products and services to the other EU member states.

The creation of the Air Operations Branch on 1 April 2018 will contribute to a broader background of RAF personnel working in space-related roles. Ongoing developments in international collaboration will progress with the UK reaping the benefits while also looking ahead to future integration. Additional RAF personnel filling key space roles overseas will enable better working relationships and improved information exchange as the RAF space cadre continues to grow. With the 100th anniversary of the RAF, the Royal Flying Corps' 1912 motto *Per Ardua ad Astra* – "through adversity to the stars" – has never been more appropriate than it is today.

SUPPORTERS AND AFFILIATES

CIVIL AVIATION

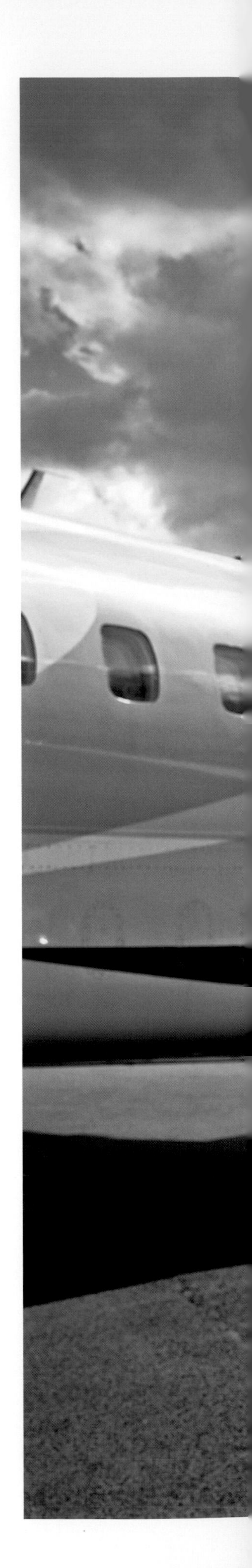

CHARTER OF CHANGE

PrivateFly

"As a pilot, part of your job is to enjoy the experience of flying," says PrivateFly CEO Adam Twidell. "But, as a passenger on an airline, that's often the hellish bit – the worst aspect of getting to or from a fabulous holiday or work trip. With a private jet, the trip is all part of the experience; the journey is the reward."

Former RAF pilot Twidell launched PrivateFly with his wife Carol Cork (pictured, opposite) in 2008, and over the past 10 years the award-winning jet brokerage has achieved incredible success. But the PrivateFly story is about much more than financial return. The company, which now has 42 staff in Britain and the US, combines technological innovation with a passion for customer service. It aims to make private jet hire increasingly efficient, more accessible and better value for passengers around the world.

Twidell's entrepreneurial appetite was whetted when he spotted a gap in the market for a fast and competitive booking service for private jets. It would use online platforms and bespoke software to compare pricing, check availability and book aircraft worldwide. The couple believed so strongly in their business concept that they sold their home to raise the funds needed to get it off the ground.

Adam Twidell spent many years flying C-130 Hercules transporters from RAF Lyneham before becoming a captain on the Citation XLS. He then led London City Airport's successful bid to build a private jet centre at RAF Northolt on the other side of the capital. He has little doubt that his Royal Air Force training and experience has been key to PrivateFly's success.

"When I think of military flying – especially operational flying – it could be very complicated," he says. "Training exercises and military operations were often linked with many other parties, coordinated with troops on the ground, and factoring in the enemy. Moving into private aviation, I could see that it should be simple to fly passengers from A to B on a timescale that suited them. But the legacy-driven industry made this process too complicated. It's simply the process of taking the customer's enquiry, finding the right aircraft for them, and enabling them to fly seamlessly on the day. That's what we set out to do: we wanted to get the technology on our side, to make booking a private jet as seamless and cost-effective as possible for customers."

As well as demystifying the jet charter business, the company has built effective partnerships with the wider supply chain. Also, by working closely with the travel industry, including travel-management companies and airports such as Manchester Airports Group (MAG), PrivateFly has been able to distribute its technology via an application programming interface (API) to travel partners, increasing private aviation awareness and extending the potential customer base. Carol Cork has also drawn on her own career experience in marketing to build a content-driven digital presence, something that has helped PrivateFly attain strong brand awareness in a very targeted way, and also to break down barriers and perceptions about private jet travel to attract a much wider audience.

The results speak for themselves. Launching PrivateFly in the middle of a recession was a risky decision. "Many people said we were mad," admits Cork, "but it proved

to be a shrewd move." Increased price sensitivity meant companies and individuals were looking for greater value and choice and were therefore open to changing their private jet supplier. Within two years PrivateFly had launched the world's first private jet-booking app, and in 2011 the company raised a further £2 million in expansion funding from external investors.

The company used the funds to grow its sales in the UK and set up online booking platforms in France, Germany and Russia in 2012. Two years later, PrivateFly took off in the USA; and in 2016 it opened an office in Fort Lauderdale, Florida in addition to its UK headquarters in St Albans, Hertfordshire. As the company recorded an impressive 50 per cent growth every year over its first decade, so the awards and recognition from the industry and further afield began to mount up.

Adam Twidell has twice been named in the annual Top 10 Leaders of European Business Innovation and is a council member of the BACA industry body. Carol was chosen as one of the Britain's top marketing visionaries in *Marketing Week*'s Vision 100. PrivateFly became the first British company to receive Argus Charter Broker status and subsequently Wyvern Broker status (both best-practice accreditations from the global aviation industry). In 2016 PrivateFly was named in the *Sunday Times*'s Export Track 100 and SME Tech Track 100 (where it appeared again in 2017 and 2018). It also ranked in the inaugural *Financial Times* FT 1000 – a list of Europe's fastest-growing companies across all sectors – in 2017.

"We've managed to make major changes to the way the sector works," says Cork. "There's now a much more blended customer base using private aircraft hire. Around 15 per cent of our customers are first-time users, and that percentage is growing. The old stereotypes of private aircraft hire being just for oligarchs and ultra-high-net-worth individuals are hopelessly outdated. It would be wrong to say that we're rivalling low-cost airlines on price, but we are helping to reduce the entry-level cost and making private jet travel more accessible. Equally, the high-profile business travellers, world leaders and government contracts that we have gained across the world demonstrate the value provided by PrivateFly, which offers transparency and efficiency underpinned by excellent customer service."

So, is PrivateFly's rate of growth maintainable? "Very much so," says Twidell. "The largest company in our sector has less than 2 per cent of the market share, so there's an opportunity to keep on growing, and indeed to accelerate growth." But to achieve this, PrivateFly will be looking at several expansion avenues as well as exploring further RAF connections to help push the business forward.

"Keeping that entrepreneurial spirit and agility alive in your business is one of the big challenges," says Twidell, "and the people you employ are the key to that. The RAF brings in young guys and girls, often straight from school or university, and empowers them by giving them the best training to be able to do a really good job. That's what we need to do to keep our business growing – recruit the right people, then really invest in them, their training and their mentoring. And at the heart of all of that is our undertaking to do everything we can for the customer."

www.privatefly.com

A RUNWAY SUCCESS

Gatwick Airport

"Gatwick is an economic hub," says Stewart Wingate, CEO of Gatwick Airport. "Our impact goes way beyond the boundary fence in attracting business and jobs, and with our new long-haul routes it just gets better." He's justifiably enthusiastic about Gatwick, which has seen an increase of 50 per cent in total passenger numbers in just seven years. Crucially, more people than ever are flying long haul to more than 60 destinations worldwide. "Gatwick now connects the UK to the world, not just to Europe," he says.

Record levels of investment, the adoption of new technology and its proactive commitment to sustainability have contributed to Gatwick being named the world's top international, low-cost airport by the Centre for Aviation in 2017. In the same year it also won Airport of the Year at the National Transport Awards; and the UK's Best Airport at the Airport Operators Association Awards.

Since Gatwick was first licensed as a public aerodrome in 1934, expansion has been spurred on by competition and innovation. As early as 1935, it introduced the ingenious, circular Beehive terminal building: the first in the world to have retractable piers at each gate to shelter passengers as they walked to their aircraft.

Such progress was suspended in 1939, when the Air Ministry requisitioned the airport. RAF Gatwick became a staging airfield for fighter and bomber squadrons being withdrawn from France at the time of Dunkirk. "The crucial role that RAF Gatwick played during the Second World War is well known among our staff and our local community," says Wingate. "It remains a source of pride and inspiration." During preparations for Operation Overlord, Spitfires, Mustangs and Typhoons flew tactical reconnaissance sorties from RAF Gatwick, amassing intelligence vital to the Allied landings.

Commercial services were resumed after Gatwick's post-war refurbishment and in 1958, Her Majesty Queen Elizabeth II reopened London's officially designated second airport. Gatwick was the first major airport to benefit from both a mainline railway station and direct motorway access to London.

Ever responsive to customer demand, Gatwick remains at the forefront of the low-cost-flight revolution that has democratised air travel over the last 20 years. With only one runway and flights increasing year on year, efficiency and cost-effectiveness have been essential in attracting low-cost, full-service and charter flights alike.

"Back in 2004, people were unsure about low-cost air travel," says Wingate, "but nobody questions the viability of low-cost carriers today. On July 4, 2014, Norwegian began to fly to JFK from Gatwick and people started to sit up and take notice. Long-haul routes have now picked up in response to demand, with transformational fares. We already have the strongest European network of any airport on the planet. Now we are adding long-haul destinations such as Seattle, Singapore, Chicago and Buenos Aires. With a catchment area of some 30 million people living within a two-hour journey of Gatwick, we can support long-haul flights to

easyJet.com

R8
HF
L

anywhere in the world." Gatwick now has the fifth largest long-haul network of any airport across Europe; a big boost to the local and national economy.

Investment in technology throughout the airport is the key to Gatwick's ongoing improvement of passenger security and experience. The freedom to implement a new investment programme came about with the break-up of the British Airports Authority's monopoly. "Gatwick was the first airport to go in the subsequent restructuring," says Wingate, who arrived in 2009 to head the new management team. "In separate ownership, we have gone out and marketed ourselves globally. We have invested £250 million per year for the last eight years and plan to do so for the next five."

While competition has forced down airfares, the low-cost culture has at times also lowered standards. "From airfield management to security processes to our retail and restaurant offerings," says Wingate, "our aim is to make the passenger's journey seamless, stress-free and enjoyable."

New self-check-in terminals and bag drops in Gatwick's north and south terminals are speeding up check-in times and giving passengers more liberty to enjoy the airport facilities. Speed isn't paramount for every traveller though.

"Focus groups tell us how stressful it can be travelling with small children, so we have assistance lanes to help families through security," says Wingate. Another new scheme, prompted by a member of staff whose son is autistic, is the provision of lanyards, which identify passengers with hidden disabilities as needing assistance. "Other airports are now following our lead," he says. "It's an example of how we can we improve continually, on the day and in the long term."

One consequence of expansion is the environmental cost. Gatwick, which achieved carbon neutrality in 2017, invests heavily in sustainable technology. It installed a photovoltaic farm; introduced long-lasting LED lighting on the runway; and built a waste-processing plant that converts waste from the planes into energy. Anti-whine devices have been retrofitted to planes, which, together with a continuous descent policy, has significantly reduced noise pollution. "We have the same carbon footprint as we did in 1999 when we served half the number of passengers," says Wingate. "Our ambition is to become Britain's most sustainable airport."

Energised by more long-haul routes, Gatwick is on course to serve a projected 50 million passengers annually. Yet, of the world's top 20 airports (measured by passenger growth), it is the only one operating a single runway. "We continue to offer the UK a financeable and deliverable second runway scheme," says Wingate, "which we stand ready to deliver should the government give us the go-ahead."

Sustained investment and the ability to attract new airlines and long-haul routes make Gatwick Airport one of the most dynamic airports in the world. "Gatwick is a national success story and the airport for the future," says Wingate. "We're proud that we have become a vital part of the country's infrastructure; and we recognise the important part we have to play in Britain's future."
www.gatwickairport.com

CENTRE OF ATTENTION

Caribbean Aviation Training Center

The Caribbean Aviation Training Center (CATC) never forgets any of its graduates. In fact, it has a method for ensuring that every pilot who passes through its doors is remembered.

"When a student completes their first solo flight, we cut the back off their shirt as a symbol," says Marketing Director Brianne Stewart. "They then have to draw a picture on the back of the shirt describing their experience on their first flight. We have an entire wall dedicated to our 'solo shirts'."

It's this kind of personal touch that makes learning to fly in Kingston, Jamaica such an enticing prospect. Of course, it doesn't hurt that Kingston is a beautiful city with glorious beaches and abundant cultural attractions. But for all of the centre's intimacy and the splendour of its setting, CATC is rooted firmly in its RAF heritage. Its founder, Captain Errol Stewart, trained at the Royal Military Academy, Sandhurst. Stewart has now graduated from pilot teacher to CEO but his fiercely high standards still infuse every aspect of the company he established back in 2000.

CATC offers a perfect grounding for training to be a leisure pilot, although – from working in commercial travel to private business transport – its courses are designed to be a foundation for aviation in all its forms. Jamaica's varied landscape offers challenges and opportunities that are ideal for learning every aspect of the profession.

"We are able to teach everything from mountain flying to learning how to manoeuvre in certain temperatures," says Stewart. "In America, pilots mainly learn over flat land so they don't have the challenge of mountain ranges where the wind can vary. Also, you'll learn to fly over sea in Jamaica – we often fly to the Caymans."

CATC is relatively small in size and, with pilots from all over the world attracted by its growing reputation, demand for places is high. The centre's management looks for certain personality types when selecting successful candidates. "Typical students are hard-working, determined people who know what their end goal is," says Stewart. "We want people who have self-discipline. People need to be goal-orientated and very hands-on."

Once on board, students can expect training of the highest quality. CATC works in partnership with Cessna, a company whose small planes are a byword for reliability. It is also looking to bring the first motion simulator to the Caribbean. Students are encouraged to learn at their own pace, tailoring their progress to their own particular abilities. What's eventually achieved is a grounding that is transferable worldwide.

Qualification levels range from Private Pilot Licences to the Airline Transport Pilot Licence. These international-standard diplomas, Stewart believes, have never been more relevant. "This is the best time there's ever been to learn to fly," she says. "Because currently the demand for pilots is increasing and the market is growing. It feels like every day there's a new fleet being launched or a new company opening up. Businesses are hiring corporate pilots. The need for pilots is increasing everywhere."

Still, however far they roam, graduates of CATC can expect to be remembered. They will always be a part of the Jamaica training centre – not just because of their commemorative 'solo shirt' – and that's exactly how the company likes it. Its pastoral care is ongoing. "We keep in contact with all of our students after they've left us," says Stewart. "We are a family here."

www.catcja.com

GATEWAY TO THE WORLD

Heathrow Airport

Heathrow is the largest international airport in Europe, where more than 200,000 passengers a day travel on 1,293 flights to any of 194 destinations in 82 countries. And it's all thanks to the Royal Air Force.

"Heathrow was originally used as an RAF base, but by the time it was completed the war was over so it was used as a commercial airfield – the first aircraft to take off from Heathrow was a converted Lancaster bomber called *Starlight* that flew to Buenos Aires," explains John Holland-Kaye, Heathrow's CEO. "Now this is where the world connects. We link so many countries around the world, so it's a real mix of people and that means we need to cater for many different cultures. For instance, we have just updated our website so it can be translated into around 50 languages."

The airport is constantly looking at ways it can expand and improve its offerings for passengers. It is consistently voted the best for shopping, and per square foot the big brand stores at Heathrow generate more income than their West End equivalents. But not everyone likes to shop, and alongside summer activities for kids and a range of restaurants, including franchises from Michelin-starred Gordon Ramsay and Heston Blumenthal, the airport is planning to open an exercise, health and well-being space. A floor beneath the Terminal 2 departure lounge will be transformed into an area for exercise and nutrition. "We are leading the way in understanding what passengers want and ensuring we provide it," says Holland-Kaye.

The importance of Heathrow is illustrated by the fact that it is the UK's largest single-site employer, with around 76,000 people having jobs at the airport. Many of these are locals. It's estimated that around 10,000 people living in the London Borough of Hounslow work at Heathrow, alongside 9,000 from the neighbouring borough of Hillingdon and 5,800 from Ealing. "It is part of their lives," says Holland-Kaye. "And that community is important to us. So we work with local schools and have a local apprenticeship scheme. We also encourage children to come into construction – we have a Primary School Challenge where we help them understand design and build mini terminals."

Yet, despite its size, history and importance to the UK, there are still aspects of Heathrow that can delight and surprise. There's the as yet unused railway station beneath Terminal 5, which was constructed in 2008 in anticipation of new rail links being added to Heathrow at some point in the future. There's also the Animal Reception Centre, where all furry and scaled new arrivals are processed, including more fish per year than human passengers. Heathrow is the biggest UK port by value for non-EU exports, used for transporting high-value, low-weight cargo, often stored in the belly of commercial aircraft. "People have no idea what travels under their feet when they fly," says Holland-Kaye. "One of our largest exports is salmon from Scotland, but it could be legal documents and jewels. Cargo is a vital part of our work, it is one of our biggest areas."

Heathrow has long-standing connections with the Royal Family, who regularly open new buildings and also use the airport on a regular basis when travelling. "The Queen touched down at Heathrow when she became Queen," says Holland-Kaye. "This is the first place her feet touched British soil." Attention is now focussed on Heathrow's future rather than its past, with the airport hoping to grow so it can become a bigger, as well as a better, place for travel in and out of the UK.

www.heathrow.com

CALL AND RESPONSE

Bristow Group

Now regarded as the world's foremost provider of industrial aviation services, Bristow Group began life as Bristow Helicopters, named for its charismatic founder, Alan Bristow. Over the period of his adventurous life, Bristow earned a host of honours, from a Royal Aeronautical Society Silver Medal to the Croix de Guerre, awarded for rescuing soldiers in Vietnam while under mortar fire.

After serving as a pilot in the Second World War, he worked as a test pilot before founding Bristow Helicopters in 1955. The firm started out in oil exploration and personnel transportation, and expanded over the following decades to provide services around the world. It evolved into the Bristow Group in 1996, and now holds the British government contract to supply search-and-rescue (SAR) helicopter services all over the UK on behalf of the Maritime and Coastguard Agency.

"We provide a service 24 hours a day, seven days a week, 365 days a year from 10 bases strategically located around the UK," says Bristow Group's Director of UK SAR Russell Torbet, who retired from a distinguished career in the RAF with the rank of Air Commodore.

Although Bristow Group works for the coastguard agency, it also covers land rescue. "In the summer, people go out exploring or biking in the mountains," says Torbet. "But, despite all the publicity warnings, some underestimate how quickly the weather can change, and get themselves into difficulties."

If an SAR team can reach those involved in an incident within an hour – known as the "Golden Hour" – then their chances of survival are increased significantly. "We have demanding response times, but fortunately our Sikorsky S-92A and AgustaWestland AW189 can transit at 145 mph, with a top speed of 165 mph," says Torbet. "Our helicopters are fully night-vision equipped, with forward-looking infrared sensors, as well as extremely effective search radar."

Bristow's contract, awarded in 2013, requires it to assimilate military crews as pilots and technical crew. As a result, having been inundated with applications, the company has been able to take on the cream of SAR pilots and crew from the RAF and the Royal Navy.

"Our ethos closely resembles that of the RAF," explains Torbet. "So Bristow Group is able to take their best practice, as well as that of the Royal Navy, to implement standards that any of the military services would be impressed by."

www.bristowgroup.com/uk-sar

CHANGE IN THE AIR

Mark Physsas Architects

Mark Physsas has always been fascinated by aircraft. Born to a British Cypriot mother and a Greek Cypriot father in Hendon, north London, he used to visit the RAF Museum in nearby Colindale as a boy. He did National Service with the Cyprus Air Force, working as a junior mechanic, and went on to study architecture. Nevertheless, he hadn't planned to design airport facilities until he happened upon a company looking to develop an airport in the Middle East.

Although Physsas and his team work on all manner of projects, including retail and residential, their work in aviation architecture is most significant. And it presents quite specific challenges, particularly as airports are often 24-hour operations. "In a lot of architectural work," says Physsas, "you can readily close down part of a building to do a renovation or an extension. You can't do that when refurbishing an airport terminal, as capacity demands need to be met throughout the build. For example, the number of check-in desks may need to be maintained throughout construction. We need to be able to develop designs that can work round most existing spaces."

The company's solution, after assessing and surveying the area in question, is to build off-site. "In some cases we build somewhere else and then install it," says Physsas. "It takes considerable time, effort and coordination to get that right. You spend more time developing solutions with manufacturers than you would in other sectors."

While a new-build airport can take between six to 12 years from conception to completion, some of the company's work involves renovating existing airports. Physsas estimates that Gatwick and Heathrow spend around £1 billion a year on airport development. Much of that is on infrastructure, so he and his team are consulted about all sorts of issues. "When security searches in departure areas became more rigorous," he says, "designers had to find a solution to that rule when you could only take 100ml vessels of liquid in a tiny little bag. Where do you put new bins in such a constrained area? How do you manage that process and educate passengers? A lot of time is spent tweaking things and working out the most efficient way."

Physsas worked as an architect for 10 years before starting his own company in 2013. He currently has five full-time staff and around 16 freelancers. For him, small is beautiful. "Building a team based primarily on freelancers definitely helps keep things fresh and alive."
www.physsas.co.uk

AIR CARE

Iberia Maintenance

A century ago, when powered flight was still in its infancy, the volume and efficiency of today's air travel market would have been inconceivable. And, as with many services we take largely for granted, the action off-stage is as important as the main event. When we take our seats, we rarely think about the attention to detail that goes into keeping several hundred tons of metal safely airborne every day. Such is the work of Maintenance, Repair and Operations (MROs). It's in the hands of these heroes hidden in the hangar that our peace of mind unconsciously lies.

For 90 years, Iberia Maintenance has undertaken skilled engineering work in the airline sector. It now employs more than 2,600 technicians, working on the full spectrum of integrated services. One of its slogans is "Fly safe, fly on time", and Iberia Maintenance is proud to be the MRO provider for the world's most punctual airlines. According to FlightStats. Iberia was the world's most punctual international network carrier in 2016 and 2017, while Iberia Express has been the world's most punctual low-cost carrier from 2014 to 2017.

The benefits to customers of Iberia technicians' expertise are incontestable. But their work is also of vital importance to the company's bottom line in a feverishly competitive market. Iberia merged with British Airways in 2010, though both continued to use their own brand under the umbrella company International Airlines Group (IAG). This move has delivered increased financial strength and opportunities for both carriers to learn from each other in their deployment of the latest technology. Through the use of lean processing and critical chain project management Iberia has been able to increase the efficiency and quality of its MRO services. It helps its customers to reduce their costs and the effort they invest in managing the maintenance of aircraft, engines and parts.

The firm's remit extends far beyond passenger and civilian planes. Iberia Maintenance works closely with OEMs (original equipment manufacturers) and major operators and has recently signed a new long-term deal to maintain DHL engines. It has also added new services such as converting passenger A330s for reconfiguration as Multirole Tanker Transports, for in-flight refuelling. The challenges continue, with a new generation of Airbuses (the A350-900 and A320neo) coming on-stream in 2018, together with the training required for technicians to be certified to repair and overhaul the aircraft.

Iberia Maintenance is currently undergoing a wide-ranging transformation to become more efficient and competitive. It is investing in staff training and equipment, hiring more people at its Madrid and Barcelona maintenance facilities and buying new digital tools to improve its productivity. It is also developing a new training scheme with the Madrid regional government to bring through the maintenance technicians of the future.

The ever-expanding commercial aviation industry brings opportunities and demands to the MRO industry in equal measure. More modern, technically complex aircraft, super-efficient engines and the expectation of bespoke, customised services to each airline on its roster. Competition might be fierce, but Iberia Maintenance is ready to meet those challenges.

www.iberia.com

IBERIA
EC-JBA

TAG
Aviation

THE PERSONAL TOUCH

TAG Aviation

Exit the M3 at junction 4a, take the A327, signposted Ively Road, drive past seven small roundabouts and, just past the Monkey Puzzle pub on your left, you'll arrive at the home of Britain's first powered flight: TAG Farnborough Airport. After you're waved through the VIP gate (the man in the hut will already have your details), the first thing you'll notice are the metallic, otherworldly buildings.

The 5,000 sq m terminal has an aluminium shingle facade and gently bends to mimic an aircraft wing; the 34 m-high control tower, with its two domed, glass-fronted offices to either side, peeps up like a submarine periscope; and the enormous 12,500 sq m hangar, split into three swooshing sections, resembles silver waves spied from a distance. It's less Heathrow, more Houston.

You won't, however, have much time to take all this in. "You'll park up and it's a 20-yard walk to the terminal," explains Graham Williamson, TAG Aviation's President of Aircraft Management and Charter. "Inside, you will be greeted by your captain and then a concierge will escort you straight to the aircraft, which will already be ready to go. It's probably another 20 yards to the ramp. Then you're in the air."

Today, Farnborough is the UK's only airport dedicated to business flights, run by the sister business of the famed Swiss watch marque. The level of discretion that it offers means it's frequently visited by singers, sports stars, state leaders and secret agents (pay attention the next time you watch *Quantum of Solace*), but increasingly it's also used by ordinary business professionals who want to save time.

"In Europe, there's the perception that this is only for billionaires," says Williamson, "but if you hire a four-seater to a short-haul destination, it'll cost €2,000–€3,000 per hour. That's not much more than a business-class seat but it gives you speed, convenience and access."

The perks aren't just about saving time, either. You're the only passengers on the plane, you choose the crew and you control the schedule. You can even dictate when the aircraft takes off. "Catering and in-flight entertainment are bespoke," adds Williamson. "Want a pizza from a particular London restaurant? A certain bottle of wine? We'll do everything we can to make it happen."

And the exit is more seamless still. "When you land at Farnborough, a customs chap walks up the steps to check your passport, and a car drives to the ramp to whisk you off to your destination."

As well as running this site, TAG offers both aircraft charter and management. If you choose the former, you'll have access to Europe's largest fleet of aircraft. There are three options: call and fly (think pay-as-you-go for private jets), TAG account (designed for frequent flyers who benefit from on-call account managers) and TAG lease (where you rent a jet and the use of a crew for a set amount of time). On the other hand, if you simply require management for your own jet, TAG can handle all of your day-to-day needs, from providing a dedicated pilot to using its pooling power to negotiate deals on fuel, insurance and hangar space.

Williamson, though, puts it all more succinctly. "This is not about champagne and caviar," he says. "It's about forming relationships with individuals and maximising the time of companies that generate jobs and wealth. Because if we don't provide that ultimate level of service, the benefits are gone. We're the custodians of Farnborough now."

www.tagaviation.com

PROP STAR

328 Support Services GmbH

The story of the turboprop-powered Dornier 328 airliner is reminiscent of the classic fable about the tortoise and the hare. The perennial back-marker has, in recent years, flown – both literally and metaphorically – past its rivals. The aircraft now boasts, among other attributes, a strong and proven reliability record within the US military service.

To begin at the beginning, German firm Dornier Flugzeugwerke was, in the 1970s, the world's oldest family-owned aircraft manufacturer. A series of takeovers decoupled the company, but the early 1990s proved a key milestone with the launch of the 328 aircraft under Deutsche Aerospace. "The 328 was so well engineered that it was actually last in its class to be released to market," says Ray Mosses, Sales Director of 328 Support Services GmbH. "The engineers were so focused on quality and cutting-edge technology that, by the time it was released, most people had already selected an alternative regional aircraft."

Deutsche Aerospace sold Dornier to US manufacturer Fairchild, which went out of business, as did its successor AvCraft between 2001 and 2005. Its type certificate – the licence needed to maintain the aircraft's airworthy condition – reverted to the German national authority and the 328, while still operational, was in limbo. In 2005 a British consortium, 328 Support Services GmbH, recognised the high-end design of the 328. Seeing its potential for refurbishment to VIP or emergency medical evacuation purposes – bid on for the type certificate, beating competition and keeping engineering jobs in Germany.

The company enjoyed a number of early successes, but it was an encounter with US-based Sierra Nevada Corporation (SNC) that proved to be a game-changer. SNC, a Tier-One Superior Supplier for the US Air Force, was seeking a transport aircraft to meet particular requirements (for example, the ability to land inside of 1,000 metres and carry 30 passengers). Of the hundreds of aircraft SNC evaluated, the best fit was the Dornier 328.

Not all 328s met SNC's highly specific requirements. The 328 team had to ensure adherence to the contract's strict demands, and each aircraft underwent six months of modifications including engine maintenance and propeller overhauls. Other modifications included Auxiliary Power Unit (APU) retrofits, ground spoilers modifications, fitting of gravel kits, avionics upgrades and high-frequency communications systems, as well as flight deck standardisation.

The initial high specification of the 328 was suddenly a major benefit. Its digital "glass" cockpit allowed for the latest avionics upgrades and the ability to integrate night vision imaging system (NVIS) capability. As 328 had its own design team, it could implement the many conversions needed to deliver 20 aircraft on budget. "All the modifications existed separately in other aircraft," says Mosses, "but SNC was the first customer to bring them together in one state-of-the-art offering to become the most advanced 328 that has ever operated."

SNC acquired 328 in 2015. While there's more military work on the horizon, future efforts may also return to the commercial sector. "All those Saabs, Bombardiers and Embraers are now 25 to 30 years old and their avionics aren't up to modern standards," says Mosses. "This means that the 328 is ideally placed to replace them." After two decades, the Dornier 328 outpaces it competitors. Its flexibility and durability – and the continued support of meticulous German engineering – have made this versatile, market-ready superstar more than a match for the competition.

www.328.eu

A REGIONAL HIGH-FLYER

Skyworld Aviation

"You can't be a jack of all trades when it comes to aviation," says Chris Beer, Managing Director of Skyworld Aviation. Beer launched the company in 1996 when he spotted the need for specialist knowledge in the world of regional aviation. "We provide a knowledgeable, high-quality service to regional operators and owners," he says. "There are a lot of brokers in the industry, but they are focused on doing a deal. They're not providing the additional expertise and services that we do."

Based in the UK, with offices in France and Canada, the independent company is now in its 22nd year of trading. It has built up an enviable global reputation for sourcing, marketing, leasing and managing regional aircraft, usually those with up to 120 seats. With satisfied clients from Kenya to Canada and Mexico to Mongolia, Skyworld Aviation has now concluded more than 540 aircraft-related transactions, with a value of around $1 billion, and the full-service professional package it provides to clients has been key to that success.

Recent transactions carried out by Skyworld Aviation underline the range and depth of this expertise. In 2015, the company was exclusively appointed by LOT Polish Airlines to market its fleet of Embraer 170s, successfully coordinating the sale and leaseback of six aircraft to a global private-investment firm. All six continued in revenue service with LOT, with some offered for sub-lease. The following year, Skyworld Aviation arranged the sale of an ATR 72–200, previously operated by Canaryfly, to Sprint Air of Poland (a Skyworld client since 2005), which became the airline's first passenger-configured aircraft of that model.

Highlights in 2017 included arranging the leases of two Saab 2000s to Skywork Airlines of Switzerland, the sale of an ATR 42-300 QC to Tennessee-based Kolob Canyons Air Services, and the sale of two Embraer ERJ 145 LRs, previously operated on lease by AeroMexico Connect.

"There's a growing market in regional aviation, particularly in Africa, parts of Asia and South America, even though the number of regional aircraft being manufactured has fallen," says Beer. "We are continuing to expand our brand – it's rare to find a company like us, with such strong expertise and experience in regional aviation."

www.skyworld.co.uk

MILITARY ADVANTAGE

Vantage Aviation

If you were looking for someone to teach you to fly, you could do a lot worse than the first Royal Navy pilot in more than 50 years to have received the Distinguished Flying Cross. Commander James Newton won this rare distinction for gallantry under fire during operations in Iraq during the second Gulf War in 2003. These days, he runs a flying school – Vantage Aviation – but one with a difference.

"Our specialism provides a link between the private and the commercial licences and those wanting to become search-and-rescue pilots, police pilots or helicopter emergency services [HEM] pilots," says Newton. "And, beyond that, skill-sets for counterterrorism."

This is where a forces background is indispensable. All of Vantage's instructors have trained on helicopters and fixed-wing aircraft, and all are ex-military. "We build three things for a client – operational capacity of captains, situational awareness and a military-type ethos," says Newton. This does not mean a boot-camp, more a state of mind. "The military is a very can-do place," he says. "You demonstrate where the benefit is in behavioural change and the civilian client sees the positives."

At its two bases – one in Wiltshire, one in Tampa, Florida – Vantage offers bespoke training packages, tailored to client needs. "We supply accommodation, housekeeping, chefs and English-language training if required," says Newton. "We conduct cultural tours and we integrate students with social activities in the UK or US, so they can grow and understand a different culture."

Vantage launched in 2007, while Newton was still serving. It has since caught the eye of numerous governments, leading to work across the Americas, the Middle East and Asia. "There's a huge appetite in Asia, even for basic training," says Newton. "But for more advanced operations, there's an inordinate amount of money being spent on high-grade military pilots training on the job, which is costly and time-consuming. We close that gap, training civilian pilots so they're ready for more advanced roles from day one."

Vantage's front-foot ethos was evident in September 2017, when Hurricane Irma hit Florida. Far from seeking to protect valuable aircraft, Newton and his staff ferried families to safety and helped with search-and-rescue. "I had experience from Hurricane Mitch in 1998, so made some provision – then it's about doing what you can." It's a mantra that serves Vantage – and an expanding list of clients – very well indeed.

www.vantageaviation.co.uk

BLUE-SKY THINKING

Baines Simmons Ltd

"A one-stop-shop for all things aviation safety," is how founder Bob Simmons, former RAF aircraft technician and civil aviation surveyor, describes his company, Baines Simmons. Founded in 2001, the firm specialises in aviation regulations and safety management, partnering with leading civil and military aviation organisations worldwide. In 2015, it became part of the global aviation services group Air Partner plc.

"Our safety philosophy is that things be practical, progressive and objective," says Simmons. "It's all about filling the gap between the regulated and the regulators. We want to make a real and lasting impact on aviation safety." This means improving everything from reliability of parts, availability of aircraft and error reporting, to risk-based decision-making, performance of flight crews and cost controls.

"Our experience across civil and military aviation, together with our range of consultancy and training services, makes us unique," says Simmons. "A good example is our work with the Ministry of Defence. We helped them build a positive and proactive safety culture that would contribute to the prevention of aircraft accidents."

Another defence contract involved assessing the error management of the Fleet Air Arm of the Royal Navy, which operates around 200 combat aircraft. The project team used an "Error Management Diagnostic", which involved 793 surveys, 150 interviews and visiting two Royal Navy air stations, one aircraft carrier and one Type 23 destroyer. The firm has also recently won a four-year contract with the European Defence Agency to provide consultancy and training services.

Baines Simmons also works with numerous national carriers, including Malaysia Airlines, Air Greenland, Qantas and Air New Zealand. "For KLM, we implemented an entire safety culture and management system," says Simmons. "We developed a strategic-level safety-management road map to lead the way forward." It was a great success with many new initiatives implemented, and KLM was voted Europe's safest airline in 2014.

Baines Simmons is known for its cutting-edge thinking. "Working alongside such a range of aviation organisations has provided us with unique insights into emerging regulatory initiatives," says Simmons. "It has resulted in an extraordinary wealth of knowledge which we apply across the whole of the industry." The firm's ultimate goal is to make the skies safer, by helping organisations with their safety challenges, and to help decrease the accident rate. The sky is genuinely the limit.

www.bainessimmons.com

WINGING THE CHANGES

Bristol Airport

Air travel is central to the world we inhabit. The sights, experiences, opportunities and connections that were closed to most only a few decades ago are now accessible to millions of people.

"Forecasts suggest that, in the future, the world's growing population will include more people who travel," says Simon Earles, Bristol Airport's Planning and Sustainability Director. "And, with demographic shifts, global air passengers could double in 20 years. It will be a changing, more connected population."

Since it opened in 1930 on its original site at Whitchurch, Bristol Airport has been in the vanguard of aviation's relentless forward march. It moved to Lulsgate, north Somerset, in 1957 to accommodate increasing traffic. Today it is on the verge of further major expansion.

At the moment, Britain's third-largest regional airport is the ninth busiest in the country. As the primary international gateway for the South West of England and South Wales, its significance to the region cannot be underestimated. It supports an estimated 15,000 local jobs and generates £1.3 billion for the local economy.

It serves a vibrant area, too. Bristol is home to world-class universities, major multinational businesses and a wealth of tourist attractions. "The local economy is thriving, and Bristol Airport is playing its part," says Earles. "We are more connected than ever, with over 120 destinations. We have invested £160 million in facilities since 2010, to ensure that customers have an amazing journey."

With the increasing demand for air travel. Britain's place in the world is changing. "The pace of change in this globalised world is not going to slow," says Earles. "New aircraft technology, the automation of passenger processes and digitalisation will present new demands and opportunities." The challenges of changing technology and climate change will usher in more fuel-efficient – and even electric – aircraft.

Having celebrated its 60th anniversary last year, the focus is now set firmly on the future. This year the airport is preparing to make public its expansion plan, looking towards handling up to 20 million passengers a year by the mid-2040s. Given that in 2018 its airline partners will fly more than 8.7 million passengers to over 120 destinations across 34 countries, that is indeed impressive growth. Bristol Airport's future, then, looks every bit as rosy as its past.

www.bristolairport.co.uk

THE CITY-CENTRE AIRPORT

London City Airport

For many air passengers, there's nothing to match the experience of swooping over the river and landing amid the skyscrapers at London City Airport (LCY). This international airport has been in operation since 1987, built on reclaimed dockland next to the Thames close to London's financial centre. As it embarks on a £480 million development, the airport is determined to shake off perceptions of London's "best kept secret".

"We are unique in London in terms of the size of our runway, but we don't let that stop our ambitions," says Alison FitzGerald, London City Airport's Chief Operating Officer. "Where historically we have been predominantly business, we have recently tipped to predominantly leisure, and we want to maximise the space we have to take larger aeroplanes. Because of our location, we need to be very innovative in the way we manage our operation and for that we can turn to the latest technology."

LCY's expansion includes the construction of a new digital air-traffic-control tower, due to come into operation in 2020 to replace the original tower built in 1987. The airport was constructed on what were formerly the world's largest man-made docks, heavily defended by the RAF during the Second World War. Those RAF connections remain in place today. When the Royal Family have used LCY they have flown on an RAF-operated BAE146 aircraft, part of 32 Royal Squadron. The Duke of Edinburgh, who became a Marshal of the Royal Air Force in 1953, once made the journey from Buckingham Palace to LCY in 19 minutes, and unsurprisingly announced that this was "wonderfully convenient".

This sense of convenience is something that City prides itself on. In its three decades, the airport has grown from 133,000 annual passengers to 4.5 million, but can still process passengers in 20 minutes or less, and had the best On Time Performance of any UK airport in 2017. This is partly born of necessity. As FitzGerald points out, if passengers were delayed then queues would begin inside the adjacent DLR train station. "That's the reality of the challenge," she says. "So we continually look at passenger volumes and try to maintain these levels. We have invested in technology like new common-use bag drops, and will ultimately have these planted in places like Canary Wharf and ExCel for remote processing. Speed is a priority and we do that without compromising safety."

The new 50-metre control tower is a case in point. Groundbreaking and gamechanging, it features 14 high-definition cameras providing a 360-degree view of the airfield, which is translated into a 270-degree view on the screens, thereby allowing controllers to see the whole airfield without turning round. "It's all right in front of them," says FitzGerald. "We can augment the view with aircraft call signs, tag and track moving objects and add on-screen labels. These tools enhance the safety and efficiency of operations – controllers have more information at their fingertips."

Given LCY's central location, it is also important to ensure the control tower is aesthetically appealing, and City takes its neighbours very seriously. "We work a lot with local schools and residents, as we recognise we have neighbours and want a happy coexistence," says FitzGerald. A big part of the regeneration of east London since the 1980s, the airport is still growing. "We now have significant development with eight new aircraft stands, a parallel taxiway and a passenger terminal quadrupling in size. We are also certifying aircraft that are quieter, more efficient, travel further and carry more passengers. There's a lot to give us optimism for the next 30 years."

www.londoncityairport.com

SMOOTH OPERATOR

Signature Flight Support

"We treat the military with the same service as anyone who owns or runs a private aircraft," says Evie Freeman, Managing Director (Europe, Middle East, Africa) of Signature Flight Support. Signature is a company known in the aviation industry as an FBO, or fixed-base operator.

FBOs work with a range of customers: charter operators, corporate flight and travel departments, individual owners and, indeed, departments of defence. They do not own or operate aircraft, but they supply support services to those who do. "We provide everything they need when they're not flying," says Freeman. In other words, the aircraft are hangered and maintained in a state of readiness, with high-level ground services on offer to passengers and crew.

Signature can also assist with flight plans through its partner Gama Aviation, meaning the service is genuinely end-to-end. "We call it 'on-demand aviation'," says Freeman. "And it is this level of personalised service that sets us apart. We really take the time to get to know our customers."

Under its parent company BBA Aviation, Signature has spent a number of years helping the RAF, both in the UK – where it has 14 bases, including London Biggin Hill in Kent – and on joint-training missions in the United States and Canada. "We're exceedingly proud to be able to support the RAF," says Freeman.

From its inception in 1992, when it had 20 bases globally, the firm now boasts more than 200 fixed-base operations worldwide. Part of this expansion relies on a programme called Signature Select, where smaller, independent FBOs come under a larger firm's umbrella, either retaining their own branding or adopting Signature's. Either way, the relationship helps both parties.

"It's 'franchise-lite', if you like," says Freeman. "It gives us the ability to be relevant to our customer by providing more locations and, individually, it helps them achieve their business goals as well. Independent brands like Menzies Executive in Barcelona or Magnum FBO in Vienna are good examples. It allows us to provide a very consistent and cohesive customer experience no matter which location our customers visit around our network."

The service is undeniably high-end – and designed to be so – but Signature also takes its commitment to corporate social responsibility very seriously. The firm has partnered with Air BP to ensure that anyone using its sterling credit card to buy jet fuel will have the carbon generated by that fuel offset with no cost to the customer. The customer also receives carbon credits, which are tallied at the end of the year, and a certificate that can be used for their own CSR requirements. This means that they are using private aviation in an environmentally responsible manner.

In addition, many of the company's ground buildings are powered by solar array, while much of the ground service equipment (such as tugs) is electric or driven by clean propane. Freeman notes that the Green Building Council – the UK arm of a global network promoting sustainability – offers certification of buildings (silver, gold and platinum) according to their environmental credentials. "All of the facilities that Signature is building or renovating will have at least a silver rating, if not platinum, in their design," she says. "For us, sustainability is a core performance indicator."

Whether in the military or civilian arena, Signature Flight Support is dedicated to the highest of standards and providing a service that is as tailored and individual as its name suggests.

www.signatureflight.com

DANGER
KEEP CLEAR
DANGER
KEEP CLEAR

BUSINESS AND INDUSTRY

"Not only does the Royal Air Force play an essential role in the defence of the UK and its overseas territories, but it also contributes enormously to the nation's stability, prosperity and standing on the global stage

MARKET FORCES

Bank of America Merrill Lynch

"While serving as an RAF Tornado pilot in Afghanistan, I advised senior military commanders on making decisions and solved complex problems based on the information available," says Richard Aboboto. "In a way, working at Bank of America Merrill Lynch isn't markedly different from being in the cockpit of a Tornado GR4. I'm using a lot of the skills I learned in the military."

Aboboto works in research marketing at Bank of America Merrill Lynch and is a member of the Military Network, one of the bank's 11 employee networks designed to nurture and strengthen a sense of community among its employees. Diversity and inclusion are key values for the bank, and the Military Network won a Gold Award in the Ministry of Defence's 2016 Defence Employer Recognition Scheme.

The network supports those serving in the forces, past and present, and their families. It promotes the value of service, teamwork and leadership – values common to both employment fields. It also recruits and mentors some of the finest veteran talent. "There are a lot of similarities and transferable skills," says Aboboto. "Both jobs involve multitasking, working in a high-pressure environment and in small teams."

As a global leader in research marketing, it is essential that Bank of America Merrill Lynch delivers a consistent and inclusive message to its clients. "As a firm," says Aboboto, "we will typically produce around 150 to 200 pieces of overnight research, globally. In my marketing role, I am inundated with research, content and trading ideas. My job is to distil that into two or three high-conviction ideas so that the bank's voice and message are coherent for our clients."

In a fast-moving world, working in the financial sector at this level requires multi-skilled employees who can adapt quickly to different situations. "We work hard to make sure our messages are both clear and relevant," says Aboboto, "without being influenced by temporary or sudden changes in market sentiment." There is also the need to stay objective, especially in today's volatile and often divisive political climate. "The main challenge is putting out an informed view backed up by research," says Aboboto, "but also not being seen to take one side or the other, because there are political and reputational risks at stake. Our primary goal is to provide relevant independent analysis and insightful research to our clients."

www.bofaml.com

LAND, SEA AND SKY

BMT

"Risk management is a big part of what we do," says Guy Tomlinson, Capability and Strategy Director of the multi-disciplinary consultancy BMT. "Our specialists are well placed to help understand and manage the consequences of certain decisions and choices." In this capacity, the company has played a key role in some landmark events, including the investigation into the tragic 1987 capsizing of the *Herald of Free Enterprise*. On land, BMT has helped test and improve the design of everything from some of the world's tallest buildings to its fastest racing cars. It is even part of the European Space Agency development team.

BMT is an international design, engineering, science and risk-management consultancy with a reputation for engineering excellence. It was formed as the British Maritime Technology Group in 1985 from the merger of the British Shipbuilding Research Association and the National Maritime Institute.

BMT has a special, but not necessarily well-known, place in Royal Air Force history. The organisation ran the ship tanks at Feltham in west London, where Barnes Wallis tested the concept of the bouncing bomb, and BMT's heritage is traceable back to that. The bouncing bomb was, of course, used by 617 Squadron – better known as the Dam Busters – to destroy Hitler's dams in Operation Chastise in 1943.

"Ship tanks are long, instrumented tanks of water through which you can propel a scale model of a hull," says Tomlinson. "You can test the hydrodynamics of designs, see how buoyant they are in water, look at how much wake they're creating, and examine their resistance through the water and the flow of water around them. These ship tanks were what our predecessor organisations used for designing future maritime platforms. Nowadays, much of this work is done with computational fluid dynamics (CFD) and in emulating those sorts of facilities." BMT's designers were responsible for creating the new QEC aircraft carrier. In a pleasing revival of the old Dam Busters connection, 617 Squadron will be the first Royal Air Force crews to fly Lightning II aircraft from that carrier.

The company's connection with water is well-known but possibly over-emphasised. "In the UK, people view us as a naval architecture business," says Tomlinson. "We've certainly got plenty of pedigree in specialist vessel design." But BMT has also worked extensively with the RAF on a variety of aircraft, including the Tornado, Nimrod and Hawk. "The Tornado work is interesting," says Tomlinson, who himself served in the RAF for 23 years. "Our specialist project-management team helped to define its user and system requirements. They supported the customer in understanding how to define what they needed to deliver the capability."

BMT also has a contract with the Ministry of Defence to support the Air Defence & Electronic Warfare Systems Delivery Team. Often based in remote locations, these specialists are responsible for the through-life capability management of air defence and ground-based electronic warfare systems.

BMT has supported the RAF on the Airbus A400M programme, developing its strategy to deliver the aircraft fleet; and providing through-life logistical maintenance. "The A400M Atlas is a key platform," says Tomlinson, "delivering tactical airlift and strategic oversize lift capabilities for the RAF. We help support the project team in development of the value-for-money benchmark for the in-service support phase, helping understand and define those requirements and understanding the consequences of taking those decisions.

"Defence is a significant part of our business," continues Tomlinson. "It probably accounts for over half our revenue. And given the fact that we are a specialist consultancy in engineering, there's a design, an engineering, a science and a risk-management skill set that we bring to a lot of different areas of defence. But we're much broader even than that. We have a commercial shipping focus, an environmental focus and a critical infrastructure focus."

BMT is involved throughout the life cycle of a defence project. "Where there's a mid-life update," says Tomlinson, "or an issue with a platform that needs resolving, we have the expertise and credibility. We understand the consequences of changes to design. The more specialisation and skill you use at the front end of a project, the more you can reduce the risk down the line; and the more you can foresee the operational consequences of decisions that are being taken."

Sarah Kenny, who was appointed Chief Executive of BMT in 2017, aims to optimise this breadth by drawing together the expertise of the company's 1,500 staff, based in 20 locations around the globe. "We want to bring together collective capabilities across the organisation that will hone our competitive edge," she says. "When you look at the breadth of capabilities we have, one of the challenges for us is how we translate some of those skills into the many areas where we have a presence. We are a consultancy and we like to bring our diverse skills and experience to bear to address our clients' most challenging issues.

"As an Employee Benefit Trust, we have a degree of autonomy and we are independent." Kenny continues. "For our customers, that's an attractive proposition. There's no hidden agenda from any external influence, and we pride ourselves on taking a long-term view."

Both Tomlinson and Kenny are STEM ambassadors, volunteering to help enthuse young people in science, technology, engineering and mathematics. One of their priorities at BMT is to get young people to play a bigger role within the organisation via its Young Professionals network.

"They are the future of the company," says Tomlinson. "We have some incredible skills. And part of the objective of our Young Professionals network is to raise awareness of what different parts of the business do. So, when our customers come to us looking for support with challenging problems, we can draw on the best of what BMT can offer, no matter where it sits in the world."

www.bmt.org

£ 14000
LGY 8

DRIVEN TO SUCCEED

Arnold Clark Automobiles

Europe's largest independently owned car retailer, Arnold Clark Automobiles, was founded in 1954 by a teenage mechanic fresh out of the Royal Air Force. The company's eponymous Scottish founder used his £167 demob money to buy and restore a Morris Ten Four, which he sold on for a profit before opening his first dealership on Park Road in Glasgow's West End. The company now has 180 branches in England and Scotland, over 11,000 employees and an annual turnover of more than £3 billion.

Sir Arnold Clark passed away in 2017, but his spirit lives on in the business he created. "Sir Arnold believed in value for money, he wanted customers to come back again and again," says Chief Executive and Group Managing Director Eddie Hawthorne. "That is an ethos that runs through the company – value for money and customer satisfaction. Sir Arnold reinvested all his earnings into the business, which allowed the company to grow and put us in a very strong financial position. We are still a family business and a private limited company and, if your origins are rooted in an entrepreneurial spirit, then you will have learnt over the years to adapt to different situations."

Arnold Clark operates right across the car industry. Each year, it sells over 300,000 vehicles, but it also repairs more than a million in its 40 body shops. It has a large car-hire division and also an independent training business, which helps maintain high standards of customer service. Many of its innovations came directly from Sir Arnold.

"We are one of the few companies that has cars with dual control, so parents can teach their children to drive," says Hawthorne. "That was one of Sir Arnold's great ideas. We charge £11 an hour, and after 10 hours, the new driver gets £350 off the purchase of their first car. It's all about giving customers a reason to return."

This creative approach is fostered by the group's £30 million training academy, GTG Training, which instils the virtues that Sir Arnold most valued in his staff. Hawthorne's job is to ensure that this is maintained. He cites as an example the firm's digital policy. "It's very exciting," he says. "We have a DPD policy – digital, physical, digital. The customer starts with the digital environment, then we get them into the physical, and then back to the digital for the final paperwork. But it's important to create a physical environment that people want to come into."

As Hawthorne explains, the key isn't to simply replicate Sir Arnold's style but to remain faithful to his spirit. "Sir Arnold did management by walkabout," says Hawthorne. "He didn't have an office. He believed in making himself available and that was a unique style that we try to emulate as the company gets bigger. We use modern methods of communicating, so all staff have an app that keeps them informed with company information and updates. I have an office but I'm only in it once or twice a week. I get out and meet staff as much as possible."

As the company moves onwards and upwards, Hawthorne is confident that Sir Arnold's style will continue to define the business. "Every senior manager knew Sir Arnold personally. We were brought up by him, born and bred in Arnold Clark, and that makes it easy for us to keep it going."

www.arnoldclark.com

CONNECTIONS THAT MATTER

JuMelia Ltd

When Julia Faulkes and Mel Redding decided to start their own business consultancy, JuMelia Ltd, they knew they wanted to deliver a service that was both agile *and* had a strong personal ethos. "We approached it with a sense of fun – the opposite to a corporate business tradition," says Redding. "We are two strong women with fantastic connections and a lot of business knowledge which we wanted to capitalise on."

With the pair's combined 45 years of experience in the defence, space and national security sector to draw upon, JuMelia has gone from strength to strength, more than doubling its turnover since it was set up in 2014. The company helps both large companies and forward-thinking SMEs to fine tune their growth strategies, win profitable new business and make mutually beneficial connections.

Innovation in the supply chain is important in the defence and security industry, as the Ministry of Defence typically contracts with first-tier suppliers. "We try to introduce smaller cutting-edge enterprises to larger suppliers and original equipment manufacturers to help them market their business offering," says Faulkes. "We introduce fresh thinking and technology from other market sectors to the larger players for the benefit of the defence customer."

For instance, JuMelia connected one of its clients – a niche firm that specialises in security cameras – to a major defence opportunity, and a cyber-security client to the Centre for the Protection of National Infrastructure. "When we work with a company," says Redding, "we will always look out for them, and will go back to them if we come across any suitable new opportunities." The services that JuMelia provides also include business growth strategy and facilitation, business development support and service delivery improvement. This includes mobilisation and transition into service of strategic defence programmes.

The company works with firms in local government, health, the emergency services and the private sector, but a large proportion of its work and clientele are connected with the defence and security sector. As well as their military business experience, both directors also have proud personal connections to the RAF spanning three generations. Faulkes retired as a Group Captain in 2007 following a 26-year career that included serving as Officer Commanding Administrative Wing at RAF Lyneham before completing a short tour in Afghanistan providing logistic support to counter-narcotic operations. Her father, Brian, served as a pilot from 1952–56 flying Vampires, Venoms and Hunters. Redding's grandfather, John Scrivener (pictured above), was a Flight Lieutenant in Bomber Command's 156 Squadron during the Second World War and was awarded the Distinguished Flying Cross for his 54 operational flights.

Last year, JuMelia took part in its first exhibition, Defence and Security Equipment International 2017 – the world's largest defence and security event. With an ever-growing client list, Faulkes and Redding are now focused on the next stage of their plan. "We want to continue to grow the business, build trust with our regular customers and enjoy what we are doing," says Redding. "We are loving building a business together that reflects our values and personal strengths. It is about getting the balance right between doing what we enjoy whilst offering a highly professional service."

www.jumelia.com

WHEEL APPEAL

CCM Motorcycles

When the CCM SkunkwerX Design Team were scouting around for a name for their new machine, they settled on Spitfire as being evocative of the stylish, speedy, British-designed attitude they wished to promote. And the new bike struck a chord with the public. The first 150 units sold out with seven days of launch in February 2017, leading to four other variants – the Spitfire Scrambler, Café Racer, the FlatTracker and the latest, the classic Bobber – all inspired by 1960s bike culture. More models are planned to follow in 2019, all playing on an aviation theme.

"We've found with the Spitfire that there is a long waiting list because there is such great demand," says Gary Harthern, Co-Director of CCM Motorcycles. "All the models we've designed are quite different in their appearance so we are able to give customers something that's retro, and futuristic, and unique – all at the same time."

For inspiration and guidance, CCM's SkunkwerX designers, turned to the rich history created by Alan Clews when he founded the company in 1971. Clews, who is Harthern's father-in-law, was a keen motorcyclist who built his own bikes with such success that he was able to turn it into business – called Clews Competition Machines, or CCM – gaining multiple success in motocross, flat-track, supermoto and road racing competition through the '70s and '80s.

Many of these races took place on former Royal Air Force airfields, which found a new use after the Second World War had ended. Clews's early designs even utilised airplane engineering in the form of the 531 high-tensile Reynolds steel tubing, originally designed for the Spitfire fuselage, which he used to construct his frames.

Following three decades of success, Clews lost control of the company in the late 1990s. Corporate governance took over but, by late 2004, the company was bankrupt. Refusing to give in, the family purchased CCM from the liquidators and set it on course for a second life, working from the original 1970s factory in Bolton to design and hand-build bikes.

"We love being part of this heritage and it's at our very core," says Austin Clews, another Co-Director of CCM Motorcycles and the eldest son of Alan Clews. "We identified that we needed to revert to the core principles that my father founded, which is limited-edition, hand-built, bespoke bikes."

Since its dramatic rebirth in 2005, CCM has continued to innovate while respecting tradition. "We've gone through periods of high-tech development with an aluminium-bonded chassis, breaking new ground," says Chris Ratcliffe, who leads the SkunkwerX design team. "We created a number of new bikes but were looking for something that would capture the public imagination, which is where the Spitfire was born." The Spitfire prototype utilised the same Reynolds 531 tubing originally designed for the Spitfire aircraft, and also called on the skills of veteran welder, Ted Unwin, who was one of Alan Clews's original team in the 1970s.

agv

CCM

"The Spitfire bike itself is very minimalistic," says Harthern. "It's stripped back of all the usual accessories you'd find on a typical Euro-compliant motorcycle." The appearance reflects this approach and has found favour with a number of prominent people, including the singer and former British Army officer James Blunt. "It's a bike that looks entirely retro and almost futuristic at the same time," says Blunt. "It looks like nothing I've ever seen before."

The decision to name the bike Spitfire came quite by accident. "When preparing the prototype for its London launch in February 2017, the bike was fired up for the first time late one night, outside in the dark, at our factory in Bolton," says Harthern. "We still had no name for the bike in the weeks before the launch but, as the bike roared into life for the first time, the straight-through exhausts were not fully tuned into the fuelling map that the engine had as standard. As a result, the exhaust literally spat out fire! And thus the name Spitfire was born."

As it happens, the Spitfire name also chimes with CCM's links to the Royal Air Force. CCM is now part of the RAF 100 Appeal group and has teamed up with the April Fools Club, the charity that supports the RAF Benevolent Fund. "Initially our decision to join the RAF 100 Appeal as a partner was based on our desire to support a worthy cause, especially as CCM's founding member Gail Clews, wife of Alan Clews, had lost her father in the Second World War," says Harthern. "He was Flight Sergeant Sydney Hennan of 466 Squadron and flew in a Halifax HY312 Bomber. He lost his life on 22 January 1944 returning from a bombing raid on Magdenburg, Germany."

Along with all of his four fellow crew members Sergeant Sydney Hennan is buried in the Dutch village of De Lutte. His grave has been visited many times by three generations of the Clews family, all of whom are active members of CCM Motorcycles. Gail and Alan Clews, the founding members of CCM in 1971, have also visited the Bomber Command memorial in Green Park, London.

Over the course of the year, CCM will be playing a part in many fundraising activities, including support for the April Fools Club's latest fund-raising venture – a cycle trip from RAF Scampton in Lincolnshire to the Möhne Dam in Germany, following the original route of the Dambusters. CCM will also be creating 100 limited-edition series of the Spitfire bike, inspired by the infamous Royal Air Force pilot, archaeologist, military officer and motorbike enthusiast TE Lawrence, better known as Lawrence of Arabia.

"We'll be donating £1,000 from every sale of these Spitfires to the RAF 100 Appeal," says Harthern, "We are sure that these will capture the attention of 100 very special owners who in turn will see their contribution to the RAF 100 Appeal as a valued and worthy gesture."

www.ccm-motorcycles.com

MARKS OF DISTINCTION

Marks & Spencer

"We can hold our heads high in these testing times, and say in time-honoured words: be strong and of good courage." So wrote Marks & Spencer Chairman Simon Marks (pictured opposite) to his employees during the Second World War, proud of all they were doing to support the war effort. As Chairman of the business that his father Michael had founded as a humble Penny Bazaar market stall in Leeds in 1884, it was Simon who successfully led M&S through the challenges of both world wars.

Simon Marks is renowned as a "retail revolutionary", who transformed M&S into a national chain of department stores and an iconic British retailer. But his connection with the Royal Air Force is less well known. It dates back to 1938 when Simon, as a respected businessman, was approached by Air Commodore J.A. Chamier, who was raising money to set up an air cadet corps to attract aviation-minded young men into the RAF. This scheme would cost £25,000. With £7,000 already pledged, Simon Marks met the balance personally. He joined the working committee as Honorary Treasurer and many meetings took place at M&S head office.

While his financial donation helped to establish the Air Defence Cadet Corps, the Air Ministry felt that Simon's most valuable contribution was his "business acumen". After the Cadet Corps became the Air Training Corps in 1941 (before later becoming the RAF Air Cadets), Simon was appointed to its Board of Finance and Welfare Council. His contribution was recognised by Air Minister Archibald Sinclair, who thanked him for his "indefatigable help", and by Air Commodore Chamier who wrote: "Dear Mr Marks, you were the man who made the Air Cadets possible!" By the end of the war, almost 100,000 cadets had joined the RAF. Simon maintained his interest in the Air Cadets throughout his life.

By 1943, over 300 M&S employees were serving in the RAF and the links did not end there. In early 1941, M&S employees raised £5,000 to pay for a Mark Vb Spitfire, serial number W3215, aptly named *The Marksman* (pictured above). It joined "B" Flight of the 609 West Riding Squadron at Biggin Hill in June and is best known for Sergeant "Tommy" Rigler's successful mission on 22 June 1941 when, on squadron patrol east of Dunkirk at 20,000 feet, Rigler shot down three German fighters, despite being hit by enemy fire. It earned Rigler the Distinguished Flying Medal. In October 1941, *The Marksman* was transferred to 411 "Grizzly Bear" Squadron of the Royal Canadian Airforce, but was shot down in France in March 1942 with the loss of Canadian pilot John Sills, aged 21.

The M&S Second World War Roll of Honour is displayed at its head office, including the names of 34 RAF servicemen, and M&S has continued to support the RAF through fundraising. Innovation and technology have transformed both organisations, while their strong sense of tradition and pride remains, alongside shared commitments to integrity and excellence.

"M&S and the RAF have made a mark on one another's histories since 1938, when Simon Marks, our Chairman and the son of our founder, helped create the RAF Cadets," says M&S CEO Steve Rowe. "But our connection with the RAF runs deeper than our shared history, the RAF's values of integrity and service mirror our own. On behalf of our customers and colleagues we are proud to be celebrating the RAF's history and its vital contribution to our nation."

www.marksandspencer.com

FULLY INSURED

Aviva plc

"It's amazing to think that people went from working at desks outside the office where I'm sitting now to flying planes and fighting in the Battle of Britain," says Anna Stone, the archivist for insurance company Aviva Plc. "Many members of our staff joined the RAF in the first and second world wars. We've got 11 Battle of Britain pilots, and a couple of our insurance clerks even became air aces. And we've got somebody who was involved in the first capture of a submarine from the air."

This latter war hero was William Coleman, who had worked for Commercial Union – a company that later became a part of Aviva – as an insurance clerk before he joined the RAF. Flying Officer Coleman was awarded the Distinguished Flying Cross for his role in overpowering a German U-Boat in rough seas south of Iceland on 27 August 1941. The submarine's capture was an important coup – it provided the Allies with a wealth of vital information, and the vessel itself was commandeered by the Royal Navy.

Today Aviva employs around 17,000 people in the UK and 25,000 worldwide. "When Aviva as it is now was formed, there was an amalgamation of General Accident and Commercial Union in 1998, and then Norwich Union merged with that company in 2000," says Stone. "So they were the three big companies – but there are hundreds of smaller companies in the group."

Some of Aviva's ancestor companies can trace their origins back several centuries. The oldest was originally called the Contributors for Insuring Houses, Chambers or Rooms from Loss by Fire, by Amicable Contribution before shortening its name to the Hand in Hand Fire & Life Insurance Society, named after its logo of clasped hands. Established in 1696, the Hand in Hand was one of world's first insurance companies. Norwich Union didn't come along until 1797 – a relative newcomer.

"We cover life insurance, general insurance, travel insurance – the whole remit of insurance," says John Franklin, Aviva's press officer. "We cover 17 different territories worldwide. We do investments as well." But the founding principles of these venerable old companies have remained intact until the present day.

"I think it does survive," says Stone. "Insurance is about sharing risk. The Hand in Hand was established so that a group of people could share out the risk if a fire broke out in any of their properties, and that principle is exactly what underpins insurance today."

Over time, Aviva's antecedent companies developed special policies for aviators and members of the RAF. "The earliest RAF-specific policy I've found is a 'protector policy' from 1931, issued by Sun Life (pictured, above), whose business we acquired in 2015," says Stone. "That was specifically for members of the RAF. But you can also see the development of aviation from looking at our other policies, things like travel insurance, and when the policies start to include flying. When flying became more common, policies changed to reflect this. Early policies might have excluded flying, when it was something that very few people did. And then, over time, it became more common and was no longer excluded."

Historically it has tended to be smaller companies that have innovated by creating policies for niche fields. "For example, with burglary insurance it would have been smaller companies that decided to specialise in that type of business," says Stone. "Then larger, more established companies realised that it was a popular type of insurance. And then they started issuing those kinds of policies as well. Or they took over companies which had become specialists in, say, plate-glass insurance, for instance. And then they built up their business that way. So you get certain people who are innovators and who want to go in different directions."

Innovation is not always associated with the insurance industry. "By nature people in insurance are cautious," says Stone, "but there are plenty of examples of innovative thinking in our group. The first company to issue a burglary policy is one of our companies. Another of our companies issued the first employer's liability policy and another the first accident insurance policy. One of our companies was a pioneer of motor insurance, back in 1896."

Among Aviva's innovations have been a range of insurance policies specifically designed for the Armed Forces. "We've also got policies providing very specific cover for things like regimental regalia," says Stone. "One of our companies was asked to a insure a regimental camel that belonged to an RAF unit in the 1950s. They wanted it insured 'against normal risks, including loss by theft and accident'. So all kinds of things get insured!"

Aviva has displayed its commitment to the future prosperity of the Armed Forces in the most practical way it can by signing the Armed Forces Covenant. "It's the right thing to do," says Franklin. "For our service personnel customers, we will waive cancellation fees and let them keep their no-claims discount on their motor insurance when they're posted overseas. Being posted overseas means you will generally need to cancel these policies. The last thing you want to do is have a cancellation fee on top of that. So you've got to try and help them out on that front. Also, for our reservists, we offer an extra 10 days' annual leave to attend training camps and provide tailored HR support for them as well."

As an insurance company, Aviva well understands the risks taken by the UK's Armed Forces, says Stone. "We should be doing whatever we can to support our servicemen and women who are risking their lives for our country."

www.aviva.com

TRAINING AND CAREERS

A HIGH-FLYING EDUCATION

Pearson

The Royal Air Force was founded at 80 Strand in London on 1 April 1918 in a building whose site is now occupied by Pearson – a company which maintains several links to the Royal Air Force and other parts of the UK's Ministry of Defence through the provision of training and education services.

Pearson began life during the industrial revolution as a construction firm before moving into publishing. It is now the world's leading education company, operating from a building that sits on the site of the former Hotel Cecil and the new building features a plaque to celebrate its connection to the birth of the Royal Air Force. Weetman Pearson, the grandson of Pearson's founder and later to become Viscount Cowdray, became President of the Air Board while based at Hotel Cecil in 1917 – the year before the founding of the Royal Air Force.

The company maintains strong education connections with the Royal Air Force, and the MoD in general, through the management of education services and the delivery of STEM (science, technology, engineering and maths) education to 16-18 year olds on A Level courses at Welbeck, The Defence Sixth Form College based near Loughborough. Young people here undertake a STEM based academic curriculum alongside a programme that seeks also to develop them as individuals better able to take up technological and engineering leadership roles in the Royal Air Force, the other Armed Services and the UK's Civil Service.

In the words of the Principal, Peter Middleton: "The college is committed to creating an environment where young men and young women grow in self-confidence, thrive academically and make the most of the many opportunities on offer. We pride ourselves on the collective pursuit of excellence. Every experience needs to make a difference, and will form part of a journey that shapes the lives of our students."

Pearson's UK President, Rod Bristow, sees other parallels between the RAF and Pearson. "We're an education company and our mission is to help people make progress in their lives through learning," he says. "All the things we do are about developing people, and one of the things I've learnt about the Royal Air Force is how much it cares about its people and how much investment it makes in their professional development."

Bristow also has personal connections to the RAF. His father was a civil engineer who built runways for the RAF around the world, while Bristow himself is an Honorary Group Captain in 601 Squadron, which was reactivated in 2017 so that a small group of ambassadors – from the worlds of industry, academia and research – could help to advise, shape and support the RAF.

Welbeck The Defence Sixth Form College at Loughborough is one of Pearson UK's flagship projects. The college takes around 350 learners and prepares them for a career in a technical leadership role in the Ministry of Defence. On average, around 35 per cent of A Level graduates from the college head off to join

STUDENT
College
Student

the Royal Air Force after first taking a STEM-based degree at university, and about 70 per cent of current RAF officers in engineering roles have come through the Welbeck route.

"The college is the first step for students who are enrolled on the UK MoD's Defence Technical Officer Engineering Entry Scheme (DTOEES)," explains Martyn Leader, Vice-President of Pearson TQ, the business unit in Pearson responsible for the education services at the college. "On leaving Welbeck, students progress to degree courses at partner universities in the UK and from there they start their professional careers in their chosen service. The college gets very good A level results, and secures university places for all its students on completion of those A level courses."

In addition, students also benefit from a curriculum that focuses heavily on their development as people and leaders, with one eye firmly on their forthcoming role as a leader in one of the armed services or the Ministry of Defence's civil service. "The unique aspect of Welbeck is that because the students already know the job they will be doing in the future, they are able to give their STEM learning at A level a solid vocational context, allowing them to leave with an understanding of how to apply their academic studies in the working world" says Leader. "In addition, unlike most sixth formers who will hardly ever come across their schoolmates in the workplace, students at Welbeck have the benefit of forging strong friendships whilst at the college which endure throughout their professional careers, as they will often be working with one another as their careers progress."

"The role of technology is absolutely central to the functioning of a successful modern air force," says Bristow. "The Royal Air Force relies heavily on innovative, technology-based ideas and solutions and today the investment that goes into aircraft and the systems that support them is extraordinary. You need incredibly well-qualified people to ensure that those investments are deployed to best effect. It's not just about being qualified in STEM subjects but being equipped to ensure the Royal Air Force can innovate. The more innovative the Royal Air Force is, the more effective it can be."

Bristow also believes that there's a false dichotomy between knowledge and skills. "Pearson supports the development of both," he says. "We work in 70 countries in 100 languages and use technology to support and deliver the best teaching. Our future strategy is about digital transformation, to provide students and teachers with more engaging, accessible resources and information. That's an important part of what we are doing and it's something we have in common with the Royal Air Force as technological transformation is so important to them."

www.pearson.com/uk

THE SIXTH SENSE

The Cheadle and Marple Sixth Form College

"Students benefit from being part of a distinct community," says Jenny Singleton, Principal at Cheadle & Marple Sixth Form College (CAMSFC). "We put great emphasis on meeting the defined needs of individuals within a supportive yet challenging environment." A strong community spirit is certainly apparent across the two campuses (the Cheadle College and the Marple College), set nine miles apart. This is underpinned by a house system, through which the individual and group needs of the students are met and a sense of identity is nurtured.

Sixteen-year-olds attending CAMSFC choose the educational path that best suits them from a variety of learning options. It is one of the few sixth-form colleges in the country that offers all three possible pathways, with students taking A-levels, classroom-based vocational courses such as BTECs and apprenticeships.

The course range is extremely broad, contributing to the college's diverse learning environment. The catchment area, too, is one of the widest in the country. It stretches all the way from south Manchester to Derbyshire and Buxton.

On the subject of inclusivity, Singleton describes a curriculum broad enough to span "the whole range of abilities". It runs the gamut from the Choices programme, designed for students with learning difficulties, to the A-level courses pursued by those whose sights are set on the best universities in the country.

The college's academic results speak for themselves, with a 99 per cent A-level pass rate. This rises to 100 per cent on vocational programmes – Singleton attributes this success in part to the supportive structure of the house system. Many of the students go on to higher education, including Oxbridge and Russell Group universities; and the college counts Olympic gold medallist Dame Sarah Storey and *Guardian* columnist Owen Jones among its alumni.

The college is also proactive in alerting learners to the new opportunities offered by higher apprenticeships and degree apprenticeships. "These are becoming an attractive alternative to university for an increasing number of young people," says Singleton.

Extra-curricular activities are an important aspect of everyday life at CAMSFC. Students explore a range of different athletic pursuits, take part in the Duke of Edinburgh Award and sign up for foreign trips. Last year, groups of students headed off to Russia, South Africa and New York.

There is also a busy calendar of events taking place throughout the year, including a recent opportunity to see an RAF helicopter up close as it landed in the grounds of the Cheadle College. The display took place in recognition of the fundraising efforts of the Public Service students, who have worked closely with the RAF since 2014 and raised over £4,000 for local children's hospitals.

A particular highlight in the college calendar is the awards evening held every year before Christmas, where students and staff come together to celebrate the achievements of those who graduated the previous summer.

"It's a chance to share memories and to relive happy times spent in one another's company," says Singleton. "Many students reflect fondly on their time at college. They frequently speak of the support provided by teachers, and of how the environment enabled them to bridge the gap between school and university or work."

Above all else, it's the friendly atmosphere and enriching educational experience that makes CAMSFC stand out. Students feel cared for and supported by a learning environment that helps them reach the goals they set for themselves. "Every student here is a name," says Singleton, "not a number."

www.camsfc.ac.uk

SERVE AND STUDY

London South Bank University

"It turned out to be a real pleasure," says Professor Paul Ivey, Pro-Vice-Chancellor of London South Bank University (LSBU), speaking of its commitment in 2017 to the Armed Forces Covenant. "We ended up being awarded 'Silver' by the Defence Employers Recognition Scheme. In terms of the values and principles that we hold dear, it's probably the most rewarding work that we've done at the university."

The Armed Forces Covenant is an agreement to support the needs of servicemen and women, reservists and veterans at the university and when seeking graduate employment. Professor Ivey sees it as an extension of LSBU's existing commitment to support the specific needs of students from all backgrounds. "It's recognising that students come with histories and a past life," he says. "It's recognising that and adjusting the university to accommodate it – and actually, to value it."

Business Support Officer Nicola Bourke says there are up to 30 reservist volunteers among LSBU staff and students. "It's our hope that that number will increase as we continue to do good work," she says.

Adrian Tindall, Tenant Manager of Research, Enterprise and Innovation, says that effective support of servicemen and women means an equal commitment to their families. "Unfortunately, the husband or the wife goes out on deployment and it's the partners who are left behind that need support," he says. "That's where we can fulfil a role to make sure they've got social mobility, and not just those serving." As the RAF celebrates its centenary – and LSBU, originally Borough Polytechnic Institute, marks its 126th year – ex-servicemen and women are making an important contribution to university life. "We value the soft skills that the Armed Forces can bring to the university," says Tindall.

Professor Ivey, Chair of the University of London Military Education Committee, thinks that the university benefits from the ethos of service personnel. "Throughout your career in the Armed Forces you are encouraged to look at the team, look at others around you and be supportive of one another," he says. "It's exactly the skills that are needed for employment after graduation."

LSBU has a long history of vocational learning, giving students the skills that employers demand. "Of course every individual has to have a skill set," says Professor Ivey. "But the training and development that people will have had in the Armed Forces matches the world of work more closely than the teaching approach used in some universities."

www.lsbu.ac.uk

SCHOOL OF THOUGHT

The Alice Smith School, Kuala Lumpur

"Students here are encouraged to enjoy and value their education," says Roger Schultz, Head of School at the Alice Smith School in Kuala Lumpur. "It's vital to instil a passion for lifelong learning that continues outside the classroom."

Schultz's strategy is reflected in the school's enriched curriculum and excellent facilities, a highlight of each student's experience here. "The environment is an important learning tool," he says. "We plan our learning experiences to promote and develop the whole child, their character and personality and their social and emotional welfare." A nurturing community atmosphere is another asset. From the age of three, students settle in quickly and are encouraged to develop their individual strengths and abilities as they move through the school to 18.

As one of the oldest and most prestigious British schools in Asia, the Alice Smith School takes great pride in its past while focusing clearly on the future. It has brought an education planner on board to ensure that the current facilities and environment are evolving in line with the rapidly changing teaching and learning requirements of the 21st century. The school is now looking to ensure it stays up to date with the latest developments. Building on core values that have engendered a reputation for excellence since its formation in 1946, the school incorporates the best of today's innovations in learning to provide students with a well rounded education.

Schultz describes a diverse extracurricular programme that fosters new skills and creates scope for character development. Through the Duke of Edinburgh Awards scheme, wide-ranging charity work and the school's partnership with the United Nations High Commission for Refugees (UNHCR), students explore valuable ways of contributing to society.

This inspiring and supportive environment is reflected in the school's academic results, with 75 per cent of students achieving grades A* to B at A Level; and 80 per cent of graduates securing places at Russell Group and top-ranking universities last year. The school offers an enriched National Curriculum for England through to IGCSE and A Level; and is committed to providing students with an excellent British education.

"British education has a worldwide reputation for quality," says Schultz, "which is recognised and respected around the world. With a significant and increasing number of British curriculum schools worldwide, transferability is certainly one of its huge benefits."
www.alice-smith.edu.my

ENQUIRING MINDS

Byron College, Greece

It is quite an achievement to be both the smallest international school in Athens and yet also the city's most diverse. However, that is the profile of Byron College, a school that is registered with the UK's Department for Education and named after the brooding 19th century English poet. There's nothing brooding about Byron College, though. It's a warm, welcoming and engaging school, passionately committed to providing its multicultural community with outstanding education that creates independent, critical global leaders.

"Our pupils reach the highest academic standards, well above international and UK standards," says Konstantinos Koutsantonis, Chairman of the school's board. "On average, more than 50 per cent of our students achieve A and A*s at GCSEs, while our sixth-form pupils head to world-renowned UK and international universities – such as Cambridge, Oxford and MIT – as a matter of course."

The school enriches and expands the UK curriculum to discover the talents inherent in every child, to inspire creativity and to encourage individuality. "We never lose sight of the pupil as an individual learner," says Koutsantonis, "whose consistent hard work and wellbeing is at the heart of every success story."

Byron College imparts a style of education that aims to build up the resilience, independence, critical thinking and communication skills of its students; all essential qualities for active and successful global citizens of the future. "We bring education to life," says Koutsantonis. "A recent geography field trip to Iceland, for instance, included a lesson that was delivered on top of a volcano, while philosophical discussions take place on Pnyx Hill – the birthplace of democracy." International mindedness is deeply embedded in the curriculum with multiple collaborations between national and international schools in tournaments, competitions and conferences. These include Model United Nations conferences and Erasmus+ projects.

Byron takes the best of British values and British education, and the best of its multiculturalism. "It is a microcosm of how wonderful the world could be," says Koutsantonis, "celebrating diversity and achievement, rewarding kindness and responsibility, and promoting excellent leadership and citizenship skills." Byron pupils, both past and present, are individuals who benefit their community, society and the world of tomorrow. They are living testimony to the school's success.

www.byroncollege.gr

LIFE AFTER SERVICE

University of Derby

Many of the 2.6 million Armed Forces veterans in the UK are reluctant to ask for help, even when they need it. With this in mind, the University of Derby, one of the largest employers in the East Midlands, is taking steps to support veterans in a number of areas of mental health. In 2016, the university ran several workshops with Health Education England to help health professionals gain a greater understanding of veterans' needs.

"Doctors, nurses and allied health professionals need to treat veterans slightly differently," says Dr Paula Holt, Pro Vice-Chancellor Dean at the university's College of Health and Social Care. She herself is a former mental health nurse who served as a British Army officer for nine years. "When soldiers, sailors and air-force personnel go through training, they may be tired, hungry or have sore feet, but they're expected to not complain. They're expected to get on with it. That kind of stoicism is deeply rooted and many veterans don't feel they should be asking for help or support. It's really important that, if someone is a veteran, we establish whether they have any issues relating to their service."

As a sign of its commitment to the welfare of Armed Forces personnel, veterans and their families, the university signed the Armed Forces Covenant in 2017. Since a number of staff and students previously served in the Armed Forces the university is keen to promote itself as an "Armed Forces-friendly organisation". This includes supporting employees who are members of the Reserve Forces, helping local cadet units and working to establish a tailored employment pathway for veterans.

"We believe that everyone should have the opportunity to engage with and access education, so we were delighted to sign the Armed Forces Covenant, supporting veterans and their families to do this," says Professor Kathryn Mitchell, Vice-Chancellor of the University of Derby. "Through our support of RAF100, we can ensure that our commitment to reaching a wide and diverse audience continues."

The university is a Gold-rated institution for teaching and learning (Teaching Excellence Framework, 2017), with a team of lecturers and professors that combine extensive industry experience with first-rate teaching and support. This commitment to teaching excellence is enhanced by the opportunity to learn in first-class facilities and undertake work placements, ensuring students leave Derby with the skills, knowledge and expertise required by employers.

www.derby.ac.uk

A War of Nerves
MINDS AT WAR
FIGHTER WRITER

ARC OF THE COVENANT

Edinburgh Napier University

"The RAF has always been very strong technically on education and learning," says Dr John Thomson, Senior Lecturer in Marketing at Edinburgh Napier's Business School. "Learning is absolutely at the heart of the RAF, at every level. So for them to gain a platform where they could take all that education and experience and convert it into degree programmes was very attractive."

The university is a forces-friendly employer. This applies not only to people leaving the services but also to those who want to continue to learn using their past qualifications and experience. "We have a lot of ex-military personnel on the staff," says Dr Thomson, "from porters and security right up to the strategic level." He himself joined the university as a serving reserve lieutenant colonel and continued serving, becoming the UK's Deputy Inspector General Territorial Army, reaching the rank of brigadier.

The Business School is based at Craiglockhart campus, which was built as a hydropathic in 1880 – and used during the First World War as a military hospital for shell-shocked soldiers. Among its patients were the poets Wilfred Owen and Siegfried Sassoon, who actually met there. Their work is celebrated at the War Poets Collection, a permanent exhibition at the campus. "People can gain a unique insight into the personal and social experiences of war," says Dr Thomson. "The collection uses words, memories, voices and objects to make people aware of the horror, the reality of war as described by Owen. Perhaps at the time it was over-glamourised; the collection provides insight into its real effect and impact."

In 2017 the university won the silver award for its contribution to the Armed Forces Corporate Covenant. This was in recognition for the help and support it gives to servicemen and women in transition from the military into civilian life. "We have a range of flexible entry points based on their previous education, their skills and experience," says Dr Thomson. "We're crediting what they have done in practice; and helping them turn their learning and experience into civilian-recognised qualifications."

The Armed Forces have strong links with Edinburgh. "There are three military barracks in the Colinton area, where the Business School is based," says Dr Thomson, "and a garrison headquarters in Edinburgh Castle. So this is very much a garrison city, rather like Aldershot or Catterick. There is a military community embedded within the civil community."

The university conducts valuable research into the Armed Forces and has an outreach programme that allows local military schoolchildren to visit, giving them the opportunity to see and experience student life. It also conducts valuable research into life in the Armed Forces. "The military wants to undertake research into human dynamics and feelings," says Dr Thomson, "not just those of its personnel but also their families. Because families are integral and a vital part of how soldiers, airmen and sailors operate."

The university's assistance in offsetting the challenges facing military and ex-military personnel now extends to Rock 2 Recovery, a life-saving arm of the Royal Marines Charity which provides support to veterans and their families experiencing stress-related illness. "This support is part of the Armed Forces Corporate Covenant," says Dr Thomson. "We offer the charity access to our facilities and our experts. So it's really advice and encouragement. Of course, they will join us on our future journey in support of the covenant; and of service personnel past and present."

www.napier.ac.uk

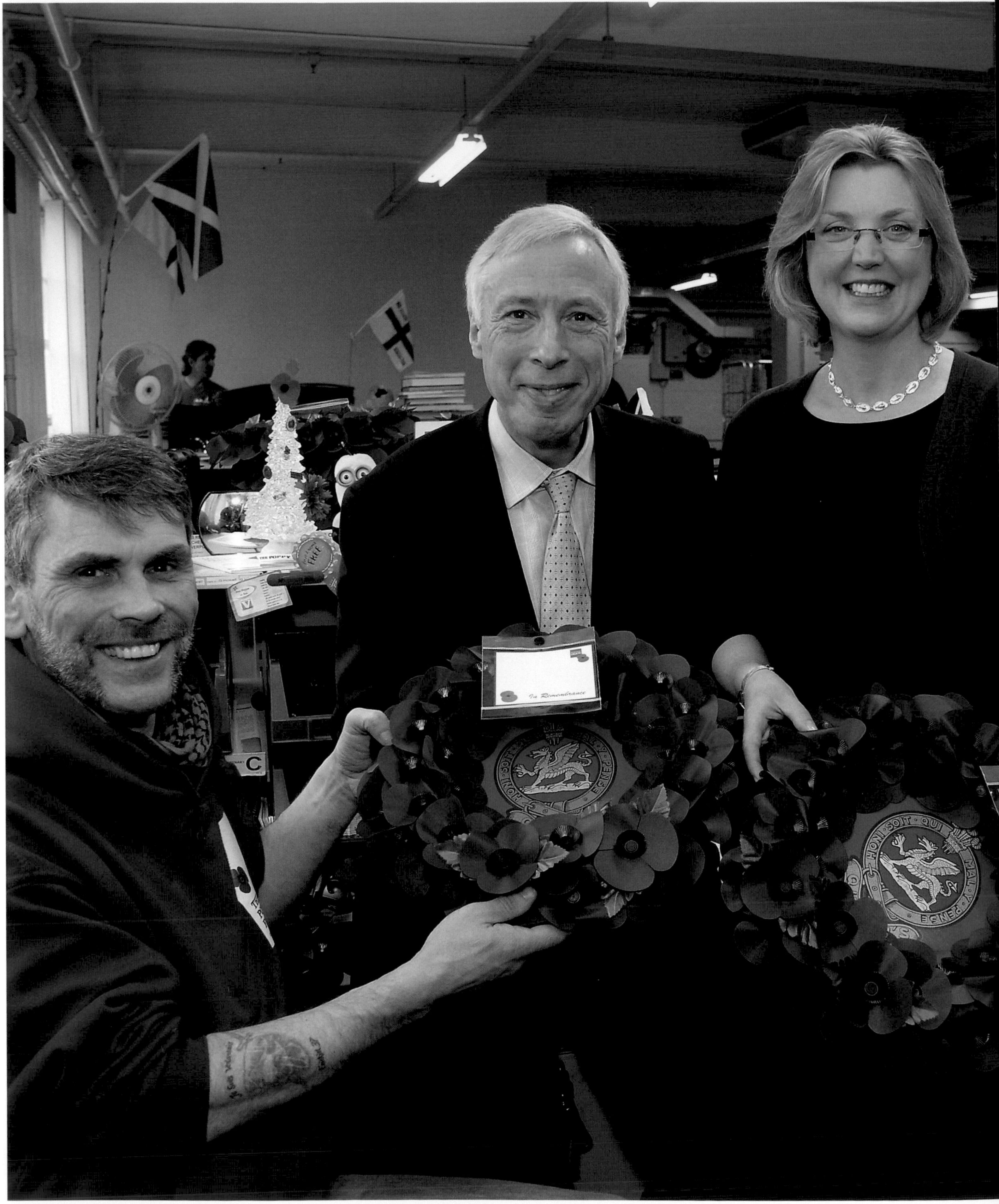
In Remembrance
HONI SOIT QUI MAL Y PENSE

A WORKING SOLUTION

The Poppy Factory

"If it weren't for The Poppy Factory," says Mark, "I'd be dead." Mark is a former soldier who was discharged from the Army after suffering a brain injury, which has also left him with mental health problems. "I'd got up and brushed myself off so many times, I'd just had enough."

Despondent, and facing the loss of his home and marriage, Mark was on Facebook when he saw a link to The Poppy Factory (TPF), the country's leading employment charity for ex-service personnel with health conditions or impairments. The charity put him in touch with one of its Employability Consultants, who understood his problems, and helped him to revamp his CV and brush up on his skills. Now, with the ongoing support of TPF, Mark has a new career, with a 50 per cent stake in a new café in a sports centre specialising in rehabilitation.

Mark is one of over 800 wounded, injured or sick veterans who have been helped back into employment by the charity since it launched its award-winning Getting You Back to Work initiative in 2010. TPF was founded in 1922 as a factory where Remembrance Day poppies were produced, "to give the disabled a chance", following The Great War. It still makes millions of plastic-and-paper poppies for the Royal British Legion's Poppy Appeal from its factory in Richmond, Surrey. In 2010, it expanded its remit to provide an employment service to veterans across the country.

This year alone, nearly 800 veterans registered with the charity for support, and TPF is already on track to provide help to almost 250 individuals. The veterans – both male and female – come from across the British Armed Forces, with about 10 per cent being former RAF personnel. Around half of the individuals self-refer, while others are referred by organisations including the NHS and JobCentrePlus. For its achievements TPF was awarded the Ministry of Defence's Employer Recognition Silver Award in 2016.

Chief Executive Deirdre Mills (pictured opposite, right, with Poppy Factory worker Gregg and Minister of State for Defence Earl Howe) says that veterans leaving the Armed Forces have a lot of skills to offer employers and their local communities, but their health issues and lack of experience in the civilian workforce can make getting, or staying in, a job difficult. "Of our veterans, 77.5 per cent report mental health conditions, such as depression or PTSD and 72 per cent report physical health conditions, from limb loss to visual or hearing impairments," she says. "As well as helping veterans to get and stay in jobs, we're working on a larger scale to change the way employers view disabled veterans and the value they can bring. With that in mind, TPF chairs the WIS Veterans Employment Group – a collection of charities that works with veterans to ensure best practice and collaborative working."

TPF uses the highly personalised IPS (individual placement and support) method of employment assistance. Each veteran is assigned their own consultant who gets to know them, their needs and their career preferences, and then helps create a plan to achieve their goals.

"We are seeing increasing demand for our services," says Mills. "Some of the stigma around seeking help for mental health problems has gone, and there's more awareness of the need to support veterans. Veterans make great employees – they're loyal, reliable, very good at leadership roles and adaptable to any situation. Many just need to get their confidence back."

www.poppyfactory.org

LEADERSHIP IN ACTION

The Institute of Leadership and Management

"Institutions like the RAF are known for their leadership prowess," says Phil James, the CEO of The Institute of Leadership and Management. "They're fantastic breeding grounds for great leaders, so a good part of our heritage includes the military services."

The institute exists to inspire and advance great leadership everywhere – so it's no surprise that it has a long and proud relationship with the RAF. Now in its 70th year, the institute is a professional community that represents more than 31,000 leaders and managers across all sectors. As well as providing networking and learning opportunities, it also offers recognition and accreditation of leaders' and managers' achievements. It also recognises military experience and rank as entry criteria to its membership grades. "Leadership and management is something you have to continually keep working on," says James. "We conduct an on-going research programme into the experience of service leavers in the workplace and run a Leadership Redeployed support group."

This is certainly the case for Squadron Leader Alison Russell-Brookes, who is Chief of Staff in the training wing at RAF Halton. She's been in the air force for 17 years, and became a member of The Institute of Leadership and Management in 2009, while working as an instructor at RAF College Cranwell. "A couple of the courses I took at Cranwell were accredited by the ILM," she says, "and I could tell there was real depth in what the organisation was doing." Seven years later, in 2016, Russell-Brookes was accepted as a fellow, and says the institute is one of her go-to resources for professional development. "It's important to learn something new every day," she says. "The blogs, webinars, articles, and research all help you to keep topping up your knowledge."

Airmen and women can earn Institute of Leadership and Management recognition right the way through their careers, and the institute also acts as a bridge for military leaders transitioning out of the forces.

"It's such a well-recognised badge of authority," says Russell-Brookes. I think that's particularly important when you're trying to translate your knowledge and experience into a language that's understood by the civilian sector. It's not just about developing into civilian employment though; it's also about developing yourself while you're in the services. What I value so much is the different perspective I get from chatting to leaders and managers in completely different sectors of work. It really broadens my horizons, and helps make me a better leader and manager."

www.institutelm.com

SOLDIERING ON

Ex-Mil Recruitment

"In the military, you can plan," says Jean-Claude Hedouin, Managing Director of Ex-Mil Recruitment, "but at the first contact with the enemy, those plans go out of the window. So your battle plan is only as good as your first contact. After that, you have to react properly and correctly, otherwise you'll lose the battle." It's a very specific skill; and not necessarily one that is easily transferable to Civvy Street.

Ex-Mil is one of Britain's leading recruitment consultancies for the placement of ex-military personnel. Hedouin founded the company after experiencing difficulty making his own transition from the Armed Forces to civilian life. "When I left the military back in 1994, there was no real help available," he says. "My first job was being a security guard on a construction site. I knew I was worth more than that."

Since it started business in 2005, Ex-Mil Recruitment has helped thousands of ex-military personnel overcome barriers to finding work. "People contact me out of the blue saying, 'Help, I need a job'," says Hedouin. "I sit down with a candidate and try to find ways of highlighting their skills and experience." His company has 28,000 people on its books, drawn from all three services. They range in rank from privates to generals, brigadiers, wing commanders and squadron leaders. "I feel honour-bound," he says, "to give my candidates the best advice, support and assistance I can."

Among the many challenges that face ex-service personnel looking for work is the lack of recognition of military qualifications among prospective employers. "The majority of companies out on Civvy Street have nothing to do with the military," says Hedouin, "so they don't understand. One of the biggest problems I've had is getting companies to appreciate what we can bring to the table."

Former servicemen and women often have skills and experience other jobseekers may lack, especially in management and general flexibility. And they are not afraid of hard work."One of their strongest assets is their work ethic," says Hedouin. "Soldiers try to get the job done, get it right the first time, and as quickly as they can. So if they see that something needs doing, they'll do it. They won't sit around."

Partly because of this, their prospects are good. "The majority of people I place are promoted above their peers in the company quite quickly," says Hedouin. "They've got the right ethos."

www.ex-mil.co.uk

INTEGRATED MISSION TRAINING

CAE

As the world's oldest independent air force, the Royal Air Force has, in many ways, set the standard for all other air forces, and that includes training philosophy and practice. CAE is proud to have supported the RAF in delivering world-class simulation-based training for many years. Like every other facet of aircraft and aircrew development, simulation has changed dramatically from those early days. In fact, the RAF and CAE enjoy some pioneering developments together that have led the way in military aviation training.

In the mid-1990s, the RAF Support Helicopter Force articulated a vision for mission training with different helicopter types that could be fully networked in a virtual environment. That vision led to the world's first military training private finance initiative and the Medium Support Helicopter Aircrew Training Facility (MSHATF) at RAF Benson, which continues to be recognised globally as one of the premier advanced helicopter synthetic training facilities.

The RAF was also the launch customer for the C-130J aircraft in the 1990s and CAE has played a role in helping train all the RAF's C-130J aircrews. Since then, CAE has developed training systems for all the world's C-130J operators. More recently, CAE contributed to the synthetic training system for Typhoon and delivered the training service for RAF Reaper crews as part of the USAF's MQ-9 aircrew training programme.

In 2017, CAE celebrated its 70th anniversary and, over much of this time, its relationship and experience with the RAF has been invaluable. Customers ranging from the US Special Operations Command to the Royal Canadian Air Force have been jointly hosted by the RAF and CAE at the Tactical Control Centre at the MSHATF, where the value of joint and networked pre-deployment mission training has been demonstrated. Many have then used what the RAF is doing as a model for their own advanced synthetic training.

As the RAF embarks upon its second century of operations, CAE is excited to continue its strong and successful training partnership. All future RAF aircrews will touch CAE in one way or another, based on CAE's range of training systems and services. It looks forward to innovating and delivering world-class training solutions that will help create the force of the future and support RAF mission readiness over the next 100 years.

www.cae.com

CREATING A LEGACY

Leighton Academy

"We do a lot of things that other schools don't do," says Joanna Young, Principal of Leighton Academy. This large primary school in Crewe has a focus on science, technology, engineering and maths (STEM), with students working on projects that link closely with local industry.

This includes work with the nearby car giant Bentley. After acquiring two Goblin electric kit cars in recent years with support from the Institution for Mechanical Engineers, Leighton Academy students work with staff from Bentley to design, build and race electric cars at Goodwood and Stafford against teams from other schools. "The children jump through hoops to be involved," says STEM Co-ordinator Jo Hall.

Such opportunities run through the academy. A group of students reached the national finals of the Bloodhound Race For The Line competition in 2017, building and racing model solid-fuel rocket cars made from foam. "Our girls, who were only nine years old, eventually lost out to a university technical college," says Hall.

Day to day, children might build and fly gliders, learn about manufacturing using K'nex construction toys, or explore robotics and computer programming with Lego. "A group in Year 4 recently created an artificial hand with a grabbing mechanism, refining it to pick up very small objects," says Hall. "These projects are not about abstract concepts. We're showing our children how the skills they're learning are used in the real world."

Year 3 and 6 students have also sharpened their maths and geography skills by collaborating with a local company, Gist, on stock control for Marks & Spencer. "The children go to their warehouses," says Hall. "It's a rich learning experience." It's one that's extended throughout the school as part of the My World project, a Cheshire initiative where children spend time at local businesses, from Tatton Park to Barclays.

"We are always considering potential areas of employment," says Young. "We noticed that there is a shortage of people going into the horticultural industry, so all our children now grow and harvest food in our garden and orchard. That learning feeds into the curriculum and links to future job opportunities." Leighton Academy has earned a Royal Horticultural Society Gold Award for gardening.

It's about making learning real and unforgettable, Young concludes, doing things that other schools don't do. "We're creating a legacy, planting seeds now that we hope will grow in the future."
www.leightonacademy.com

SUPPORTING CHANCE

Hornsey School for Girls

Goldilocks, Red Riding Hood and the Gingerbread Man are familiar characters for the pupils at north London's Hornsey School for Girls. This owes less to the girls' childhood grounding in fairy tales and more to their study of forensic science. As part of the school's dynamic curriculum, its students learn about solving crime and are presented with these characters as "suspects".

"The school motto translates as 'the better prepared, the stronger'," says Chimène Peddie, Head of Enterprise, "and our focus is on preparing students for the outside world when they leave. Problem solving is an essential skill in today's ever-changing jobs market that relies on technology and innovation. We encourage their intellectual curiosity, team working, using their imaginations and building resilience so they can handle any challenge."

The school was founded 130 years ago and now takes boys in the sixth form. For its 950 students, a conscious curriculum shift emphasised science, technology, engineering and maths (STEM) education to help its girls gain access to careers where they are under-represented. In March this year, the RAF, BAE Systems and the Royal Navy gave Year 8 pupils presentations on topics including the uses of virtual reality and developments in facial recognition technology. "People still think the RAF is just about flying planes," says Peddie, "but it could offer our pupils a job in radio microphone technology, for example. We impress upon all our pupils that there are no barriers to what they want to do."

Sixth-form students are supported by mentors who are not exclusively from STEM industries. One female teenager who wanted to pursue a career in motor racing benefited enormously from this arrangement with specialist advisors. She is now on her way to achieving her goal.

Hornsey's commitment to its pupils is demonstrated by their achievements. Their progress between the end of Key Stage 2 and Key Stage 4 is rated well above average (+0.66). This makes Hornsey the highest performing secondary school in Haringey. Excellent outcomes in English put it in the top five schools in the country for that subject. Hornsey's results also rank it in the top 10 per cent of schools in Britain.

Thanks to Peddie and her colleagues' dedication to helping their pupils' wishes come true, no career is out of reach for pupils at Hornsey School for Girls.

www.hsg.haringey.sch.uk

TRAIN OF THOUGHT

KP Training & Consulting Ltd

"It's that journey from nothing to something," says Kanta Pindoria, founder of KP Training & Consulting Ltd. "That's where we bring the best out at every stage." Since Pindoria started the company in 2007, she and her colleagues have trained thousands of people, at various levels, for more than 250 companies.

"Our slogan is 'Bring the best out of people'," she says. "We do this by respecting and understanding the customer; by nurturing them into what they want to become. Bringing the best out of people is seeing the potential within, and for them to see it themselves, no matter which walk of life or discipline they come from."

Based in Park Royal, north west London, KP Training & Consulting Ltd is a small company that works on an international level. It is now offering courses specifically tailored for service personnel and veterans leaving the armed forces. "Some of our trainers and consultants have retired from the armed forces," says Pindoria. "Various disciplines are looking to use their transferable skills to make a life after the armed forces. That's about setting up a business, and then providing them with a necessary skill-set."

The firm set up armed forces training programmes in response to demand. "We had a few inquiries, and then tailored the courses so that they had the right skill-set, and designed the training programme to help them set up a business," says Pindoria. "We also support those leaving the armed forces to face the challenge of adapting to a civilian work-life. It's a change in environment, from control-and-command to a softer, relaxed, civilian life. That's one of the adjustments they have to make. We try to encourage and nurture them using training methods to allow them to progress and fit in with the aftermath of being in the armed forces."

For Pindoria, people who have experience of military service tend to have qualities that are extremely valuable. "Number one is the respect factor," she says. "But there's also the integrity, the quality of the management and leadership skills that they have, the self-discipline and resilience of wanting to achieve and the willingness to learn. Those skill sets were great fits to some of the training we provided. It enhanced it, actually."

www.kptraining.com

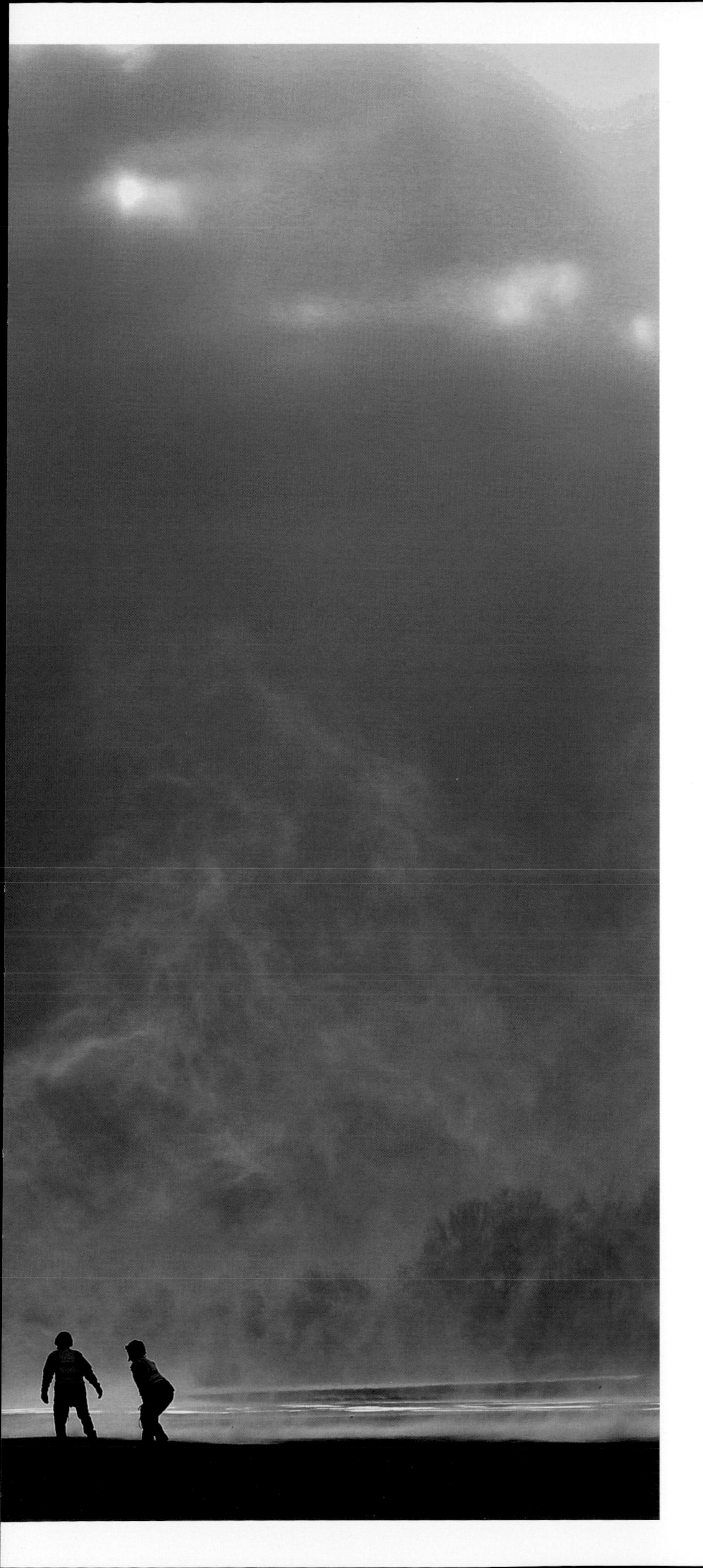

DEFENCE

"The vision of 1918 that air warfare would become decisive had been vindicated in the most emphatic terms possible, and has continued to be in every conflict since"

STRIKE PARTNER

MBDA

While it is now well known as Europe's leading manufacturer of complex weapons, MBDA and its predecessor companies have enjoyed a long and successful partnership with the RAF that even predates the modern concept of the missile. For example, in the Second World War, MBDA's predecessors were the UK's main manufacturers of propellers, making a vital contribution to the Battle of Britain and later campaigns.

The first guided weapon borne from the partnership between the RAF and a predecessor of MBDA was De Havilland Propeller's Firestreak missile, which entered service in 1957 and armed RAF fighters such as the English Electric Lightning and Gloster Javelin as well as the Fleet Air Arm's De Havilland Sea Vixen. This was followed by Red Top, the third British indigenous air-to-air missile to enter service in 1964, and the Blue Steel nuclear missile, which equipped the RAF's "V" bomber force until 1970. From the 1950s to the 1980s the UK was protected by the RAF's ground-based Bloodhound missiles, designed by another predecessor of MBDA – the Bristol Aeroplane Company. These were later augmented in the air defence role by the Rapier missile systems used by the RAF Regiment.

Matra's Martel was the next important missile to enter service with the RAF in 1972 and its fuselage contributed to the development of the Sea Eagle anti-ship missile which began operational service in 1982. Following the creation of BAE Dynamics in 1978, the RAF introduced the Skyflash missile which provided the cutting edge of RAF fighter capability on the Phantom and Tornado F3 throughout the tense Cold War period.

In the build-up to the first Gulf War and beyond, ALARM provided the ability to suppress enemy air defences in Iraq, Kosovo and Libya, whilst ASRAAM underpins the RAF's short range air-to-air capability and the Storm Shadow cruise missile provides a unique long range attack capability used in Afghanistan and later in Operation Shader in operations against ISIS from 2013 onwards. MBDA's Brimstone missile currently provides the RAF with a world-beating, precise, low-collateral strike capability and has seen extensive operational service in Iraq, Afghanistan, Libya and Syria, with an unmatched success rate.

MBDA's revolutionary new Meteor air-to-air missile is entering service on Typhoon and Lightning II, whilst the new Spear surface attack weapon will give the RAF a vital and unrivalled ability to strike even the most difficult and well-protected targets at range. MBDA and the RAF have built a trusted partnership that is set to continue for years to come.
www.mbda-systems.com

X
E
28V DC

FESTIVAL OF FLIGHT

Cobham PLC

Cobham plc is the UK's third-biggest defence company and enjoys both an incredibly close working relationship with the Royal Air Force and a shared, rich aviation history. The company was founded by, and takes its name from, the legendary aviation pioneer, Sir Alan Cobham. Sir Alan was both a pilot in the Royal Flying Corps during the Great War and an aviation pioneer who did so much to raise the profile of aviation between the wars.

When Sir Alan left the newly formed Royal Air Force at the end of the First World War he became a great advocate and pioneer for the potential commercial application of aviation. He embarked on a number of long-distance flights, including to India, South Africa and Australia. In 1926, he became the first person to fly from London to Cape Town and back, for which he received the Air Force Cross, and the first to fly from London to Australia and back, for which he was knighted by King George V.

"Sir Alan became a household name for his pioneering work," says David Lockwood, CEO of Cobham PLC. "He did much to promote aviation to the masses with 'Cobham's Flying Circus', an aircraft show that toured the UK, giving pleasure flights to thousands, which focused on the nation's youth especially. He would certainly applaud and support RAF100's aim today of promoting STEM (science, technology, engineering and mathematics) subjects and the aviation agenda among the younger generation."

As part of his long-distance flying, Sir Alan was quick to recognise the potential of air-to-air refuelling. Even today, Cobham plc is synonymous with aerial refuelling, with its drogue systems flying on most of the world's advanced tankers.

It is now a global company that has a diverse product line across aerospace, land, space and maritime domains, but Cobham continues to be – at its very heart – a defence and aerospace company. Its product line now includes a range of diverse items, including vital equipment for NASA's Mars Science Laboratory Mission, sophisticated electronic assemblies for the EA-28G Growler, F-35 and UAVs and ground-penetrating radar to enhance counter-IED detecting. "Our emphasis on electronic warfare, radars and communications make us highly relevant in today's contested and data-rich military environment," says Lockwood.

Cobham now provides a range of high-specification products and systems that are used on multiple aircraft types throughout the world, in both the commercial and military sector. But as deep and diverse as its product line is, the most visible sign of Cobham's work with the RAF today is in its world-class training support. Cobham's Falcon aircraft provide invaluable electronic warfare training to both RAF and Royal Navy personnel, both at home and on deployed exercises. RAF aircrew train with Cobham every day, brief and debrief with them, and fly alongside them in some of the most complex and challenging scenarios. Cobham also provides electronic warfare training to NATO, the USAF and some customers in the Middle East.

For the past 20 years, Cobham has also provided the Ministry of Defence's helicopter training at the Defence Helicopter Flying School at RAF Shawbury. Here, aircrew from all three services have benefited from the expertise that Cobham has provided both in the cockpit and in the maintenance hangars. Cobham provides helicopter services around the globe, but it is most proud of its support of the MoD for so many years. Cobham is now moving to a new era of international training provision at its newly opened helicopter academy at Newquay Airport in Cornwall. Here Cobham provides world-class specialist training in every helicopter skill necessary for today's military and paramilitary or emergency services.

So, while Cobham is an international company with 11,000 employees worldwide including a major business in the United States, it maintains an exceptionally close relationship with the Royal Air Force. In addition to providing all manner of systems, services and support across the RAF, it has embraced and embodied the whole force approach, both at home and abroad. From Reaper to Sentry, Typhoon to F35, Cyprus to deployed exercises in Oman, Cobham has stood shoulder to shoulder with its RAF colleagues, delivering operational excellence at every turn.

"We fly and operate with the Royal Air Force on a daily basis," says Lockwood. "But we also employ a high number of ex-military and RAF personnel that both retains and reinvests their expertise. We are signatories of the Armed Forces Covenant, and we are keen to expand and deepen our extremely close working relationship with the military and the RAF in particular. We actively recruit veterans, not least because they're great people who do great things, but also, their experience is invaluable in some of the roles and services that we provide back. Also, we plan to increase our proportion of reservists so that we can cement even further our psychological contract with the service."

Lockwood expects aerospace technology to continue to be vital to Britain's security. "Air power is such an important arm of UK military power, and with aerospace being such a key part of the UK's future prosperity and maintaining her technological edge, the partnership between the UK's aerospace industry and the RAF is as vital today as it was in 1918," he says. "As the RAF marks its centenary, Cobham is just a few years behind, but our history, heritage and future remain in lock step, as they have for the past 100 years. Cobham wishes the RAF and all her personnel our warmest congratulations on reaching such an important milestone, and looks forward to the next 100 years of pioneering and innovation."

www.cobham.com

G-FRAI
G-FRAI

100 YEARS OF INNOVATION

BAE Systems

"We pride ourselves on our close and enduring partnership with the Royal Air Force, which has delivered leading-edge technology and helped maintain operational advantage throughout the RAF's illustrious 100-year history," says Jane Butler, UK Government & Customer Relations Director, BAE Systems.

BAE Systems continues to deliver aircraft at the forefront of technology, from icons of the past such as the Supermarine Spitfire and the Harrier, to the aircraft of today such as the Panavia Tornado and the Eurofighter Typhoon – the multi-role backbone of the modern-day air force.

When the RAF was formed on April 1, 1918, it already used a number of highly effective aircraft, many designed by companies that would later become BAE Systems. Manoeuvrability was a byword for the Sopwith Camel, whilst other First World War aircraft such as the Bristol F.2B Fighter and De Havilland DH.9A were employed in a variety of air roles.

During the Second World War, the Supermarine Spitfire became the symbol of the RAF as a fighter, as well as undertaking roles such as reconnaissance and aircraft carrier operations. Aircraft like the Avro Lancaster and the De Havilland Mosquito – which was built in such a number of versions it was a true multi-role aircraft – were employed in precision-strike roles from 1943.

From the 1950s onwards, more icons of the air, such as the English Electric Canberra jet bomber, the Hawker Hunter fighter and the delta-winged Avro Vulcan were introduced into RAF service, followed by the English Electric Lightning – the only all-British supersonic aircraft.

By 1969 the world's first Vertical/Short Take-Off and Landing (V/STOL) aircraft, the Harrier, entered RAF service. Seven years later, the Hawk trainer, the latest version of which is still being manufactured by BAE Systems today, appeared – and was adopted by the Red Arrows in 1979. Each development, each capability provided inspiration for what followed next – and the echoes of these innovations in military aviation can be clearly seen in today's current and next generation aircraft.

Advances in flight controls and aerodynamics in the 1970s and 1980s resulted in the Jaguar Active Control Technology and Experimental Aircraft Programme demonstrators, which ultimately led to the four-nation Eurofighter Typhoon – the main expeditionary aircraft of today's RAF. Typhoon enjoys a significant upgrade path, which is continually being developed, ensuring the aircraft will continue to provide relevant operational capability for many decades to come.

BAE Systems is also proud to have continually developed novel support solutions for the RAF. Its experiences with Harrier and Tornado have led to the innovative TyTAN (Typhoon Total Availability eNterprise) agreement, which is delivering significant savings in through-life cost.

The developments in technology continue. The V/STOL capabilities of the Harrier aircraft were a clear precursor to the next generation Lockheed Martin F-35B Lightning II jets, in which BAE Systems is a key partner and, just like the Sopwith Camels, the Hawker Sea Fury and the British Aerospace Harriers before it, will soon take off at sea, from the UK's flagship Queen Elizabeth-class aircraft carriers, where the company is also a leading partner.

Looking to the future, the company's work on technology demonstrators such as Taranis will inform new developments – including future unmanned programmes and the next generation of fighter aircraft. BAE Systems remains committed to investing in tomorrow, to developing the technologies to protect what matters most – and to ensuring its proud and longstanding relationship with the RAF.

www.baesystems.com

KM W
KM Y

babcock

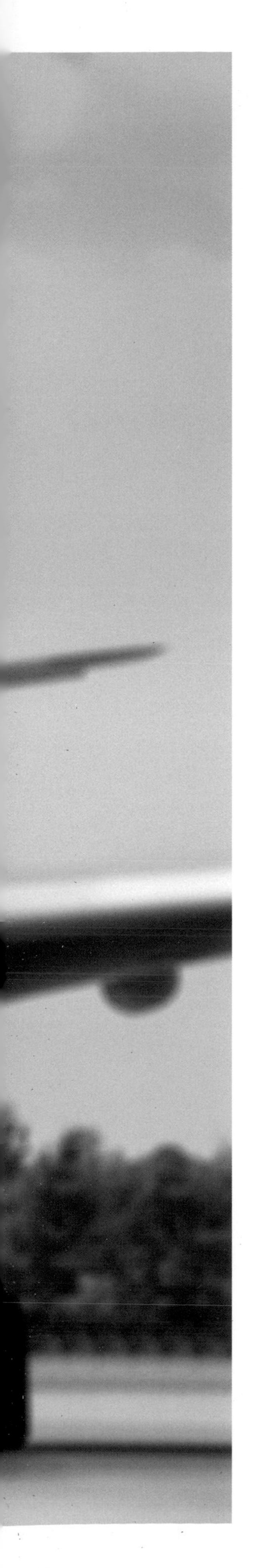

AVIATION EXCELLENCE

Babcock International Group

Babcock is a long-standing industry partner to the Royal Air Force. The two have worked together for almost 100 years, delivering support to air power in defence of the UK.

From supporting the No.3 Maintenance Unit at RAF Milton, to helping build the iconic Merlin engine used in legendary aircraft such as the Spitfire and Lancaster during the Second World War, through to the flying training, aircraft maintenance and airbase support it provides today, Babcock has unique expertise and is a long-standing provider of aviation support.

"Babcock is proud of its 100-year relationship with the Royal Air Force," says Babcock International Group CEO Archie Bethel. "We are looking forward to another century of working together, delivering air power and building another proud legacy for air-minded young people joining the Royal Air Force of the future."

Today, Babcock has a rich aviation heritage, with more than 1,300 pilots, over 4,000 engineers and support specialists delivering vital support to the aviation sector. Within its aviation business it owns, manages and operates a diverse fleet of more than 500 fixed and rotary wing aircraft for both defence and civil customers. It is the second-largest civil aircraft operator in Europe.

Babcock maintains 25 per cent of the Ministry of Defence's fixed wing aircraft and supports more than 70 per cent of all Ministry of Defence flying training hours – representing more than 500,000 hours during the past 14 years alone on the Light Aircraft Flying Task (LAFT).

Babcock is a partner in both the Ascent joint-venture responsible for Military Flying Training Services and AirTanker consortium for Voyager, delivering a world-class flying training system and air-to-air refuelling capability. Babcock also supports the Tucano and Hawk aircraft, as well as owning the fleet of Grob aircraft vital to flying training. It is also pivotal to the operation of many Royal Air Force stations, from infrastructure management to air traffic control, technical support to workshops and logistics.

Babcock invests in the brightest talent supporting all three armed services. Its Aviation STEM (science, technology, engineering, maths) programme is led by employee "ambassadors" who interact with schools, colleges and universities to actively promote both STEM subjects and the opportunities within its aviation business. Additionally, it has active apprenticeship and graduate programmes within the business. Babcock's commitment also applies to Air Cadets, to whom it provides glider and light-aircraft flying experience. With a strong alignment to its customers many Babcock employees are ex-RAF personnel and it also provides a number of reserves to the Royal Air Force.

As the UK's largest engineering support services company, and the second-largest supplier to the UK Ministry of Defence, Babcock is experienced at delivering world-class engineering on a large scale having gained extensive technical experience from supporting the Royal Navy, British Army and the Royal Air Force. Additionally, Babcock's global aviation operations in aerial emergency medical services, search and rescue, and aerial firefighting ensure that it can deliver a wide breadth of practical aviation experience to the continuing support of the Royal Air Force.

www.babcockinternational.com/aviation

A PROVEN PARTNERSHIP

Marshall Aerospace and Defence Group

Marshall Aerospace and Defence Group has proudly supported the Royal Air Force since the service was formed in April 1918. Headquartered in Cambridge, Marshall is now one of the largest independent aerospace and defence companies in the UK.

In 1938, just before the Second World War, a major flying training school for the RAF Volunteer Reserves was established by Marshall at Cambridge Airport, which enabled 600 new RAF pilots to be trained for the Battle of Britain. By the end of the war, the company had trained more than 20,000 aircrew. This training scheme was universally adopted by the RAF in 1941 and continues in part today.

The air support of the Expeditionary Forces during the Falklands conflict in 1982 was made possible due to the installation by Marshall air-to-air refuelling receiver equipment in the RAF Hercules aircraft. The Falklands campaign identified the requirement for a long-range strategic tanker for the RAF and, in 1983, Marshall built its largest hangar to convert civil TriStars for the RAF as both freighter and tanker aircraft for which Marshall became the Sister Design Authority.

In 2013, severe hailstorm damage to five RAF C-130J aircraft raised an Urgent Operational Requirement (UOR) for Marshall to return the aircraft to service. In recognition of the exceptional response by Marshall to the UOR, the RAF awarded Marshall a Chief of the Air Staff's Commendation. These are just some of the challenges that Marshall has faced together in partnership with the RAF.

The strength and trust of the relationship was marked in 2016 by the 50th year of Marshall supporting the RAF's C-130 fleet which today supports Armed Forces around the world. Marshall has always risen to technical and logistical challenges over the decades with the RAF.

It is through Marshall's reputation for supporting the RAF that has led to the company also supporting 11 other air forces and having delivered more than 300 aircraft; an export capability that was a contributing factor to the company winning a 2016 Queen's Award for Enterprise in the International Trade category.

Alistair McPhee, CEO of Marshall Aerospace and Defence Group, commented: "I am incredibly proud that as a business we have supported the Royal Air Force throughout its rich history over the last 100 years and I look forward to how we will support the Royal Air Force in its second century."

www.marshalladg.com

THE PLANE TRUTH

Airbus

During its 100 years of operation, the Royal Air Force has played a critical role in ensuring the safety and wellbeing of not only the people of the UK, but of millions of people around the world. Airbus is proud to support the RAF, and looks forward to its aircraft continuing to play a vital role for the service for many more decades to come.

Airbus is a global leader in aerospace employing a workforce of more than 133,000 worldwide, including approximately 15,000 in the UK. The RAF is currently the only air force in the world to operate all three of Airbus's flagship military aircraft – the A330 MRTT Voyager, the A400M and the Eurofighter Typhoon. In addition to fixed-wing aircraft, the RAF also operates more than 20 Airbus Puma II helicopters. The A400M is the newest Airbus product to join the RAF fleet, providing numbers XXIV, LXX and 206 Squadrons with the world's most advanced and versatile tactical airlifter.

Following delivery of its first A400M in November 2014, aircraft are being delivered to reach a total fleet of 22 aircraft. The A400M is operated from a newly constructed state-of-the-art hanger at RAF Brize Norton, and has been used by the RAF in humanitarian missions to the Caribbean and operational test flights all over the world.

With a unique ability to carry payloads of up to 37 tonnes, at speeds comparable with pure-jet military transports, while taking off and landing from soft unpaved runways, the A400M gives the RAF the capability to deliver troops, equipment and supplies where they are needed most.

The aircraft's two-pilot flight deck crew benefit from 21st century state-of-the-art technologies including an integrated, digital avionics system and fly-by-wire controls. These systems, combined with the aircraft's night-vision-compatible glass cockpit, greatly reduce crew workload and the aircraft's ability to fly at altitudes and speeds comparable to a jet transporter significantly increase the comfort for those on board compared to previous generation airlifters.

Already a firm favourite at air shows, wowing crowds with its spectacular manoeuvrability, the RAF A400Ms have further captured the imagination of the general public through Airbus's A400M Photography Competition, which attracted more than a thousand entries and provided the stunning imagery used in this tribute to the world's oldest air force.

www.airbus.com

A WORLD OF INNOVATION

Lockheed Martin

Both in its current incarnation and through its heritage companies, Lockheed Martin has a rich history with the Royal Air Force that spans more than 75 years. Iconic aircraft such as the Hudson, Martin B-26 Marauder and Consolidated B-24 Liberator have seen distinguished service with the RAF in peacetime and in times of global conflict. In more recent times, the C-130 Hercules has been the backbone of the RAF's tactical air transport fleet and the F-35, the RAFs first fifth-generation aircraft and the world's most advanced combat aircraft, will continue Lockheed Martin's relationship for the next 50 years.

As well as being the centenary of the RAF, 2018 will be a significant year for the UK's F-35 fleet as the iconic 617 "Dambusters" Squadron reforms to be the first Lightning Force Squadron. Lockheed Martin is working closely with the Ministry of Defence to prepare the infrastructure at RAF Marham for the aircraft's arrival in summer 2018.

In the UK, Lockheed Martin employs approximately 1,700 people across 11 key facilities, from Faslane in Scotland to Culdrose in Cornwall. Beyond aircraft, Lockheed Martin delivers critical capability to the RAF including military flight training (through Ascent; a Joint Venture with Babcock), air surveillance radar, cyber and weapons capabilities. And, as the importance of space and cyber capabilities grow, the company is working with the RAF to provide world leading and cost-effective capabilities to further enhance the RAF's ability to continue to defend the UK.

Lockheed Martin is committed to inspiring the next generation of engineers, space explorers and astronauts and it regularly engages in STEM (science, technology, engineering, maths) activities. Its Generation Beyond programme, developed with Discovery Education, provides interactive resources to teachers at schools across the country to help them educate pupils about space. Lockheed Martin has STEM ambassadors at its key locations who work with local schools to encourage young people to think about the opportunities that STEM careers can offer. It is proud to sponsor the TechnoZone at the Royal International Air Tattoo in Fairford where Lockheed Martin teams guide young people through activities such as virtual-reality tours of Mars and F-35 building blocks and help them learn new skills in a fun and innovative way.

Lockheed Martin is proud of its close relationship with the RAF and is a proud to be a supporter of RAF100.
www.lockheedmartin.com

SURVEILLANCE SPECIALIST

General Atomics Aeronautical Systems, Inc. (GA-ASI)

General Atomics Aeronautical Systems, Inc. (GA-ASI) is the world's leader in the development and deployment of remotely piloted aircraft (RPA), supporting allied forces throughout the world. Over the past 10 years, the Royal Air Force and GA-ASI have formed a vital partnership, delivering game-changing surveillance and strike capabilities that have helped ensure the safety and security of the United Kingdom.

Flying more than 100,000 hours over the past decade, the MQ-9 Reaper RPA has been a key asset of the Royal Air Force, being flown by the RAF's XIII and 39 Squadrons in support of operations in Afghanistan and the Middle East, alongside Britain's allies in the United States, Australia, France and Italy.

The endurance and flexibility of the MQ-9 Reaper makes it a pivotal component in the RAF's arsenal. In addition to its kinetic ability, the Reaper provides unsurpassed intelligence, surveillance and reconnaissance (ISR), with payloads that include electro-optical/infrared (EO/IR), Lynx multi-mode radar, electronic support measures (ESM), laser designators, as well as various weapons packages.

During this long-standing partnership, the RAF and GA-ASI have established a relationship built on trust, problem solving and delivering solutions that anticipate the needs of the Armed Forces. "GA-ASI is a proud supporter of the Royal Air Force," says Linden Blue, CEO, GA-ASI. "For the past 10 years, the UK's MQ-9 Reaper fleet has provided persistent, armed surveillance of the battlefield that assists military leaders in making informed operational decisions, and protects allied forces on the ground. GA-ASI looks forward to delivering the next generation of the storied MQ-9 to the RAF in the form of the new MQ-9B Protector."

As it looks to the future, GA-ASI will support the continued success of the RAF with the rapid deployment of a new generation of RPA called the MQ-9B Protector. With greater range, persistence, and strike capability, the Protector will set a new global standard for RPA. In keeping with the partnership's goal to lead, the new Protector will become the first RPA to be certified to fly in civilian airspace in Europe and throughout world.

"GA-ASI thanks the Royal Air Force for its confidence, support, partnership and forward thinking," says Linden Blue. "We look forward to the next decade and beyond of game-changing aeronautical technology."
www.ga-asi.com

MAKING A SHOW OF IT

Defence and Security Equipment International

In 1868, the world's first aeronautical exhibition was held at Crystal Palace, in the south London suburb that now bears its name. This was one of many events that followed Prince Albert's inaugural International Trade Exhibition, staged in the original Crystal Palace in 1851. Known as the Great Exhibition, it was designed to bring together customers, researchers and manufacturers to excite innovative new ideas and establish global trade.

Such gatherings added impetus to the early attempts at powered flight that culminated in the Wright brothers' success in 1903. Within 11 years, air power was being deployed globally as the First World War unfolded, and – 15 years after the Wright brothers' first flight – the Royal Air Force was established. From the start, it engaged both the public and industry. In the 1920s the RAF participated in events such as the Wembley Exhibition and the British Empire Exhibition. This set a path of public and industry engagement which the RAF has continued to follow throughout its first century.

Air power rapidly developed in the crucible of the First World War, when aspiration and imagination often led technology. This has been a constant feature of air power's development – the challenge of harnessing the energy and drive needed to bring new ideas to life outside the imperatives of conflict. The RAF has intuitively understood this challenge and sought every opportunity to bring those wearing flight-suits, lab coats and overalls together in partnership.

Exhibitions, like the remarkable showcase first staged by Prince Albert, serve to encourage and promote exceptional innovation. As its contemporary equivalent for the defence, aerospace, and security sectors, Defence and Security Equipment International (DSEI) takes on this mantle biennially at the UK's flagship exhibition centre, ExCeL London. DSEI has grown to be a pivotal point in the industry's calendar, an event that displays British manufacturing at its best and brightest.

International cooperation and collaboration remains the key to developing and sustaining defence capabilities in the future. Through industry events and exhibitions, pioneering ideas can prosper, alliances are secured, and business thrives. DSEI is proud to work in partnership with the RAF and the RAF's sister services to reflect this global outlook in the years to come.

www.dsei.co.uk

AN ENDURING RELATIONSHIP

Boeing

From the Harvard to the Chinook, Boeing and its legacy companies have supported the Royal Air Force and the United Kingdom for 80 years. In 1938, the Air Ministry contracted with North American Aviation for the supply of Harvard training aircraft, beginning the relationship between the UK and Boeing's family of companies. In 1939 Pan American began first airmail, then passenger services, across the Atlantic with Boeing aeroplanes. Shortly after this, Winston Churchill became the first world leader to fly across the Atlantic in a Boeing 314 Clipper.

Boeing was founded in Seattle by William E Boeing in 1916 and its international headquarters are now in Chicago, but the corporation has strong roots in the UK. Indeed, 2018 marks the 80th anniversary of Boeing's links with the RAF – in June 1938, the British Air Ministry agreed to buy 200 Harvard training aircraft from Boeing legacy company North American.

It started a relationship that has included the supply of many Boeing aircraft to the RAF – from Boeing 314 Clippers to 787 Dreamliners, from Harvards to Chinooks, from A-20 Boston bombers to Douglas DC-3s and C-47s. While celebrating the history of the RAF, Boeing also commemorates the long-lasting partnership and the strong, shared future together with the UK that is on the horizon.

Boeing is the world's largest aerospace and defence company, developing capabilities for its customers from beneath the waves to outer space. It connects, protects, explores and inspires the world. The company has doubled its direct employment in the UK since 2011 and tripled its spending with the UK supply chain over the same period. Boeing spent £2.1 billion with UK suppliers in 2016 and 18,700 people in the UK work at Boeing and the company's tier one supply chain.

Today the C-17 Globemaster III and CH-47 Chinook provide the backbone of the RAF's fleet, with services and support at home and overseas from the Boeing team helping the RAF stay mission ready. Boeing's Information Services team support the Ministry of Defence's Support Chain Information Services and the company's defence training business continues to grow in the UK too. Additional growth by Boeing in the UK is planned, including support for the Boeing P-8A Poseidon for the RAF at Lossiemouth.

www.boeing.co.uk

SHARED HERITAGE

Leonardo

Throughout the past century, the Royal Air Force has been at the leading edge of aerospace capability. "We are proud, as Leonardo and on behalf of our predecessor companies, to have been able to bring our skills to bear in supporting the RAF across such a period of extraordinary growth in innovative technology," says Norman Bone, Chairman and Managing Director of Leonardo in the UK. "We have pride in our shared heritage, and we are committed to our shared future."

The constant throughout this period has been the importance of the partnership between the men and women of the British Armed Forces who commit themselves to the service of the United Kingdom, and those in the industrial aerospace sector who create the advances in technology and manufacturing to bring new capabilities to the front line.

From the earliest aeroplanes to the sophistication of today's aircraft, from the Spitfire's gyro gunsight to the electronically scanned radars, advanced targeting pods and the aircraft protection systems in modern fixed and rotary wing fleets, Leonardo has researched, designed, built and supported technology in the United Kingdom.

Today Leonardo remains one of the UK's largest hi-tech engineering companies, with 7,000 highly skilled people across the country in Basildon, Bristol, Edinburgh, Luton, Southampton and Yeovil. It continues to place innovation and adaptability at the core of all it does, and to place those capabilities at the service of the Royal Air Force, its sister services and of Leonardo's export customers around the world. This brings value to every region of the UK through Leonardo's supply partnerships with 2,300 companies including around 1,500 small and medium-sized enterprises.

As operational demands continue to evolve, Leonardo has placed partnerships at the heart of its approach to help deliver to the RAF and its overseas customers the deployed capability they need, in a timely and cost-effective way. To build for the future, Leonardo engineers run varied Science, Technology, Engineering and Maths (STEM) programmes to inspire the next generation. By imparting its passion for engineering and demonstrating the creativity at the heart of British capabilities, Leonardo looks to ensure that UK aerospace can continue to thrive into the RAF's second century.

www.uk.leonardocompany.com

LEADER IN FLIGHT CONTROL

Moog Aircraft Group

Over the last 66 years, Moog has built a reputation throughout the world as a company whose people and products are at the forefront of the aerospace industry. Company sales exceed $2.5 billion with over 11,000 employees operating in 28 countries. "Our success is down to the unparalleled commitment of our people, and a strong focus on advanced control systems and product technologies," says Mark Trabert, President of Moog Aircraft Group. This commitment has been at Moog's core since the company's founding in 1951. The growth in Moog's stick-to-tail aircraft flight-control systems capability has enabled them to become an industry-leading Tier 1 supplier to the world's aircraft manufacturers. Its products are on nearly every military and commercial platform in the marketplace

Moog has built its reputation on its wide variety of aircraft motion-control systems, ranging from high-precision primary and secondary flight controls to sophisticated engine mechanisms, such as the complex Three Bearing Swivel Nozzle System on the RAF's new F-35B Lightning II. This system controls the engine nozzle to transition the aircraft from horizontal to vertical flight.

Aircraft engine fuel and geometry control has to be flawless in a hot, high-vibration environment. Moog's extensive pedigree in fueldraulic technology is widely utilised within both civil and military engines, such as the EJ200 that powers the RAF's Typhoon.

Moog has invested heavily in its UK operations, with more than 1,000 employees providing production and product support for a variety of historic, current and future RAF aircraft and engines. Including the Hawk, Tornado, Typhoon, F-35, and Voyager. This continued investment and innovation has seen the emergence of new technologies such as the electro-hydrostatic actuators used on the F-35. As the flight-control system prime integrator, Moog developed a new architecture, with a self-contained hydraulic supply integrated into an electronically controlled fly-by-wire actuator system, minimising overall system geometry and reducing weight. A similar approach was used on Atlas, the RAF's new A400M transport aircraft

Moog's control applications also extend to helicopters and missiles, utilising either hydraulic, pneumatic or electric technologies, and unmanned aircraft, such as Mantis, which had one of the first lightweight all-electric flight-control systems. Moog Aircraft Group is determined to stay at the forefront of control system technology, focusing on even better performance technology whilst driving down the overall cost of ownership.
www.moog.co.uk

AN AEROSPACE ACE

Saab

For nearly 40 years, Swedish defence company Saab has been a dedicated partner to the UK and the Royal Air Force. It has collaborated on a variety of advanced defence and security solutions, and built a strong relationship that has empowered British forces.

Saab's values are rooted in trust, reliability, innovation and loyalty, producing systems that are underpinned by a commitment to meeting the needs of the service. The company has delivered several systems that have been in use by the RAF for many years, with each product supporting different roles across the air power spectrum.

At the forefront of these is Gripen, one of the most advanced multi-role fighters in the world. It is currently used at the Empire Test Pilots' School in Wiltshire, providing future test pilots with world-class training. Saab is proud that 35 per cent of this advanced aircraft's content is sourced in the UK, providing an economic benefit of up to £3 billion and some 5,000 to 6,000 jobs over the next 10 years.

In addition, Saab has been protecting RAF aircraft from hostile threats with its counter-measure dispensing technologies for decades. Aircraft that are currently, or have been, equipped with Saab platform protection systems include the Harrier, the Tornado and the Typhoon, and Saab will continue to develop innovative solutions to support the Typhoon for many years to come.

Saab has also supported defence and surveillance operations by providing the ground-based surveillance and air defence radar Giraffe AMB to 16 Regiment Royal Artillery, which has used it on operations and at key events such as the 2012 Summer Olympics in London. The radar is able to classify and track a wide range of challenging air threats and offers warning of incoming rocket, artillery and mortar rounds.

Innovation is key to the RAF's continued success, and Saab is renowned for its innovative approach to technological solutions. Around 25 per cent of Saab's revenue is reinvested in internal R&D, producing products and systems adapted to face modern challenges.

Saab is also a regular supporter of the RAF Charitable Trust and Benevolent Fund, participating at various airshows and events to support these charities. The company's extensive experience of developing advanced technology for military aerospace has enabled a long-term partnership with the UK and the RAF, helping to create a stronger, safer Britain of today and tomorrow.

www.saab.com

POWER SUPPLY

Pratt & Whitney

For more than 80 years, Pratt & Whitney – a world leader in the design, manufacture and service of aircraft engines and auxiliary power units – has been proud to power the Royal Air Force fleet.

The company was founded by Frederick Rentschler in Connecticut in the US in 1925. Since it started working with the service, Pratt & Whitney has been a driving force behind the RAF's operational ability – from the iconic air-cooled Wasp engine in the 1930s to today's F117 and F135 propulsion systems, which power the C-17 Globemaster III military transport and the fifth-generation F-35 Lightning II, respectively.

These engines deliver cutting-edge technology to address the complex and diverse needs of the Royal Air Force. Indeed, Pratt & Whitney remains committed to delivering world-class propulsion systems to power its customers now and into the future.

The F135 is the world's most advanced fighter engine, delivering more than 40,000 lbs of thrust and unmatched advances in safety, design, performance and reliability. The F135 propulsion system for the F-35 incorporates the LiftFan. In 2001, this piece of technology earned Pratt & Whitney the prestigious Collier Trophy, an aviation award administered by the US National Aeronautic Association. The LiftFan provides short take-off and vertical landing (STOVL) capability to the UK's military.

Coupled with an adaptive control system that allows the aircraft to transition from hover to flight mode at the push of a button, these technologies enable the F-35B to operate from land bases, as well as the new Queen Elizabeth-class aircraft carriers. The engine also leverages unique fifth-generation thermal management and stealth capabilities, which make the aircraft more survivable against increasingly sophisticated threats.

Pratt & Whitney is working closely with the Royal Air Force as it progresses toward initial operational capability (IOC) in 2018. The company feels privileged to be delivering an engine that will be the power behind the United Kingdom's future land and carrier fighter force. It is also very proud to help the world's longest serving air force commemorate its historic milestone of 100 years and counting.

www.pw.utc.com

A HISTORY OF INNOVATION

Thales

Since its inception in 1918, the Royal Air Force has explored and extended the frontiers of human skill, endurance and technology. Thales is proud of its legacy of close cooperation with the world's first independent air force.

This legacy is inherited from its precursor companies. Big names in British technology like Marconi, Shorts, Thorn EMI, Vinten, Racal and Rediffusion all cooperated with the RAF during two world wars, providing – for instance – innovations in optical equipment for delivering weapons and hydrostatic fuses used in the bouncing bomb.

Today, Thales continues that tradition as the RAF faces unprecedented challenges that place new demands on people and equipment. Thales is supporting the RAF's technological transformation: for example, Chinook and A400M Atlas aircraft are equipped with Thales cockpits and, under the Marshall Programme, the company provides key air-traffic management capabilities to support RAF operations at home and overseas.

It is also partnering on the construction of a new High G-force Centrifuge pilot training facility at RAF Cranwell and will provide the instructors and maintainers to prepare future generations of RAF fast jet pilots for the rigours of G-force.

However, the company's relationship with the RAF is primarily about people. The RAF is transforming its training and Thales is designing, building and servicing a new generation of synthetic training services. Its instructors and engineers also work alongside uniformed colleagues at every stage of a young pilot's progress, which ranges from basic flying tuition to advanced mission training in simulated environments.

In addition, the Thales Charity Trust has close links with several RAF charities and is a proud sponsor of the RAF100 Appeal. Many of the company's people also support the RAF directly as uniformed reservists, and it actively backs the Armed Forces Covenant.

As well as commemorating 100 years of achievement, Thales also celebrates the RAF's current work, which serves to inspire its own people to continue delivering extraordinary hi-tech solutions that enable the RAF to shape its second century, protecting UK citizens and projecting the UK's influence around the world.

www.thalesgroup.com

INSPIRING THE FUTURE

Northrop Grumman

Northrop Grumman has a well-established presence in the UK and is involved in a range of future game-changing defence and security programmes. Whether this is as a partner in the F-35 Lightning II, as a specialist in large intelligence datasets, as the pre-eminent provider of High-Altitude Long Endurance unmanned air systems, or as the go-to company for truly open system architectures for battlespace networks – Northrop Grumman has built an unparalleled reputation as an innovator.

"Partnerships are extremely important for us and we have a long history of collaboration with the RAF helping ensure that they have the technologies and capabilities they need," says Andrew Tyler, Chief Executive, Northrop Grumman Europe. "We are proud to be working alongside the RAF and to support the centenary celebrations."

Northrop Grumman is fully integrated with RAF operations through providing whole-life support, including maintenance and modernisation services, for the RAF's fleet of Sentry E-3D AWACS aircraft based at RAF Waddington. The company is also a principal partner on the F-35 Lightning II programme with key roles in providing the centre fuselage, and much of the aircraft's situational awareness, communications and battlespace networking capabilities.

As F-35 squadrons deploy onto the new aircraft carrier, HMS *Queen Elizabeth*, supporting the aircraft is a major focus. "With the UK providing global component maintenance, repair, overhaul and upgrade services for F-35," says Tyler, "we are excited to be part of the innovative industry–government partnership together with BAE Systems and the Defence Electronics and Components Agency (DECA) that will provide these services."

Looking to the future, Northrop Grumman is deeply committed to promoting science, technology, engineering and mathematics (STEM), and to nurturing the next generation of talent not only in cyber security, but also in aerospace engineering. This year, Northrop Grumman will launch its Summer Time Advanced Aerospace Residency (STAAR) summer camp at RAF Cosford for 14 and 15 year olds, developed in partnership with the RAF Museum and RAF Cosford to inspire young people and provide a unique experience to help them understand more about advanced aerospace systems engineering. "2018 will be a landmark year for the RAF," says Tyler, "and we at Northrop Grumman look forward to contributing to its success, providing inspiration for the future and to deepening our partnership over many years to come."

www.northropgrumman.com/europe

CUTTING-EDGE SUPPORT

Raytheon

Raytheon is proud to be a sponsor of the Royal Air Force's 100th anniversary celebrations. Raytheon's roots in the UK stretch back over a century to when Cossor Electronics (which Raytheon acquired in 1961) was established in Clerkenwell, London, in 1896. The company's association with the RAF dates back to the early 1930s, when it used its specific engineering expertise to develop the radar receiver for the Chain Home defence system and its associated radio communications network, which provided Fighter Command with a decisive technological edge in the Battle of Britain.

Deployed in 1937, it was Cossor's pioneering radar technology that provided Fighter Command with intelligence on approaching Luftwaffe formations. And it was Cossor's radios that then enabled this information to be "networked" so that the RAF's outnumbered pilots could be directed accurately and rapidly towards enemy bombers and their escorts, thereby allowing them to engage with maximum impact.

Today, Raytheon is proud to continue to provide the RAF with a technological edge on operations, through the provision and support of two innovative, world-leading intelligence, surveillance and reconnaissance (ISR) aircraft: the Sentinel (in service with 5 Squadron) and the Shadow (in service with 14 Squadron). Both aircraft are key UK ISR assets that have been consistently deployed on NATO and coalition operations around the world, and provide vital intelligence to the UK's Armed Forces across a wide range of different operations.

Raytheon also provides the RAF with the Paveway IV, its primary air-to-ground precision-guided strike weapon on operations, and the AMRAAM, its beyond-visual-range air-to-air missile. Integrated on the Tornado GR4, the Typhoon and the F-35 Lightning II, the Paveway IV provides unrivalled operational flexibility, while the AMRAAM gives the Typhoon a first-class air-intercept capability.

"The RAF is a very important customer for Raytheon," says Richard Daniel, Chief Executive and Managing Director, Raytheon UK. "Many of our 1,700 employees in the UK and our colleagues in the US are honoured to work alongside the RAF to support and maintain its aircraft and weapons on a daily basis. We extend our congratulations to the RAF as it marks a historic milestone and send our best wishes for its 100th anniversary celebrations. We look forward to supporting the RAF100 Appeal as Technology Sponsors of the Baton Relay and Primary Sponsor of the RAF Engineering Challenge, and to continuing our association with the service for many years to come."

www.raytheon.co.uk

A CENTURY OF PIONEERING

Rolls-Royce

"Rolls-Royce is immensely proud to have powered the Royal Air Force throughout its illustrious history," says Tom Bell, Rolls-Royce President – Defence. "We have shared a century of innovation, partnering to break new ground in the field of aviation, and are committed to continuing that pioneering spirit to enable future generations to reach for the skies."

Rolls-Royce has been partnering with the RAF since it first took to the skies in the Kestrel-powered Bristol fighter in 1918. Since then, the pioneering and innovative spirit of both organisations has powered an illustrious history. The development of the Merlin engine in 1933 heralded one of the most famous chapters in the story of Rolls-Royce and the RAF. It powered two of the most iconic aircraft ever to fly in RAF colours: the Spitfire and the Hurricane, both of which played such a heroic role in the Battle of Britain.

The Merlin transformed Rolls-Royce from a relatively small company into a major contender in aero propulsion. In parallel, it began the development of the aero gas turbine, pioneered by Sir Frank Whittle, which ushered in the jet age. The Welland engine entered service in the Gloster Meteor fighter in 1944 and gave the company the confidence to commit itself to the gas turbine, in which it had a technological lead. Jet power enabled the RAF to further push the boundaries of flight, and the partnership with Rolls-Royce continue to flourish as the Avon engine powered the Canberra and Hunter into service, while the Olympus first earned its spurs in the distinctive Avro Vulcan.

This pioneering spirit continued with the entry into service of the world's first vertical take-off and landing aircraft, the Harrier – its Pegasus engine providing unmatched manoeuvrability for a fast jet fighter. Today, short take-off and vertical landing (STOVL) performance has been taken to the next level in the RAF's newest aircraft, the F-35B Lightning II, thanks to the Rolls-Royce LiftSystem.

Elsewhere, Rolls-Royce technology and innovation are enabling RAF operations around the globe, around the clock – delivering the power behind the combat, transport and patrol, and humanitarian missions of today, and training the pilots of tomorrow.

One hundred years after Rolls-Royce and the RAF's first flight together, the partnership is continuing its rich tradition in setting new standards for innovation and operational excellence.

www.rolls-royce.com

NUCLEAR INTELLIGENCE

AWE

The business of nuclear deterrence is subject to a uniquely challenging set of circumstances. As a signatory to the 1996 Comprehensive Nuclear Test Ban Treaty (CTBT), the UK cannot conduct tests of nuclear warheads. Yet to maintain the country's nuclear defences safely and effectively, they must be tested. So how? The answer is big science.

AWE (Atomic Weapons Establishment) has spent more than 60 years developing and maintaining the warheads for Britain's nuclear deterrent, for the Ministry of Defence. Its team of scientists and engineers provide and maintain warheads for Trident, but also offers government innovative solutions to combat nuclear threats, proliferation and terrorism, with 24/7 emergency response support.

"The thing that inspires me is the vision that people have at AWE," says CEO Iain Coucher. "These are people who can conceive of experiments or technical solutions to anything – from the tiniest of measurement systems, to warheads and to buildings. Few people get to do something so technically challenging and so important."

With no nuclear testing permitted, analysis and verification of capability is carried out by staggeringly complicated computer simulation. AWE has three of the UK's most powerful supercomputing systems, each capable of two thousand million million (10^{15}) floating point operations per second (or 2 petaflop), with another 4.3 petaflop system – the Damson supercomputer – becoming operational this year.

Specialist code simulates the complex science at the heart of a nuclear warhead, while these codes are then validated by empirical evidence drawn from plasma physics and hydrodynamic experiments. AWE's Orion laser creates super-dense matter at temperatures in excess of 10 million degrees Celsius, while large-scale radiography tests the parameters of simulated explosive shock.

As well as testing, AWE's work includes lifecycle responsibility for materials, accounting for all of the environments that the warhead will experience, such as remaining in storage for many years, road transport, and deployment undersea. The physics of sustained acceleration, vibration, temperature changes, stress and many others have to be understood over timescales of seconds to years.

Under the 1958 Mutual Defence Agreement, AWE collaborates with equivalent weapons laboratories in the US, gaining vast benefit from shared expertise as well as access to facilities and test data. There is also a mutual relationship with academia. "Up to 15 per cent of Orion's system time is available to international academics and researchers," says AWE's head of physics, Professor Andrew Randewich. "In UK universities, around 140 sponsored PhD studentships are currently in place and undergraduate student placements encourage recruitment and employability at a time when UK graduate STEM (science, technology, engineering, maths) skills are in short supply."

In uncertain times that throughput of expertise is vital to UK national security and AWE is on the front foot to foster those skills to tackle the diverse and developing threats in 21st century defence.

"I am incredibly proud to be leading this great company," says Coucher. "A company with a long history and a rich heritage of supporting the UK's nuclear deterrent and keeping our country safe."

www.awe.co.uk

LIFESTYLE

THE FACE OF AVIATION

Hamilton

For over a century, the Hamilton watch company has been a byword for precision in a variety of different areas. In its very early days, the Hamilton pocket watch was regarded as an impeccably trustworthy timepiece on the railroads of America – in fact, it was chosen as the "Watch of Railroad Accuracy" in 1912. Its close links with military heritage were epitomised in the Second World War when it briefly stopped making watches for consumers and instead provided a million items for US troops. Since then, however, the Hamilton brand has been most affiliated with the worlds of celluloid – its products have featured in more than 450 movies since 1951 – and, above all, aviation.

Hamilton's links with the skies began in 1918, when it became the official timekeeper for US airmail flights between the cities of Washington DC, New York and Philadelphia. The brand was also of invaluable help to Admiral Richard E Byrd in 1926, when he used it for his pioneering flight over the North Pole. By the 1930s, TWA, Eastern, Northwest and United Airlines had adopted it as an official timepiece. Indeed, United Airlines selected Hamilton especially for its first coast-to-coast flights between New York and San Francisco, a journey that lasted 15 hours and 20 minutes.

These days, Hamilton watches are used as aviation equipment all over the world. "Maintaining our partnerships with squadrons or outstanding pilots is key to the enhancing of future models and staying up-to-date," says Sylvain Dolla, CEO of Hamilton Watch International. "These watches are born from a strong legacy in air travel and a desire to serve the working pilot, as well as the consumer interested in aviation, or just those who admire the purpose-built, yet supremely attractive, designs."

Pilots and squadrons have provided the watchmaker with a wealth of feedback over the years and, as a consequence, the company has introduced a number of new functions to its timepieces, such as two time zones, and the ability to calculate land speed and drift angle or fuel required, convert units of measurement and log information for up to 20 flights. For Dolla, the link with aviation professionals has been vital to Hamilton's enduring success. "Understanding the world of aviation and keeping a close relationship with its practitioners helps us to understand their expectations and what they really require," he says, "not only in terms of design but also technology."

The company's many clients have included Air Zermatt in Switzerland and the Patrulla Aspa in Spain. Hamilton also provided watches to the Royal Air Force, including asymmetrical chronographs with a black dial and large white hands and indexes for higher visibility. Hamilton became the official timekeeper of the Red Bull Air Race in 2005, when it began collaborating with one of the race's participants, the aerobatic pilot Nicolas Ivanoff, who is now its brand ambassador. "In 2010, the competition stopped for a few years to fine-tune the concept," says Dolla. "Now it's back, with Hamilton as

SAT
CHRONOMETER

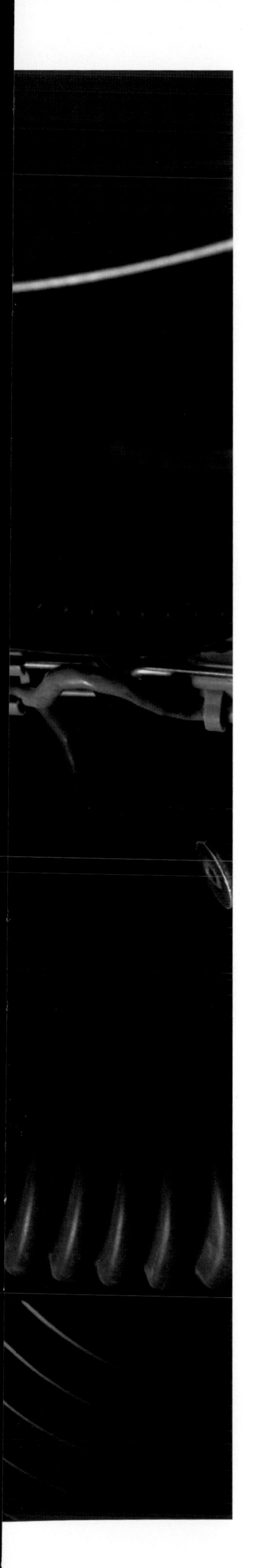

its main partner, and with more passion than ever to make this championship a globally eminent event."

With its sister company ETA providing collaborative technical expertise, Hamilton has consulted closely with pilots over the years. Throughout 2018 it is placing pilots at the heart of its centenary celebrations in aviation in a number of different ways.

"It's all about understanding pilots' needs in aviation watches," says Dolla. "Firstly, racing pilots – we are strengthening our partnership as Official Timekeeper of the Red Bull Air Race World Championship by supporting more pilots than ever. Secondly, rescue pilots – our long-standing partner Air Zermatt is marking its 50th anniversary this year, and we're celebrating our fourth watch collaboration together so far. Finally, the young generation of pilots – Hamilton is the official watch sponsor for the Air Force Academy of the United States."

In addition, Hamilton has marked its centenary of timing the skies by developing a limited-edition version – exactly 1,918 individually numbered pieces – of its Khaki X-Wind Auto Chrono watch (pictured, page 185). "We wanted the most precise Hamilton mechanical movement ever made," says Dolla. "Celebrating 100 years of timing the skies was the perfect milestone to launch this watch. Being an aviation piece, it had to be highly technical and packed with aviation features." Hamilton has also recently extended the Khaki X-Wind line to include a modern, edgy automatic Day Date version (pictured, opposite), with large glow-in-the-dark Roman numerals, a sporty dial and typical pilot hands.

The original, groundbreaking incarnation of the Khaki X-Wind Auto Chrono watch appeared in 2005, with a drift-angle calculator. Highly useful for pilots, the calculator has enabled them to calculate and record crosswinds on their journey in the skies. When they enter details of the wind speed and direction into the rotating bezels of the device, they can establish not only the angle of drift but also the crosswind component too. The 2018 enhanced, limited-edition version of the watch is even more special than the original incarnation. It comes in its own robust, 45 mm steel case, and also has improved readability: it sports newly shaped hands, and sand-coloured Super-LumiNova numerals, which glow neon-green when in darkness.

It boasts one extra feature of remarkable precision. "It is the first Hamilton chronograph movement with a silicon hairspring," says Dolla, "which makes the movement more precise, as silicon is non-magnetic and less sensitive to shocks – an important factor for pilots as they are often in environments with high magnetic fields, such as airports."

As Hamilton clocks up a full century of combining aviation with technology, it intends to continue developing exciting new watch models with high-performing movements and exclusive new designs. "Hamilton produces watches that are technical, authentic and unique," says Dolla, "for people looking for something special and daring."

www.hamiltonwatch.com

THE FABRIC OF A NATION

AW Hainsworth

AW Hainsworth & Sons has been manufacturing premium woollen cloth from its mill in Farsley, Yorkshire since 1783. Today the mill sits on 4.5 acres of land and is led by the seventh generation of the Hainsworth family.

Using a fully vertical mill, AW Hainsworth manages the production process from start to finish, processing 6,700kg of wool every week. It has developed an expertise in selecting the appropriate fibres and understands the importance of fibre placement. "As well as carefully selecting the best raw wool, our diligence at every stage allows us to manage the quality of our cloth to standards envied by mills globally," says Managing Director Tom Hainsworth. "Our specialised departments have the experience to drive performance and improve products by using timeless processes perfected by modern technology."

AW Hainsworth's cloth has played a part in some of the most iconic moments in military history. The red uniforms worn by the British Army at the Battle of Waterloo in 1815 were made from Hainsworth's signature scarlet cloth which is still worn by the Royal Guards outside Buckingham Palace and seen every year at the Trooping the Colour ceremony. From 1899, the cloth for the first official Khaki uniforms worn by the entire British military was developed by AW Hainsworth in conjunction with the University of Leeds, and its special five-colour mix and unique blend process is still used today.

When the Royal Air Force was formed in 1918 it was AW Hainsworth that proposed the distinctive Wedgwood-blue uniform that is still worn today and known as "RAF blue". It has inspired air regiments from numerous other countries to copy the exact fabric. The company has developed an understanding for the stringent demands of the military when it comes to structure, durability and wearability, and these skills are now applied to the cloth that it delivers to each of its many and varied markets.

Today, AW Hainsworth is a market leader in high-performing textiles and innovative fibre solutions. "Our in-house lab, accredited by the UK Accreditation Service, allows us to be innovative and apply modern technology to our traditional manufacturing process," says Tom Hainsworth. "It ensures consistency at all stages of the manufacturing process but also develops textile solutions that incorporate the natural benefits of wool."

The company's range of innovative solutions and cutting-edge fabrics protect firefighters, police officers and military personnel worldwide. Its passion for protecting people who face hazardous situations as part of their profession drove AW Hainsworth to create the first inherently heat- and flame-retardant fabric in the UK, when the market demands for firefighter uniforms changed from the historic woollen tunics in 1982.

Hainsworth's product ranges don't end at uniform and protective fabrics, however. Its cloth also graces the catwalks of fashion houses such as Chanel, Valentino and Prada, and is worn by the likes of Karl Lagerfeld, Harry Styles and the Duchess of Cambridge. It also offers a comprehensive range of high-quality interior fabrics to the aviation and rail industry, premium piano components to Steinway and the world's fastest snooker baize. "We take a long-term view to making cloth," says Tom Hainsworth. "You don't just pick up a craft. It takes time to develop."

www.awhainsworth.co.uk

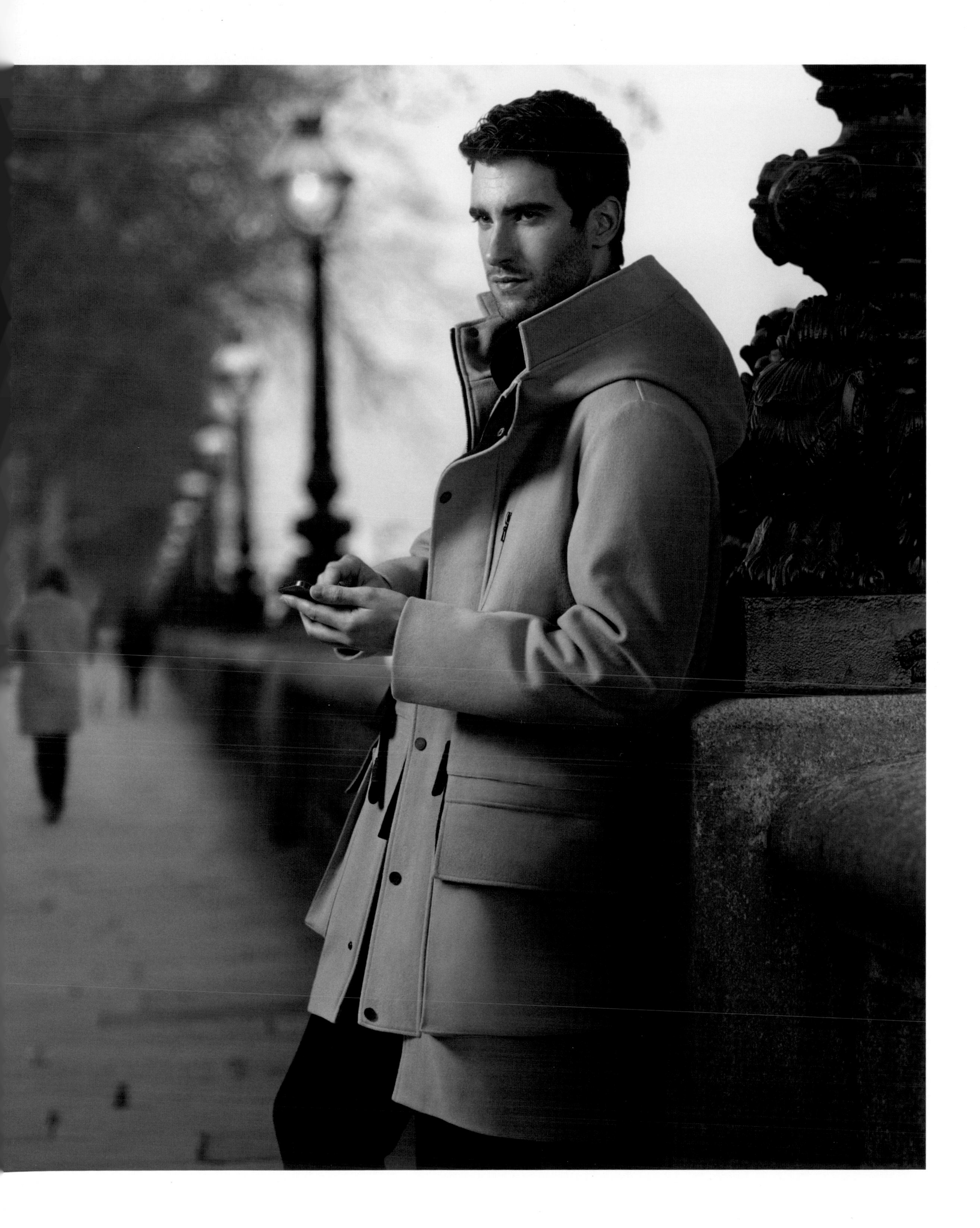

DESIGN FOR LIFE

Martin Kemp Design

"We'd like to be seen as purveyors of a new British interior design – denizens of ultimate style and chic," says Martin Kemp, founder of London-based Martin Kemp Design (MKD). "We'd like to become the first British company to court such a same cachet."

His eponymous company is only six years old, but Kemp is already close to fulfilling that dream, with the world's elite calling on his services. They include Kylie Minogue, for whom MKD recently designed an apartment. "Kylie explained: 'You've done such lovely things for me, I'm happy to do the same for you!' " he says. "But, usually, we are immensely discrete about our celebrity clients."

These include a famous fashion icon who was impressed by a private jet that MKD had designed and refitted. "He said it was the only plane on which he's travelled that suits him and his style," says Kemp. "We thought this was immensely kind and flattering." The plane – designed for a client with a meticulous eye for detail, with a tailored colour-scheme of taupes and greys – has, remarkably, since been sold at a profit.

Kemp started his company in February 2012, after working for various design studios in both the UK and the US. Born in Wales, he showed artistic ability at an early age and studied three-dimensional design at the Cardiff School of Art & Design, before moving to London to work in retail design and then relocating to Los Angeles, where he designed celebrity homes. After his return to London, he saw a gap in the market for a high-end interior design company. "There were many interior decorators, but very few super-prime residential interior designers," he says.

More than just an interior design company, however, MKD now brands itself as a "lifestyle service", producing creative solutions for interiors, architecture, yachts, cars, furniture and products. Focus is largely on the super-prime residential market, but also embraces high-end retail, office and restaurant design.

"We can cover almost everything, from the architecture right through to putting the bed linen on the beds," explains Kemp. "We source artwork – from Renoirs to high-street prints – and classic motor cars, and we even suggest holiday destinations to our clients. They like to be discerning. They like to be different. That's why building a relationship is so important, and why projects can take three years or more. We travel with our clients, go out to dinner and occasionally on holiday with them. We are invited to spend time together understanding how they live and what they like." The company undertakes projects right around the world, from London to Monaco, Courchevel to Beijing, New York to Mumbai. Clients tend to be entrepreneurs, global business owners and celebrities. Recommendations come by word of mouth and through very discreet networking opportunities.

MKD's designs are always bespoke, and range from understated country elegance to dynamic city chic. The studio uses the best-quality materials and employs top craftsmen, both locally and internationally, to create "heritage designs" that will endure. Future plans include the launch of an MKD product range, comprising homewares such as candles, soap pumps and tissue boxes.

"When we accessorise our clients' homes we find that there's a gap in the market for high-designed pieces that match the interiors we create, so we've decided to supply our own." And, for Kemp, MKD is an inherently British company. "We're not about bulldogs, Winston Churchill or Union Flags. We are reinventing the British design vernacular."

www.martinkempdesign.com

OLD FIRM, YOUNG HEART

Grenson

Tim Little is talking through the moment in 1997 when he quit his job in advertising to start his own shoemaking business. Shoemaking was an industry, he admits, of which he had no experience. "I remember handing over the keys to my Porsche and the next day walking from my house to Chiswick to buy stationery at WH Smith," he explains. "I went from director of an agency to absolutely nothing. But then again, aren't all the best passions irrational?"

Well, maybe not so irrational. The decision wasn't so much taken on a whim but because he sensed an opportunity. He loved the great Northamptonshire shoe marques and their traditional approach to craftsmanship, but thought that many of their designs were similarly stuck in the past. Little's customers clearly agreed, and it wasn't long before his small King's Road store in Fulham, west London, was supplying not only Selfridges in the capital, but also Barneys in New York.

Fast forward eight years, and Little had made quite a name for himself. Grenson, one of Britain's most famous shoemaking labels, founded in 1866 by William Green (pictured, above), asked him to revitalise its business as CEO and Creative Director. "In 2005, when I started, Grenson's average customer was probably 60 plus," he says. "But many were 70 or 80 years old. Its rivals were elite and snobby, too. I thought it was a missed opportunity for a wonderful craft."

So Little set to work, using his early experiences with the label as a blueprint. "My first proper pair of shoes were actually Grensons," he says. "I always felt that Grenson had a slightly quirky, younger edge that some of its rivals lacked. So we decided to keep the craftsmanship but have more fun with the design. We call it 'an old company with a young heart'."

Today, this ethos runs throughout the business, which has grown to be 100 staff strong and now has six of its own stores, including one in New York. A typical example is one of Little's early hits, which came when he experimented with using a white wedge sole, normally seen on workwear boots, on to a classic wingtip brogue. It soon became a common sight among thirtysomethings in east London. Yet at the same time, Grenson always kept its traditional super-strong Goodyear welting construction – a technique pioneered by the label in the 1870s – that sees the upper stitched to a leather band, which is then stitched to the sole.

"In the 1930s," says Little, "Grenson's tagline was simply 'The Good Shoe' and I thought, 'That's what we should be like now, understated yet confident'. Our tone of voice is more honest. We want you to wear our shoes every day and batter them. And when you do, bring them back and we'll tidy them up."

It's an approach that has been so successful that the previous owner sold the business to Little in 2010. Grenson now sells to stores all over the world and even provides shoes for the Red Arrows, whose pilots wear them when they attend events or collect medals, re-establishing a link that existed decades ago.

But why shoes? Why was Little willing to gamble everything on them? "Because you invest in them," he says. "Like denim, they shape to you the more you wear them. In five years' time you'll say, 'That's my favourite pair – don't you dare throw them away!' "

www.grenson.com

SPIRIT OF FREEDOM

Spitfire Heritage Gin

The iconic Spitfire is to be built once more – in Britain. Thanks to a consortium of British manufacturing companies led by the Spitfire Heritage Trust – and Spitfire Heritage Gin – new Spitfires are set to take to the skies. The gin – like the Spitfire, "built to be the best" – is committed to supporting a prototype Spitfire "Type 2K": a full-scale, two-pilot, next-generation aircraft built from state-of-the-art composite materials and processes.

The journey started with a chance meeting between a children's author and a pilot and a Spitfire expert. "I wrote a book, *The Ghost of Cameron Crowe*, with a Spitfire at its heart," says Ian Hewitt, founder of Spitfire Heritage Gin. "It introduced me to David Spencer Evans, who talked about Spitfires, and Lesotho – 'the Kingdom in the Sky'. In 1940 this small African country donated more money, per capita, to the Spitfire Fund than any other country, furnishing 72 Squadron with 24 aircraft. I became Vice Chairman of the Spitfire Heritage Trust in 2015."

Hewitt went a step further, with the launch of Spitfire Heritage Gin, which would go on to support the trust across various projects. "Gin is the quintessential British tipple," he says. "Like the Spitfire, ours was created to be the best: a symbol of freedom, British verve and excellence. World champion small-batch, single-estate gin producer John Walters created our botanical gin, using rosemary for remembrance, borage for courage, blood orange for the fallen, and rose petals for the Air Transport Auxiliary (ATA) pilots. Top aviation illustrator Romain Hugault created the label's 'Bunny' the ATA girl."

The trust's first international mission was to thank Lesotho (during the 50th anniversary of its independence) with a full-size Spitfire. A Basotho blanket, the country's national dress, bearing images of the Spitfire and the trust's emblem was created by royal appointment to mark the occasion. The Spitfire monument was presented to the king of Lesotho by Hewitt and Evans at the country's Armistice parade in 2016.

Spitfire Heritage Gin launched in May 2016. Two months later, at a blind tasting, Harrods' sommeliers ranked it among Britain's best artisan gins. Stocked at Harrods, RAF officers' messes and the finest restaurants and bars, Spitfire Heritage Distillers is proud to support the RAF Association during the RAF's centenary year, gifting a hefty percentage of the profits from every commemorative bottle sold. "Raise a glass," says Hewitt, "and be proud of your Spitfire Heritage."

www.spitfireheritagedistillers.com

FORM AND FUNCTION

Rimowa

"Rimowa suitcases are a record of a personal journey, a trusted travel companion," says Rimowa's CEO, Alexandre Arnault. Renowned for its lightweight, hard-wearing luggage, this German brand has traversed the globe in the hands of many, from holidaymakers to business travellers to the RAF – with a classic look inspired by aircraft design.

Founded in Cologne in 1898, Rimowa comes from a long line of innovators. "The company's founder, Paul Morszeck, began making cases from wood and leather," says Arnault. "He pioneered an approach to manufacturing that blended the utmost precision and skill with new ideas and new technologies." Inspired by the lightweight, resilient aluminium used for the first commercial aircraft, Paul's son, Richard, launched the first-ever lightweight metal suitcase in 1937. In 1950, Rimowa's suitcases gained the clean, elegant lines that have become their hallmark. These can still be found on every product the company manufactures.

Heritage and innovation lie at the centre of Rimowa's design philosophy. It is governed by the idea that form must follow the beauty of function, which is clearly seen in its suitcases. "The exterior of a Rimowa suitcase has changed little over the past six decades, but that does not mean that the suitcase itself has not altered," says Arnault. "We use the latest technological advancements to improve every feature. Can a wheel, for instance, spin more smoothly? Can a shell be made both lighter and more resilient?" However, it's not just about machinery. "Each suitcase is imbued with decades of experience and expertise at the hands of skilled craftsmen. Every detail in its over 200 parts and 90 manufacturing steps is considered and coaxed to perfection."

This has always been the company's approach and has led to some of Rimowa's most revolutionary and iconic products. This includes the best-selling sturdy aluminium Topas suitcases, launched in the 1950s. "They are the perfect encapsulation of the company's past, present and future," says Arnault. Equally popular is its suitcase range made of ultralight, resilient polycarbonate – another world first that Rimowa launched in 2000. The company's latest product is yet another innovation.

"We have introduced the Rimowa Electronic Tag, or RET, which allows customers to replace paper baggage tags on select airline partners," says Arnault. "Each of these innovations has been purposefully driven by Rimowa's heritage. It is a constant reminder of where the company has come from and where it has yet to go."

www.rimowa.com

MODEL CITIZENS

Hornby Hobbies

Although we might associate the name Hornby with trains and railways, the venerable toy company is also heavily involved with aircraft through two of its biggest brands – Airfix and Corgi. Hornby Hobbies has owned Airfix since 2006 and Corgi since 2008, and these two companies are both deeply immersed in the history of the Royal Air Force.

"The most popular models with both brands are RAF craft and we've always carried a wide range of them," says Michael Clegg, Hornby's flight specialist. "If you asked the collector, they'd say our strength was the RAF, that's what we are known for."

Airfix revolutionised the toy market when it began producing plastic self-assembly kits, beginning with the Golden Hind in 1952. This was quickly followed by the Spitfire Mk 1, which became an early best-seller as aircraft became indelibly associated with Airfix. These days, Airfix kits are more often sold to adult model-makers than schoolchildren, but the popularity of RAF aircraft has not lessened.

"Aviation has always been the most consistent part of the range," says Hornby brand manager Darrell Burge. "We have always been a British company and have always specialised in British subjects, including those aircraft flown by the RAF. The choice of models is simply phenomenal now. There are around 70 planes in the current range, spanning all eras of the RAF's 100-year history, from the Sopwith Camel up to the Eurofighter Typhoon. The Spitfire is so popular worldwide that we make just about every mark or make ever produced. The Red Arrow Hawk is the second-best seller in the UK; again it's an iconic aircraft that represents the modern RAF." The Spitfire and Hawk are still available as starter kits aimed at younger markets, making them the gateway into model-making for generations of British children.

Over at Corgi, Clegg notes that the brand's die-cast metal vehicles have also made the transition from child's toy to collectors' models. That switch occurred when Corgi introduced the Aviation Archive range in 1988. Initially, this featured beautiful scale models of civilian aircraft, but Corgi soon added a line of military aircraft, starting with the Spitfire and the Hurricane, and these proved hugely popular. The success of the range was cemented when Corgi produced the Avro Lancaster.

"This big, four-engine heavy bomber in die cast really caught the imagination and helped to established the brand," says Clegg. "We now have Cold War jets such as the Canberra and Hawker Hunter, and we also have Typhoons and Tornados. Our latest model is the Lightning F6, which is a great aircraft and collectors are going mad for it. It's the only Mach 2, fully British-designed Cold War aircraft, and is a very impressive sight." Similarly, a range of toy models is also produced, to ensure that children can still collect something that they can play with.

Both Clegg and Burge emphasise the importance of accuracy in the design of these models, not just for the sake of the collectors but also because they are responsible for representing the RAF around the world. "When we attend air shows, we work with the RAF and we try to get involved whenever we can," says Clegg. "With Airfix and Corgi we cover most of the planes in their history and we are known all over the world for producing the best models of RAF aircraft."

hornbyhobbies.com

SPARKLING SUCCESS

Greyfriars Vineyard

"Growing grapes and making wine in England is definitely different to doing it in France, Australia, Chile or anywhere else," says Michael Wagstaff, owner and winemaker at Greyfriars, the award-winning vineyard and winery on Surrey's picturesque North Downs. "We have different problems and different opportunities. It's a unique wine-growing region."

He's not wrong. Since buying Greyfriars in 2010, Mike, a former CEO of a North Sea gas company, and his wife Hilary, a former lawyer, together with their rock musician brother-in-law David, their vineyard manager, have transformed the vineyard from an acre-and-a-half plot producing around 2,000 bottles per annum, to an industry-acclaimed, 50-acre boutique producer of 75,000 bottles of English Sparkling Wine each year.

Much of this is attributable to the topography and climate of the North Downs. Greyfriars is located on the evocatively named Hog's Back at the West End of the North Downs. "The chalk hills are ideal for wine growing because they drain easily," explains Hilary. "Vines hate soggy roots." The geology is perfect for producing the classic Champagne varieties Chardonnay, Pinot Noir and Pinot Meunier. Furthermore, the south-facing slopes enhance the ripening process in September and October. No wonder Mike describes it as a "wonderful local confluence".

What this confluence brings to the wine is flavour, in particular for sparkling wine. The English climate is marginal, so grapes aren't ripe enough to make world-class still wine, but they are perfect for a stunning sparkling wine. Typically, sparkling wine needs slightly less ripe, more acidic grapes. The longer ripening period in England, as opposed to further south, provides these growing conditions.

"English vineyards have stopped trying to make a copy of Champagne and are now making something that is truly English." The result is known as English Sparkling Wine. "It's English, not British," clarifies Mike. "That's an important distinction because 'British wine' refers to wine that has just been fermented here from grapes grown abroad."

Greyfriars' rise has happily coincided with British consumers increasingly wanting to understand the provenance of their food and drink. "It's not just wine, it's craft beer, gin, local cheeses and all sorts of products," says Mike. "People are realising that Britain is now a culinary destination. We produce world-class food and drink, and we should celebrate that. The majority of people in Britain had never tried English wine until recently. So we're at an early stage, which makes it all the more exciting."

What is also thrilling is the reaction of the wine cognoscenti. Most recently, Tom Stevenson – the internationally renowned Champagne guru and author of the *World Encyclopaedia of Champagne & Sparkling Wine* – named Greyfriars' 2013 Blanc de Blancs Brut as his favourite English sparkling wine. Moreover, many restaurants and pubs that weren't interested in English Sparkling Wine a few years ago are contacting Greyfriars about stocking the label's range. "Exporting overseas is for the future – Hampshire is abroad at the moment!" says Hilary.

"Our top priority is very much the home market," concludes Mike. "We believe this is the place where people will have the strongest affinity with our wine because it is local and British."

www.greyfriarsvineyard.co.uk

PAINTING WITH GEMS

Sharon Khazzam

Jewellery designer Sharon Khazzam's studio is on a quiet, tree-lined street. But walk through the doors and it's like stepping into a Moroccan treasure trove or prising open a sunken treasure chest to reveal a spectacular horde of gems. Giant, paintbox-coloured stones sit in oyster shells on Khazzam's desk alongside piles of tiny precious gems. The walls are painted a bright orange and tacked with inspirational images, and on her drafting board are intricate work-in-progress paintings of new ideas.

The delight on discovering her eclectic studio space gives a clue as to why Khazzam has enjoyed a three-decade-long career, is honoured as a member-at-large by the American Society of Jewelry Historians and, in 2014, was inducted into the Council of Fashion Designers of America. Much like the interior of her studio, Khazzam's designs are a burst of colour that can't help but brighten the day of the women who wear them.

It took years for Khazzam to find the right source for the stones she needs, be they rare pink padparadscha sapphires or tourmalines. "The most important thing is having a relationship with your gem dealers, a friendship," she says. "Each person is strong in regions of the world or stones." Her connections with dealers were forged when she took her first job with Asprey in the 1980s and later, in 1993, when she ventured out under her own name. "Now I have a gem dealer who I know will find a stone for me, if it exists," says Khazzam. "He's extremely strong in a gem that I adore – a paraiba tourmaline. I am obsessed with it. It's very, very rare, from Brazil. It's the colour of the Caribbean waters; a deep blue that you feel you want to dive into."

Though getting to work and play with sparkling precious stones daily might be the obvious reason for Khazzam being drawn into the jewellery world, it was in fact painting that got her hooked. "It is by default that I am a jewellery designer," she explains. "I fell in love with it because, at university, you had to paint designs in miniature; that's what caught me, really. My favourite part of the process is still to sit at my drawing board and just paint."

Her approach could be considered quaint in an era of computer-assisted designs, but hand sketching affords her creations more character and expression. "It's funny," she says. "I am constantly being approached by people who keep insisting that I start working with a computer, that it's so passé to hand draw every design. But I feel that it's very important, not only to me but also to my clients. They appreciate the time it takes for me to actually draw it rather than sit at a computer and press buttons. The whole idea is to have a unique jewel. Nothing is perfect. If everything is perfect then you can duplicate the designs and I feel that loses a little bit of what I do."

Khazzam's desire to create uniqueness means that she is adventurous with the scale of her pieces – a case in point being the huge starburst she wears around her neck daily. Her stones are unusual, as are her colour combinations, and she doesn't follow any jewellery trends. There's a timelessness to her work. "I try to make pieces that will last way past my generation, my children's generation and their grandchildren," she says. With three decades of design behind her, Khazzam is well on her way.

www.sharonkhazzam.com

HOME ADVANTAGE

The Shed Inc.

"I believe that a home should be a happy, colourful and vibrant place," says Vicky Brook, CEO and founder of Gloucestershire-based homewares business, The Shed Inc.

To this end, her company produces stylish, colourful, timeless and high-quality homeware, including china, textiles (such as cushions and aprons), stationery and pet accessories. Best sellers are the luxury cotton makeup bags and wash bags, the dog accessories and pet collections. All products are designed to look great alongside other favourite labels or with other Shed products – according to Brook's "mix and match" lifestyle philosophy – and are sold online and in independent retailers. Bespoke designs can also be found decorating Britannia and Cunard cruise ships.

"Our designs are all inspired by my animals past and present, my love of flowers and by the great outdoors," says Brook. "They have a very British feel, with prints featuring dogs with Union Jack coats, hedgerows, Chelsea flowers and Cotswold paisleys. I am massively keen to keep industry here in the UK, which is why we've brought out a 'Lovingly Made in the UK' collection, made by local craftsmen and women, who bring the highest quality of workmanship."

Launched in 2012, the company was born as a collaboration between Brook and her best friend Susan Schippel. Brook had been a high-powered human resources executive until her younger daughter became seriously ill with a complex medical condition. At the same time, Susan, a renowned textile designer, was diagnosed with breast cancer. What began as a way of helping both through a difficult time became a successful business.

In 2016, Brook was awarded *Achieve* magazine's Mumpreneur Award of Excellence. She is particularly proud that, in five years in business, no customer has ever returned an order as faulty for a refund.

Sadly, Susan's breast cancer proved to be terminal, and she died in August 2016. But her legacy continues. Her daughter (and Brook's goddaughter) – textile designer Molly – has taken on her mother's role, transforming Brook's ideas into beautiful prints. As a tribute to Susan, Brook has named The Shed Inc.'s new seaside-inspired design "Susie's Beach". "Her husband and family loved the coast and it was always her dream to retire there one day," says Brook. "I want to do her proud and for her spirit to live on in our textiles."

www.theshedinc.co.uk

THE FULL ENGLISH

The Black Farmer

For 30 years, Wilfred Emmanuel-Jones fantasised about owning his own farm. But it was his last disappointing full English breakfast, one in a long succession that featured bland, bready and unsatisfying sausages, that finally gave him the impetus to kick-start his farming business. He decided to create his own, gluten-free sausages: the kind of meaty, great-tasting ones he felt were sorely lacking in the market. So The Black Farmer was born.

A multimillion-pound turnover later, and with his sausages stocked in most of the major supermarket chains, Emmanuel-Jones has more than fulfilled his dream. Since then, The Black Farmer has diversified into pork, chicken and beef products, including eggs and bacon. Now consumers have all the components they need to treat themselves to a really delicious full English.

The vision Emmanuel-Jones had for the business, however, entailed much more than just creating a superior quality sausage. It also had to represent who he was and what he stood for: "The idea of a black farmer was a total stretch for people in the early days," he says. "But I wanted to challenge the stereotype of what it is to be British, because modern Britain is incredibly diverse. I wanted The Black Farmer to champion that diversity." Celebrating Britishness is at the core of the brand. It uses 100 per cent British sources for its products, and all packaging features Emmanuel-Jones flying the Union Jack.

"I love being British," he says, "and The Black Farmer is a celebration of everything that makes us quirky and different. I just don't think enough brands do that."

Not content to simply sit back and enjoy the fruits of his labour, Emmanuel-Jones wants to reach out to other wannabe food producers and help them get their businesses off the ground. "When I get approached by budding entrepreneurs," he says, "and I believe they have a really sound business idea, I will offer them all the help and advice – and sometimes the investment – they need to develop their own brands, in return for a stake in their future businesses."

For Emmanuel-Jones, giving something back is key to the brand's legacy. "The greatest gift you can give someone is opportunity and the chance to follow their dream," he says. "I don't want to be remembered as the guy who made great sausages, I want to be remembered as a guy who made the world a better place."

www.theblackfarmer.com

ISLAND OF TREASURES

Visit Malta

This is a proud year for Malta. Its capital, Valletta, is the 2018 European Capital of Culture. The accolade has prompted a joyous celebration of the island's culture and history.

Malta has a long history suffused with stories of invasion and culture clash, of political intrigue and strategic value. Positioned near Sicily, it has been subject to the attentions of regional powers stretching back in time from the Phoenicians to the Nazis.

"We are a small country but with a very proud and vibrant population," says Peter Vella, Director UK & Ireland at the Malta Tourist Authority. "History has shaped Maltese culture from its amazing, heroic feats in the face of adversity and its wide assortment of rulers over the centuries. The nation needs to be heard by the wider world and the opportunity afforded by Valletta's status this year provides an excellent means to do so."

Valletta is a UNESCO World Heritage Site, a fortified city with glorious baroque architecture, and the capital of a modern European nation. It also has one of the most beautiful natural harbours in the world as a backdrop.

This has set the scene for a kaleidoscopic array of celebratory events, including May's Valletta Green Festival in the Piazza San Gorg, which featured an *infjorata* – a floral carpet comprising some 80,000 seasonal flowering plants. In early June, the Grand Harbour itself hosts the *Pageant of the Seas*, a colourful show of competitive races and aquatic displays.

The visual arts are represented in a multinational, island-wide exhibition called *The Island is What the Sea Surrounds*. Music, poetry and theatre combine in October for *Orfeo & Majnun*, a melding of Middle Eastern legend and Greek myth that typifies the Maltese experience.

The island has had a long relationship with Britain, beginning with a naval skirmish as Malta became a British protectorate in 1800, a status it retained until full independence in 1964. But it is for its stoicism under sustained German and Italian bombing in the Second World War – for which the entire population was awarded the George Cross – that it is often best remembered.

"More bombs fell on Malta in April 1942 than on the whole of the UK during the nine months of the Blitz," says Vella, a Maltese and British dual national. "And remember, the Maltese islands combined are still smaller than the Isle of Wight."

Malta was the subsequent jumping-off point for 1943's invasion of Sicily, the first incursion back into Western Europe for the Allies en route to victory over Nazi Germany.

"The Maltese regard the British as their closest cousins," says Vella. "The systems of government, education, business and law are all based on the British model. English is one of the two official national languages and the main one used in business. And Britain is by far the biggest tourism market, accounting for more than a quarter of all visitors."

Despite myriad cultural, gastronomic and religious influences – something of Europe, something of Africa and the Middle East and quite a bit British – Malta's identity is still very much its own. In its year of celebration and beyond, this jewel sparkles in the Med.

www.maltauk.com

PUSHING THE BOAT OUT

Hawk Yachts

The freedom of the seas has fascinated humanity through the ages. This liberty, and the ability to experience sea travel in impeccable comfort, forms the inspiration for Hawk Yachts – a world leader in luxury expedition yachts. The company draws upon the seafaring experience of its founder, Captain Matthias Bosse, who has spent more than two decades at the controls of major yachts and expedition cruise vessels. "What is the ultimate reason to own a yacht?" he says. "It is the freedom to explore the world in total luxury."

Captain Bosse, whose CV includes sailing all seven oceans and serving as the master of prestigious private yachts *Lady Moura* and *Carinthia VII*, wanted Hawk Yachts' bespoke designs to offer a synergy of sleek aesthetics and state-of-the-art technology. His team also sought to challenge the serious constraints of the "traditional" superyacht market, where costly designs and operating expenses – along with a lack of versatility – effectively curtail and stagnate the true possibilities of yacht ownership. Instead, Hawk Yachts embodies an expansive approach that is simultaneously intrepid-hearted, free-spirited and business-minded. "The tide is turning for the yachting market, as it struggles to offer new and current customers better value," says Captain Bosse. "Hawk Yachts is at the forefront of this required market shift."

Nick Lockett, the company's Managing Director, joined Hawk Yachts in 2014. "Seventy per cent of the world's yachts are based in the Mediterranean but go nowhere else," he says. "New yacht owners are often surprised to find that their vessels lack sufficient seakeeping to realise their expectations and are needy in terms of their relationship with shore management. They're expensive and complicated to maintain, and follow predictable design trends. We're designing yachts that provide far better value and broader experiences, conceived for luxury and adventure. The team wanted to design highly functional yachts while maintaining outstanding beauty: superyachts that would look outstanding in Monte Carlo marina but would also have the capability to go to the Amazon or the Antarctic – with exceptional levels of comfort in both environments."

The company's yachts are also created with ecological concerns and future emissions regulations in mind. Key elements include ocean-waste regulation, and a hybrid diesel-electric propulsion system, which enables a low-impact, highly capable electric mode.

At the heart of Hawk Yachts' seafaring vision is the creation of new benchmarks in luxury and adventure, such as the truly majestic Sea Hawk. "It's a private yacht classification vessel – a PYC, as we say – and superyachts of this size for charter are very rare," says Lockett. "It's 103 metres long and has 2,800 sq m of living space, with 18 cabins and an elegant interior."

The ultra-manoeuvrable Sea Hawk has been designed to operate with the highest levels of safety, efficiency and comfort throughout long-haul expeditions, even in the world's most remote locations. For polar regions, it has a robust ice-friendly hull shape, reinforced ice belt and heated shell door seals. It is equally in its element sailing in tropical climates, in warm temperature waters or in silty rivers, thanks to its effective cooling capacity and freshwater production, as well as insect filters and pollen barriers.

SEAHAWK

The relatively compact ocean-ready Cape Hawk 690, at 48 metres long, is also immaculately designed for "rugged luxury" and boundless voyaging possibilities, with a 5,000-mile range that allows you to enjoy almost any destination in the world. "Nature can be unpredictable," says Lockett, "and the Cape Hawk is designed to keep you safe." They're also a safe investment – designed to minimise initial costs and maximise revenue from charter through extending the season. "The yacht is designed to break even with around 100 days of charter,"says Lockett. "This includes depreciation and generous budgets for refit."

This manageability crucially extends to the maintenance of the yachts – while "conventional" superyachts entail exorbitant running costs, Hawk Yachts have ensured that equipment and propulsion technology is accessible and can be maintained by the on-board crew at sea. Remote system monitoring can also diagnose the condition of components and enable maintenance as required. Refit and general maintenance costs are also minimised through a shared company Swiss Ocean, which combines the expertise of yacht management with the commercial common sense of Columbia/Marlow, the biggest ship-management company in the world.

"Our yachts are designed for long-distance travel and what we call 'blue water', or open sea, competence," says Lockett. "This opens up a 52-week season; the average yacht is only used for five to six weeks a year. We feel that yachts should be in constant use. From the owners' point of view, that year-round, worldwide capability represents significantly increased revenue, because it allows owner use and also the potential to charter throughout the calendar – and you're now able to reach locations that appeal to both experiential holidaymakers and classic charter clients."

With all of Hawk Yachts' designs, the journey is as much part of the experience as the global destinations. Generously proportioned living and storage spaces offer extensive creative scope and potential for accommodating a wide range of guests, along with such features as an interior spa or study facilities. Cape Hawk has the capacity to include a sauna, a science laboratory or a submarine garage (with space to launch and operate a passenger submersible such as the Super Yacht Sub 3-500 LX from U-Boat Worx); separate entrances can also be designed for expedition purposes or luxury entertaining. Sea Hawk features six decks and a helicopter hangar, as well as a bar, which affords breathtaking views out to sea. With Hawk Yachts, these views could be literally anywhere, from the unforgettable Scandinavian spectacle of the Northern Lights, to a tranquil idyll off the coast of Vietnam, or Alaskan archipelagos.

"People nowadays want to genuinely experience the world," says Lockett, "and to share that inimitable experience with their family and friends." Surely there's no finer way to explore our extraordinary planet; this truly is luxury without limits.

www.hawkyachts.com

MOTIVATIONAL SPEAKER

Estelon

A small collection of battered old radios and stereos lies in a cabinet at the head office of luxury speaker manufacturer Estelon in Tallinn, Estonia. "This is the root of Estelon's history," says Alissa Vassilkova. "These belonged to our grandparents – they're how my father Alfred learnt where sound comes from. He opened them up and made them better as his love of music evolved into a curiosity for physics." They signify the start of a lifetime devoted to the dream of delivering perfect sound – a dream that led Alfred Vassilkov to found Estelon in April 2010.

Alfred Vassilkov, now 60, was born in St Petersburg and grew up surrounded by music. His father played the accordion at dances, his aunt taught piano and Alfred himself would tune into Radio Luxembourg to hear tinny renditions of his favourite Western pop songs. Soon his love of music and his inquisitive nature combined to take things in a new direction. "I wanted to understand how you could create sound from electricity," he says. "I began to take radios apart and adjust them to make them better."

After studying acoustics in St Petersburg, Alfred began to build speakers from scratch for himself and his friends, even making the speakers for his own wedding, although Soviet-era restrictions meant that materials were limited. In the early 1980s, he moved from St Petersburg to Estonia, where his mother had been born, and began designing speakers for a company that made radios. Alfred started to develop and deploy innovative techniques, not only to secure the best sound but also to make skilful use of scarce resources.

Following the collapse of the Soviet Union, Estelon faced competition from western technology giants. Alfred continued to experiment, but also visited international shows to see the latest in speaker technology and discover what consumers wanted and needed. He travelled with his daughters, Alissa and Kristiina, schooling them between shows on the science of sound. Both daughters, as well as their partners, are involved with Estelon. "We can support his ideas and bring them to the world," says Alissa. "We are helping his dream come true every day."

Alfred continued to develop his own speakers, working on a prototype for five years until he was ready to reveal it to the family. Over breakfast, they agreed to start a company and within six months the first Estelon speaker system was showcased in Denver in the US. It immediately drew acclaim thanks not only to its incredible sound quality but also to its striking appearance. "The speakers look amazing but their sculptural quality is crucial to their engineering," he says. "They are built from the inside out and the appearance creates the best conditions for all the components inside."

Awards soon followed, with Estelon continuing to push the boundaries with each new model. "The Extreme, our largest speaker system to date, contains a lifetime of experience and knowledge and can be adjusted in rooms of different sizes," says Alfred. "Our latest model is the Lynx, which is wireless and features modular hardware that can be upgraded to account for the latest technological developments."

With a presence in more than 25 countries and a reputation for cutting-edge engineering, Estelon is growing in size and prominence. Through it all, Alfred has remained the pioneering spirit at its heart, drawing on decades of experience and his fascination with the physics of sound in his determination to trailblaze new frontiers.

www.estelon.com

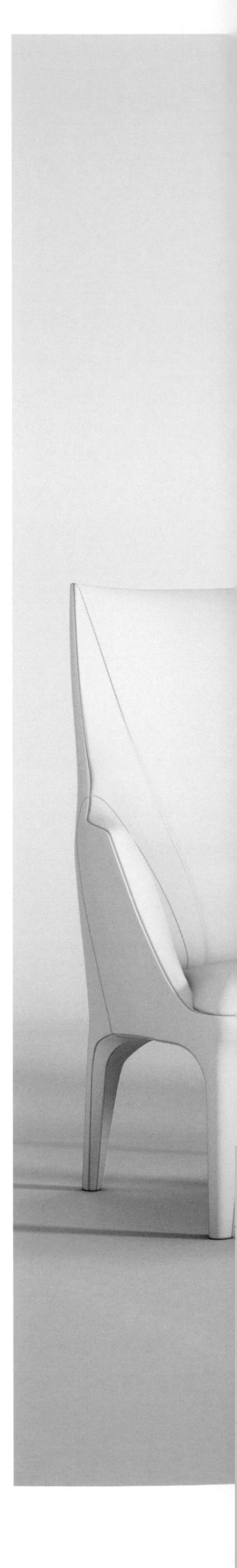

TECHNOLOGY

PLANE MAGIC

Meggitt PLC

The global aerospace and defence engineering company Meggitt has a rich history of engineering solutions for aerospace. It dates back to London in 1850, and the founding of Negretti & Zambra, a company that made the first altimeter for hot air balloons. In the Second World War the Spitfire was equipped with Lodge spark plugs, Serck Aviation radiators and Dunlop Equipment gun-firing systems – all businesses which are now part of Meggitt.

Today Meggitt continues to pioneer new technologies for military and commercial aircraft. "Our vision is *Enabling the Extraordinary*, and that is exactly what Meggitt does," says Chief Executive Tony Wood. "We deliver technologically differentiated systems and products with high certification requirements in aerospace, defence and selected energy markets."

Headquartered at Bournemouth Airport, Meggitt has 48 facilities around the world and around 11,000 employees. It places huge importance on protecting those who risk their lives for others; every day, pilots depend on Meggitt's products for their safety. "Some of the most important applications lie behind the scenes," says Wood. "Our servicemen and women operate in some of the most extreme environments on the planet, and our expertise helps protect them."

Wood points out that Meggitt's blast-resistant, crashworthy fuel tanks for military helicopters have reduced fire-related deaths to almost zero. "We're also one of the largest producers of polymer seals on aircraft," he says. "It might not sound very interesting or innovative but it is that window or door seal separating you from 600 mph speeds and minus-60 degree temperatures. Without it you couldn't breathe."

Meggitt describes its products as "plane magic" – the kind of everyday technical masterpiece that people take for granted. "It reminds us that we just observe the wonder of technology every day without really understanding it," says Wood. "These technologies and products underpin global trade and prosperity, and also the security of people's daily lives."

From advanced composite materials to state-of-the-art electronics, Meggitt is always at the forefront of innovation. For instance, it pioneered engine-health monitoring technology, enabling aero engines to operate more reliably and efficiently. And its time-domain reflectrometry measures the quantity and quality of fuel and oil in aircraft systems through cutting-edge radar-probe techniques.

"It's those sorts of concepts that are quite new," says Wood. "An aircraft fundamentally looks very similar to one of a few years ago but the digital environment around it has changed almost beyond belief over the last 15 years."

Digital technology is also at the heart of Meggitt's production process. "A significant opportunity exists in being able to track our components," says Wood, "the ability to give real-time information on our products, and provide better service." Parts have the potential to be tracked to and across the factory floor enabling technicians to build units more accurately and efficiently. "It's all part of ensuring product uniformity and eliminating variation," says Wood. "We want innovation. Enabling us to take out variation, in an aerospace world, is the only way to get to 'one in a billion and better'."

Meggitt's strength is people and technology working together to attain such results, in manufacturing, engineering and development. "Innovation doesn't just happen," says Wood. "It comes by virtue of the expert people we employ, and the way they work as teams to deliver these quite extraordinary things."

www.meggitt.com

THE INFORMATION AGE

Fujitsu

Fujitsu has supported the Royal Air Force for more than 50 years by providing administrative and, critically, operational capabilities such as ballistic missile warning and command-and-control information systems. Fujitsu has a strong emphasis on technology and innovation, and throughout the company's 81-year history it has constantly pushed the boundaries of what is possible. This has included the development of a wide range of telecommunications and computing services and products, including the fastest supercomputer in the world. All of these developments have contributed to the introduction of ever-more effective ways of working for its customers.

The digital revolution has seen the pace of change continually accelerate and organisations everywhere, both commercial and military, need to be able to capitalise on the benefits of new capabilities to stay ahead of the competition. To do otherwise introduces the threats of competitors and adversaries gaining critical, game-changing advantage. Fujitsu aims to work hand-in-hand with its customers to tackle the digital journey together.

"Organisations of all kinds are coming together to deliver a better, smarter and more engaging digital future for their customers and themselves," says Duncan Tait, Fujitsu's Head of EMEIA (Europe, Middle East, India & Africa) and the Americas. "By balancing their sometimes differing needs and priorities, they are helping to co-create something much more than just the sum of their parts."

Digital co-creation blurs traditional supplier/customer boundaries and, in adding value through this approach, Fujitsu builds on trusted relationships with customers, understanding their goals as well as their challenges. "We believe that we have a responsibility to help them to understand the art of the possible by sharing our own innovative thinking with them and going beyond simply reacting to their requirements in a transactional way," says Tait.

Examples of where Fujitsu seeks to contribute to joint thought leadership include the rapidly developing fields of artificial intelligence, machine learning and the internet of things, as well as all other aspects of an ever more connected and automated world. "Only by bringing these technologies together can one make sense of an increasingly complex world," says Tait. "A human-centric approach, empowering people with advanced technology, is the only way to deliver the full benefit of digitalisation."

Another key tenet of Fujitsu's vision for the digital age is to make coherent information available whenever and wherever it is needed. The company's extensive capabilities in networking and systems integration are used to link and enhance situational awareness – from industry through main operating base, theatre, and to the cockpit. This integrated approach extracts maximum benefit from existing investment in IT systems. Functionality can then be enhanced further by applying the latest digital innovations and developments, and by learning from other sectors.

The result is a single information environment that can transform operations by bringing pace and agility across all strategic bases and tactical theatres. "This must all be delivered in a reliable and secure way that protects our customers' critical activities," says Tait.

Fujitsu's commitment to its customers extends beyond simple commercial business and the firm is proud of its record in serving alongside the UK Armed Forces at home and on operations during both peace and conflict. Equally, it values greatly the contribution that former members of the Armed Forces make to its business as they embark on second careers. This is reflected in Fujitsu's status as a Gold Award winner in the Defence Employer Recognition Scheme.

www.fujitsu.com/uk

HI-TECH HEROES

L3 Technologies

L3 Technologies is the leading provider of a broad range of communications, electronic and sensor systems and products deployed on military, homeland security and commercial platforms. The company is also a prime contractor in aerospace systems, security and detection systems, and pilot training. In the UK, the company has seven businesses, each working to one of L3 Technologies' four global segments in the US.

"The last 18 months have been particularly important for us, both globally and in the UK," says Ron Cook, Managing Director. "The business rebranded to its new L3 Technologies name in December 2016, reflecting its evolution into a leading global provider of a broad range of technology solutions."

L3 now employs 31,000 people globally, including over 2,000 in the UK. Cook is keen to highlight the company's British success and its partnership with the UK Armed Forces. A principle feature of this relationship is the provision of the RC-135-manned electronic surveillance aircraft under the Airseeker programme. This, equipped with a variety of sensors, gives the RAF a high level of situational awareness in terms of both tactical and strategic intelligence, and performs a critical role in supporting defence-wide strategic decision-making.

Cook also highlights L3's UK Commercial Training Solutions (CTS) business. "We provide vertical, seamless and affordable solutions to support the global commercial aviation-training marketplace," he says. "CTS capabilities span the complete spectrum of commercial aviation training. This includes initial aircrew selection, cadet (ab-initio) training, resourcing and airline training, with the latter supported by hi-tech simulation products, including the RealitySeven full-flight simulator."

The company is also proud of the continuing success of L3 Maritime Systems business in the UK. Among many other services, Marine Systems supplies the Integrated Platform Management System for many Royal Navy platforms, including HMS *Queen Elizabeth* and HMS *Prince of Wales*, as well as Type 26 frigates and Astute-class attack submarines.

Other L3 businesses in the UK include ASA, the systems solutions company based in Hampshire, with core capabilities in data fusion solutions, complex information systems and mission-configurable communications. Meanwhile, WESCAM supplies its electro-optic and infra-red systems across the UK military, while TRL, based in Tewksbury, is the leading supplier of cryptographic and counter-IED technology.

www.l3t.com

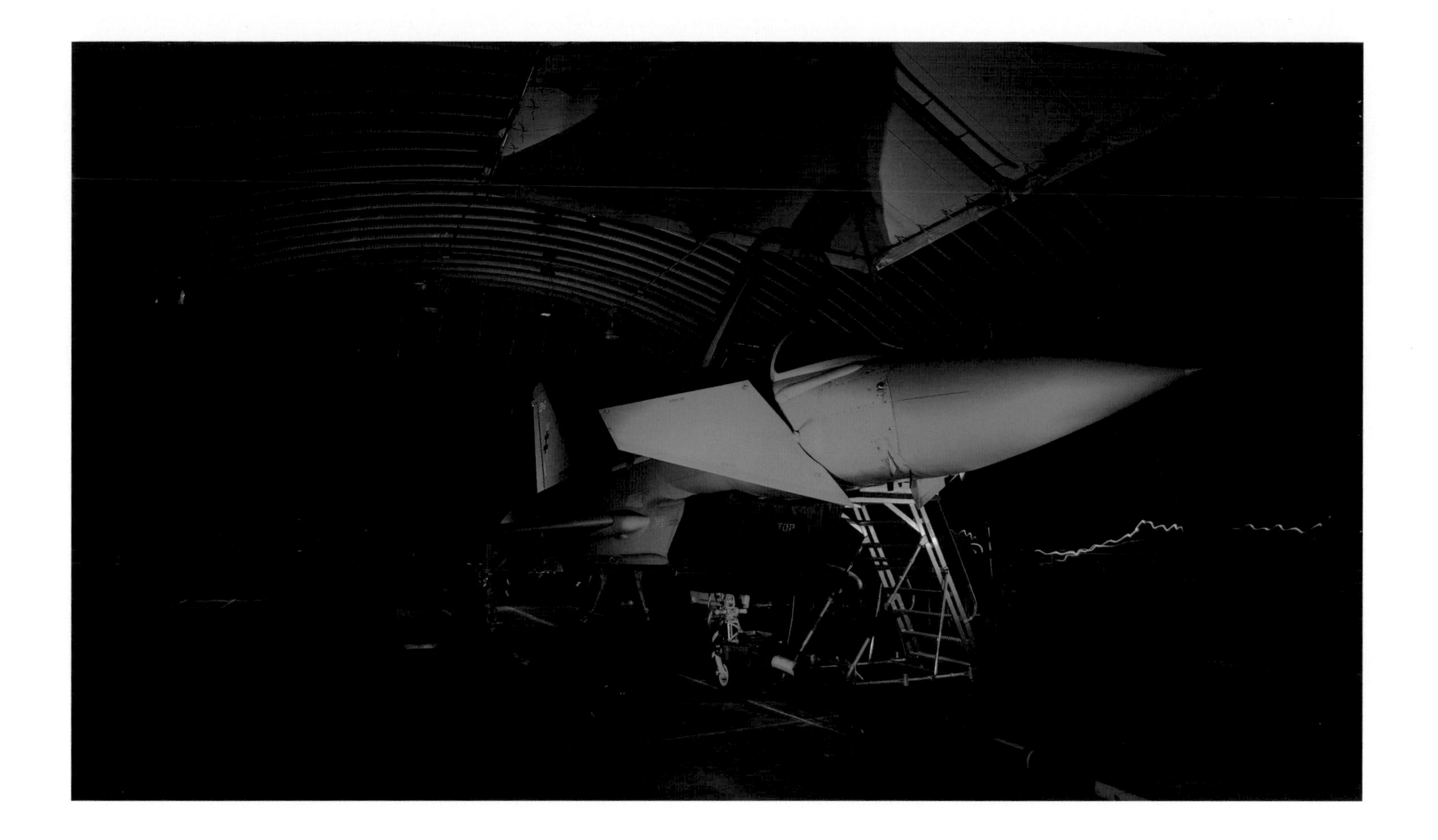

COLLABORATING FOR SUCCESS

QinetiQ

"At QinetiQ, we are immensely proud of our long-standing support of the country's Armed Forces," says a QinetiQ spokesperson, "and feel especially honoured to support the RAF as it celebrates its centenary."

QinetiQ and its predecessor organisations have been involved in the flight testing and evaluation of an extensive range of military aircraft that have entered RAF service, including the iconic Lightning, Jaguar, Hawker Hunter, Comet and Britannia. Through its heritage, the company has developed distinctive knowledge and unique facilities. Its low-speed wind tunnel is one of just three in the world and is used regularly by Boeing. Indeed, every two seconds, an aircraft whose wing design was tested in the company's wind tunnel takes off or lands.

"Our vision today is to be the 'chosen partner around the world for mission-critical solutions, innovating for our customers' advantage'," explains the spokesperson. "Collaboration is vital to understand our customers' needs, and we work in close partnership with the RAF to address its current and future challenges through technology and innovation. We are particularly proud of our close partnership with the RAF Air Warfare Centre, which brings together an exceptional combination of military operational expertise and QinetiQ's technical know-how, rigorous independent thinking and specialist test facilities, to deliver world-class test and evaluation of military aircraft and systems."

The company also helps train test pilots and engineers. Since 1943, the Empire Tests' Pilot School has trained more than 1,300 test pilots from 32 countries. Today, QinetiQ deploys innovation and investment to help the RAF address operational and efficiency challenges. For example, it is delivering a radically different approach to test aircrew training using civil registered aircraft and modular courses, and a bold programme to modernise the UK's air test range capabilities.

Reflecting the RAF centenary celebrations' ambition to inspire the next generation, QinetiQ actively supports the Armed Forces Covenant and was a proud Gold Award winner of the MoD's Defence Employer Recognition Scheme in 2016. Supporting the employment of ex-service personnel, spouses and reserves, promoting RAF recruitment, and running a highly effective STEM engagement programme are all fundamental to the company's values. "QinetiQ looks forward to helping the RAF deliver the Next Generation Air Force," concludes a spokesperson, "and achieve its next 100 years of successful operation."
www.qinetiq.com

THE BIG BLUE THEORY

IBM

Hursley House near Winchester (pictured, above) is embedded in RAF folklore as the wartime design headquarters of Vickers Supermarine. It is in this grand 18th century mansion that Vickers developed the iconic Spitfire (pictured, opposite), as well as creating early postwar jet fighters such as the Attacker, the Swift and the Scimitar.

For the past 60 years, the building has been occupied by IBM and, in a neat coincidence, it is still playing a key role in military history – this time as one of the many centres where IBM carries out crucial work in partnership with the Royal Air Force. "Effectively, IBM technology is being used to monitor the skies and protect UK airspace every second of every day," says Quentin Vaughan, European Defence Industry Leader at IBM.

IBM, known as "Big Blue", is one of the world's largest technology companies, with nearly 380,000 employees across 177 countries. It staff have included five Nobel Prize winners, six Turing Awards and five national medals of science, while its groundbreaking inventions over the last century have included dozens of things that we now use every single day, including the ATM, the personal computer, the hard-disk drive, the magnetic stripe card and the UPC barcode.

Less well known, perhaps, is the fact that IBM has long been involved in military surveillance, first developing UCMP (UKADGE Capability Maintenance Programme) and now updating it with an even more complex successor, Project Guardian. "Much of IBM's work throughout its history has been in the financial sector," says Vaughan. "Over the years, we've developed computer systems that are able to ingest large quantities of data and use that information to make informed decisions for banks and other financial institutions. What we've found is that a lot of the programmes we've pioneered in this field can also have applications in defence."

So, with UCMP and Project Guardian, instead of processing thousands of high-volume banking transactions every second, similar IBM technology is used to analyse information gleaned from hundreds of radar systems located around the UK and the world. When a French commercial aircraft lost communications with air-traffic control and strayed into UK airspace last year, IBM's technology was able to alert the MOD immediately, and RAF Typhoon jets were quickly scrambled to intercept it. "In most cases the reasons for the things we pick up are quite trivial," says Vaughan. "Usually it's because the plane's radio has packed up. But there is always the threat of hijack, and certain hostile air forces will often make provocative incursions on UK airspace, so we have to remain vigilant. We are also involved in monitoring the Falkland Islands, and in that area we have to be constantly situationally aware of any potential threats from the Argentine air force."

IBM has developed many other links with the RAF. In 2002, after acquiring Pricewaterhouse Coopers Consulting, IBM started to take on back-office functions for the RAF, using its technology to work on procurement, accounting and HR. IBM also created the RAF Logistics IT Strategy (LITS), which monitors aircraft for safety and maintenance purposes. Additionally, it is involved in a programme that has trained hundreds of ex-RAF personnel to work in cyber-security. "A lot of our staff are ex-RAF," says Vaughan. "It's important to draw from people who have knowledge in that field when we're designing and building a system that's crucial to the defence of the country."

www.ibm.com

19
19
19
19
19

THE SKY'S THE LIMIT

Ultra Electronics

If a story promised to feature The Who's drummer Keith Moon, Concorde's nose and a television, one might imagine a high-velocity death for the unfortunate appliance. But all three appear, somewhat improbably, on the timeline of Ultra Electronics, a company that began life making headphones and radios and is now home to some of the most sophisticated communications and infrastructure technology in the world.

Keith Moon's (admittedly slender) part in the story comes later. It begins with a demobbed Royal Flying Corps radio engineer, Teddy Rosen, setting up shop in 1920 in north London to manufacture loudspeakers for the burgeoning radio and gramophone market. His bestselling brand of speaker – the "Ultra" – soon became the name above the door and the company grew rapidly.

In 1939 Ultra's first television receiver went on the market for transmitting the BBC's High Definition Television Service from its studios at Alexandra Palace. At the outbreak of the Second World War, Ultra's operations drew on Rosen's military heritage, with a diversification into aircraft infrastructure for Short Stirling heavy bombers. And while the manufacture of radios and televisions continued in peacetime, so did an interest in communication and control systems for new generations of turbo-prop and jet aircraft.

Meanwhile, in 1961, 14-year-old Keith Moon left school in Alperton and enrolled at Harrow Technical College. This led to a paid apprenticeship at Ultra, where he assembled and repaired radios. He didn't stay long, but he bought his first drum kit with his wages, joined a covers band and auditioned for The Who three years later.

Ultra's Group Marketing Director, Chris Binsley explains how, back at Ultra in the same year, the TV and radio business was sold to Thorn. "The company's developments in aerospace gathered pace through the 1960s and '70s, producing a roll call of icons," says Binsley. "Concorde's famous nose was articulated with the help of Ultra tech. The Rolls-Royce engines, for which Ultra provides controls, powered RAF Hawk trainer jets and airliners including Lockheed's TriStar and the Boeing 747. Nimrod reconnaissance aircraft deployed sonobuoys developed and produced by Ultra."

The company's HiPPAG air-cooling system has assisted thermal imaging systems in Lynx helicopters and guided air-to-air missiles on Harriers and Typhoons. And finally, its targeting system – the Litening pod – has flown more than 150,000 hours in RAF service on both the Tornado and the Typhoon, achieving just under 100 per cent mission availability.

Currently, Ultra is part of a team developing products at the cutting edge of avionic tech, principally for the latest word in fighter jets: the Joint Strike Fighter. Ultra's MD of Precision Control Systems, Mike Clayton, explains why it's a step change in fighter technology. "The JSF can take you out before you know it's there," he says. "The sensor suite and its stealth capability means it'll know you're in the air a long time before you do. It takes out targets beyond visual range."

So what does Ultra provides for the Joint Strike Fighter package? The two main features are de-icing controls for the Pratt & Whitney engines, which are self-explanatory, and something a little more complicated called "stores ejection".

J1-NIM2

"Stores are anything – a missile, a bomb, chaff – that you drop out of the aircraft," says Clayton. "Traditionally, the method of pushing the stores away is like a firework. There's a pyrotechnic charge which covers the aircraft in soot and stores fall away. When an aircraft is travelling very fast, you have to push it away hard enough to defeat the boundary layer, which is the air rushing past. If you don't, the store comes back!"

Ultra's solution is compressed air, which forces the stores away more controllably and cleanly with less airframe stress. The system is currently installed in more than 300 JSFs; and Ultra has sold over 11,000 for use in aircraft around the world.

But it's not just in the air that Ultra is forging ahead. Its 19 separate businesses break into three divisions, corresponding with their areas of operation: air, land and sea. Maritime applications make up a significant proportion of the business and draw on acoustic expertise that has been an unbroken thread throughout Ultra's history.

"Maritime and underwater warfare technology represents just over 30 per cent of what we do as a group and it's growing," says Clayton. "The capability of non-friendly threats is becoming greater around the world, so our ability to deal with them requires another increase in sophistication."

Clayton cut his teeth as a software engineer, working his way up through naval radar applications before joining Ultra to run its submarine division. He's a relative newcomer to aerospace and says that, while nearly all the company's senior staff has a background in physics or engineering, he sets great store by the expertise brought by ex-forces personnel.

"It means were not just theoretically answering customers' questions," he says. "We get a lot of advice from people who have been out in the sand and the dirt using this kit, so we appreciate their knowledge and skills. We acknowledge the training the RAF and other services provide and how it helps us make better and better products."

Safety is paramount. "If a tank breaks down, you get out and fix it," says Clayton, bluntly. "If something goes wrong with a plane, you'll be sweeping up the bits with a dustpan and brush." The company applies very specific safety classifications to all its systems, discussing potential problems and their solutions with clients before projects are embarked upon.

As global threats diversify, international defence cooperation increases in importance. And the number of nations buying into JSF and many of Ultra's other applications mean it's a market unlikely to be dramatically affected by American tariffs or European uncertainty (a recently aborted takeover of US rival Sparton notwithstanding). Ultra remains as embedded in Western defence strategy as it is in the products that deliver the highest standards of technological capability to Britain and her allies.

www.ultra-electronics.com

AT THE HEART OF SAFETY

Frequentis

Think about the various services that keep us safe and there's a fair chance that Frequentis will be involved in some capacity. The Austrian company has been supplying safety-critical communication and information systems to companies for more than 70 years, with its UK and Ireland subsidiary active for more than 25 years, working with the likes of the Metropolitan Police, the Ministry of Defence (MOD), Network Rail and the NHS's Ambulance Radio Programme.

Founded in 1947, the company has its origins in postwar Vienna, where it assisted in the rebuilding of broadcast communications. Today Frequentis has expanded its initial focus on control-centre voice communications to develop cross-industry expertise in civil aviation, defence, public safety, maritime and public transportation markets.

The worldwide digital revolution has transformed Frequentis in recent years. "Traditionally this has been a hardware-driven business but, in the past 10 years, it has become progressively more software-centric," says Andy Madge, Managing Director of Frequentis UK. "There's a greater emphasis on integrating the communications into what the controllers have in front of them and we've needed to transition from pure voice communications to full control-room solutions. This means getting the best out of the digital environment – how we connect with other information and display it to the controllers. That applies to the military as much as it does to civil aviation."

For the last 20 years, Frequentis has been working closely with the MOD on military air traffic management (ATM). This includes the control of the aircraft around all of the various military airfields (including nine Royal Navy air stations, 39 UK airfields and MOD establishments and three overseas airfields) monitoring 2.4 million flights every year. Additionally, Frequentis provides essential communication for air defence, supporting UK airspaces and the airspace around overseas operations.

The relationship with the MOD thrives, Madge believes, because of the reliability of Frequentis's mission-critical solutions. "The MOD can't do without comms in either of those two roles," he says. "They are 100 per cent confident in what we provide. We've done that very well over 20-plus years and the reality is that, even as we transition to a much more digital-based service, we'll continue to provide that level of reliability."

Frequentis has been a key contributor to the MOD's Marshall air traffic services programme, refitting the ministry's air-traffic-management systems and providing long-term ATM capability for the safe operation of all main bases, airfields and air weapon rangers. Frequentis, via the MOD's prime contractor, Aquila, is delivering all voice communication systems.

This has been driven by the increasing digitalisation of services and solutions. "The challenge of wanting to use data and networks is that customers want their systems to connect seamlessly," says Madge. "They want to access multiple levels of information and communicate that across their networks. The need for enhanced situational awareness is also something we are seeing across all domains we work in, particularly for the emergency services."

This safety-critical culture is embedded in the DNA of Frequentis. Madge says that by understanding the safety-critical environment of its customers, Frequentis can support them in order to achieve their goals.

"We understand the tasks and responsibilities our customers take on a daily basis in order to maintain their safety-critical operations," he says. "We can therefore support them in a sustainable way."

www.frequentis.com

ROYA
ZZ177
090207

OPERATIONS OPTIMISED

Ocean Software

Communications have always been vital to effective military decision-making and, as threats change rapidly, systems have to keep pace. Australia-based Ocean Software has developed one such system – FlightPro – that empowers forces in a truly comprehensive way. "Our products form the core systems behind highly complex operating environments," says Ocean's Business Development Manager Jon Windover. "We go from command-and-control all the way down to individual units and people doing their daily jobs."

Existing systems for military training, logistics and operations tend to be a patchwork of processes – ageing IT systems, Microsoft tools and whiteboards – all beset by cost inefficiencies. With military budgets increasingly squeezed, the problem isn't difficult to define.

"FlightPro is the first truly mature, commercial, off-the-shelf, operations-management system," says Windover. As an enterprise-wide tool, it's been adopted by Australia, Canada, Finland, Belgium and France. "The next target is the Royal Air Force," says Windover. "We have identified significant efficiency and cost-gain opportunities through the use of our single, interoperable system, which is able to work with other mission-critical tools. Current systems and tools struggle to integrate with other systems and share data." Ocean has a UK footprint via a BAE Systems contract at RAF Coningsby and Lossiemouth, where FlightPro is used to manage training for the Typhoon force. "It's end-to-end, future-proofed and it will unify testing, training and frontline ops," says Windover. "It would align with the Chief of the Air Staff's vision for 'information, integration and innovation'."

The firm has shown it can cut costs in other areas. One of its products, PILS (Pharmaceutical Integrated Logistics System), has saved the Australian Defence Force millions of dollars by allowing pharmacies to procure and dispense in a closed-loop integrated supply chain that massively reduces waste from expiry.

The procurement picture is very fluid, says Windover, with tenders for programmes such as Air Support to Defence Operational Training (ASDOT) up for grabs, but he is confident that, given the platform, Ocean will deliver. "The RAF understands the value of information," he says. "We free up resources and valuable budget, delivering the clearest picture of capability and readiness to commanders. That's where we add value."

www.ocean.software

"The RAF has been at the forefront of technological innovation throughout its history and maintains its combat advantage through a combination of high-end technology and the quality, skill and innovation of its people"

COMMUNITY

SUPPORT SERVICES

Shropshire Council

"People are very proud to have the RAF here," says Councillor Peter Nutting, Leader of Shropshire Council. Shropshire Council works with service charities, local businesses and other public bodies, such as the NHS, to ensure that military personnel and veterans are supported in Shropshire, which is home to two RAF training bases. "There is a real respect for our RAF colleagues and the work that they do," he says.

They are right to be proud. After all, national security relies in part upon the good relationship between the Royal Air Force and the people of Shropshire, one that has existed for 100 years. "We really depend on these close links," says Squadron Leader Kim Leach of RAF Shawbury. "We have around 75 fields and clearings that landowners give us permission to use so that we can practice tactical approaches to fields. To have the freedom of movement to deliver low-level training, we rely on the support of the local people."

For its part, says Squadron Leader Leach, the RAF works hard for Shropshire, not just by providing jobs but also by contributing to community projects. "Our students will go out and work with local communities," she says. "That might mean painting a church hall, decorating the chapel of a church, clearing out a children's playground or doing some gardening in a hospice. We're always out and about, supporting the local community, and that's really important to us."

Shropshire Council, like every local authority in the UK, has signed up to the Armed Forces Covenant: a pledge to support all serving and former military personnel and their families. "We work with a number of service charities, the British Army, the Royal Navy and the RAF, and businesses," says Councillor Nutting. "Businesses may offer discounts to service personnel and veterans. They may offer free advice to people soon deployed out of the military back into civilian life. Some businesses would guarantee ex-military personnel an interview for a job, provided that they meet the criteria for that particular job."

Shropshire Council helps ensure service personnel and their families get access to local services such as education and healthcare. Indeed, it helps the county's 7,000 veterans in a variety of ways, including combating stress. Squadron Leader Chris Wilson, from RAF Cosford, also in Shropshire, says the covenant is vital. "It ensures that service personnel, who tend to move around a lot with their families throughout their career, aren't disadvantaged when they come to Shropshire," he says. "Whether it's help with housing, medical and dental facilities, or schools."

Military aircraft of the Royal Flying Corps began flying from Shawbury in 1917, a year before the formation of the RAF. Today, as well as providing tri-service flying training to pilots and rear crew at the Defence Helicopter Flying School and the Central Flying School (Helicopters), the base is home to the School of Air Operations Control. This school trains RAF and Royal Navy air traffic controllers and flight operations personnel. The base also houses the UK's largest and oldest aircraft maintenance and storage unit, which has been located at RAF Shawbury since 1938.

RAF Shawbury has a rich history. In 1944, navigation training was centred there at the Empire Air Navigation School. One of its most celebrated missions took place in 1944, when Wing Commander David Cecil McKinley flew a Lancaster PD328, codenamed Aries, in a

OXYGEN REFILLING
VALVE INSIDE

07
ZM507
DEFENCE HELICOPTER
FLYING SCHOOL

secret flight from Shawbury around the world. "The mission was to improve long-distance navigational techniques with the aim of making precision-bombing more accurate and therefore helping with the war effort," says Squadron Leader Leach. "So this was a record-breaking flight that flew unarmed round the world – at a time when London was being bombed."

RAF Cosford opened in 1938, and celebrates its 80th anniversary this year. "The base is home to Royal Air Force engineering," says Squadron Leader Wilson. "We train all the RAF's aircraft engineers, ICT technicians, physical training instructors, training officers, engineering officers and defence photographers."

The pioneering aviator Amy Johnson – the first woman to fly solo from Britain to Australia – visited Cosford many times during the Second World War. Women were not allowed to fight, but Johnson was part of an all-female pool of ferry pilots, someone who'd win over the control-tower guards by leaving packs of cigarettes for them. These Air Transport Auxilliaries (one of whom is pictured, previous spread) were highly skilled and versatile fliers whose job it was to take fighter planes to the frontline.

"Those women were just remarkable," says Squadron Leader Wilson. "They might take a Spitfire up to a frontline base and then be ferried back in another aircraft – by a woman, again. The next day they might be in a completely different aircraft type and ferry that to another unit. These women could turn their hand to flying any kind of aircraft."

RAF Cosford is also home to one of Shropshire's most popular visitor attractions, the Royal Air Force Museum. "It's a cutting-edge museum, in that it's got lots of historic aircraft from around the world," says Squadron Leader Wilson. "There are lots of RAF aircraft, but also German aircraft and Japanese aircraft from the war years. It's a really good place where kids can come and learn, not just about old aircraft, but how aircraft work." The museum, which also includes an exhibition on the history of the Cold War, has more than 70 aircraft of international importance, including the oldest Spitfire in the world.

Shropshire is playing a central role in the RAF's centenary celebrations. "We're sending a few hundred people down to The Mall in London to parade and witness the huge flypast of RAF aircraft," says Squadron Leader Wilson. "But there are lots of ceremonial events up and down the country. We're playing a big part in most of them."

Meanwhile, the future of the RAF in Shropshire looks bright. "The latest project at RAF Shawbury is the introduction of the new Military Flying Training System," says Squadron Leader Leach. "This project will introduce two new helicopters into service at RAF Shawbury – the Juno H135 (pictured, left) and Jupiter H145 – and will ensure that RAF Shawbury continues to be a world leader in delivering military helicopter flying training."

She says it will also secure the future of Shawbury as a core base, and jobs for the local community for at least another two decades. "It's really quite an auspicious start to the centenary of the Royal Air Force."

new.shropshire.gov.uk

FIRST LINE OF DEFENCE

Defence Discount Service

"The Armed Forces, past and present, are our everyday heroes," says Tom Dalby, Head of the Defence Discount Service (DDS). "They do amazing things for their community and don't ask much in return. This is not just a great way for us to give back, but also for businesses to say 'thank you'."

Defence Discount Service was launched in late 2012 and provides Armed Forces servicemen and women, along with veterans, with discounts online and in the high street. Six years since its launch, the service has been a resounding success with more than 7,500 retailers signed up across Britain. These include BA, Samsung, KFC, Cineworld, New Look and Toby Carvery, among other big-name companies and thousands of local independents.

"We're recruiting more businesses each day," says Dalby, "and we're approaching half a million sign-ups from personnel and veterans. We should surpass that this year. In 2018 we are encouraging local communities to really back the service and for local retailers to start accepting the service in store and start offering a discount."

Some local retailers can't believe how generous the terms are, wondering if the offer of free advertising is too good to be true. "They suspect hidden charges," says Dalby. "But there aren't any and there is no catch. It doesn't cost them a penny. It is a way for them to give back to the Armed Forces community."

The scheme offers two strands of savings options to members of the Armed Forces community: online, which is free of charge; or through a member's card – the Defence Privilege Card – which costs £4.99 for a five-year membership and can be used to save money on the high street. "The service for us is about volume," says Dalby. "The more members we get, the more companies come on board and vice versa."

That audience is growing fast, and not just in Britain. DDS sends cards as far as Canada, the USA and Australia. Availability is a key factor in the service's development, as is making it simple to access for those that are eligible. The DDS mobile app has attracted 200,000 downloads and is one of the top 150 British shopping apps. "We'll keep developing the mobile app," says Dalby. "We think it's the way people want to shop. If you're on the high street, you can look at 'Offers near me' and see a map of discounting retailers. And if you want a new TV, say, you can type 'TV' into the search window and it'll tell you who's giving online discounts."

Spouses and partners of serving personnel are eligible as members, and DDS takes pleasure in making the scheme so widespread. "Forces life is not easy," says Dalby. "It's often disrupted and families go through a lot. A lot more personnel are becoming veterans, too. They're not just elderly men – they can be male or female, or in their thirties. They're going through transition into civilian life and DDS provides tangible help."

Signing up is easy through the DDS app or website – or, for the less computer-literate, a phone call – is all that's needed to request an application form sent through the post. This last attention to detail is a typical of the inclusiveness that runs through the DDS philosophy: a generosity of spirit befitting a service designed for some the most deserving members of our community.

www.defencediscountservice.co.uk

HELP FROM THE SKY

Kent, Surrey and Sussex Air Ambulance Trust

The Kent, Surrey and Sussex Air Ambulance Trust (KSSAAT) is the only enhanced medical team to use a 24-hour air helicopter service in England. The charity, formed in 1989, has two helicopters in use every day and operates four shifts daily to give full 24/7 coverage. For each shift there are at least two pilots, a doctor and a paramedic on each aircraft. Recently completed operational facilities at Redhill Aerodrome, near Gatwick Airport, mean that the aircraft are now housed and maintained at the one base.

"We have full engineering support on-site," explains KSSAAT's CEO Adrian Bell, "which makes a huge difference to turnaround times, especially with unscheduled maintenance." The charity is also opening a forward-operating base at Rochester Airport in May 2018, to support rapid regional access. KSSAAT works closely with the South East Coast Ambulance Service NHS Foundation Trust. "Our own dispatch personnel work alongside ambulance service emergency call handlers in the control room," says Bell, "to identify each and every patient who would benefit from the specialist care that we provide."

The air ambulance teams fly, on average, six to eight missions every 24 hours. The doctors and paramedics, some from a military background, are trained to work in a "pre-hospital environment" where they are capable of giving anaesthetics, performing emergency surgery and administering blood product transfusions at scene or in the helicopter. "All clinical staff undergo an intense training period under close personal supervision until certified to practise on their own," says Bell.

To inaugurate a round-the-clock service in the first place was quite an achievement. "There was denial, even within the air ambulance industry, that it was needed," says Bell, "because it was thought difficult to deliver. There was concern about how we would manage ad hoc landings by night, and the capabilities of the pilots and the aircraft. But our basic premise was that, if people need us during the hours of daylight, the huge likelihood is that they still need us at night. We conducted a very thorough audit to find evidence for this premise."

The 24-hour service was introduced in 2013 and was an immediate success, treating an additional 450 patients in the first year of operation. Ever since then, KSSAAT's coverage has meant that patients across these three counties are never more than 20 minutes away from life-saving care.

www.kssairambulance.org.uk

A MEETING OF MINDS

Alzheimer's Society

Lawrence Fisher was "delightful, the perfect gentleman" – a husband, a father, a keen golfer and an RAF veteran who'd flown with the forces during the Second World War. "The best photograph I've got of him was in his RAF uniform," says his wife, Morella Kayman MBE.

But when Lawrence developed dementia in his early fifties, Morella felt totally isolated. "I was in my thirties and had no idea whatsoever – I couldn't understand why he was forgetting things," she recalls. "I was running a business, I had a young child who was at school and there really wasn't any support." Determined to ensure that no one else would struggle alone, in 1979 Kayman co-founded what is now Alzheimer's Society. "Nearly 40 years later, what's been achieved is amazing," she says. "Everybody knows what dementia is now."

Today, Alzheimer's Society supports thousands of people each year. "Around 850,000 people across the country live with dementia, and that's going to increase to over a million in the next few years," says Chief Executive Jeremy Hughes. "Our ambition is to support everyone with a dementia diagnosis by 2022." As the UK's leading dementia charity, Alzheimer's Society has three key strands: providing support to those with dementia and their carers; transforming communities so they are more inclusive and campaigning for social change; and investing in research. "Crucially," says Hughes, "everything we do is led by the wishes of people living with dementia and their carers."

Besides its helpline and online resources, Alzheimer's Society delivers local services across the UK. "One way people can get involved is as a 'Side By Side' volunteer, a new initiative that helps people with dementia to keep doing the things they enjoy with the support of a volunteer," says Hughes. "If someone's got an RAF background, for example, we'll match them with a likeminded volunteer so they can reminisce, talk about the things that interest them, or even visit the RAF Museum together."

Alzheimer's Society volunteers also run local "Singing for the Brain" groups and drop-in Memory Cafés, providing opportunities for fun and contact. There's even a dedicated veterans' café in Plymouth. "It's about giving people with dementia the space to be themselves and a part of society," says Hughes. "There's a real dementia movement growing: we've got thousands of volunteers and fundraisers, and over two million Dementia Friends, all committed to creating dementia-friendly communities. Together, we're united against dementia."

www.alzheimers.org.uk

FORCES OF NATURE

Hampshire County Council

"During the period of serious floods here, Royal Air Force Chinooks flew in all the materials needed to help divert water," says Hampshire County Councillor Andrew Joy. "Not just sandbags but structures, platforms for taking photographs, everything. At a time of crisis, our working relationship with the Royal Air Force really comes into its own."

Councillor Joy is a former flying instructor who helped bring the Chinooks into service at RAF Odiham back in 1980. It is now the Chinook force headquarters. These days he acts as Hampshire County Council's Armed Forces champion.

"My role is to draw together the efforts of Hampshire County Council in coordination with civilian agencies," he says, "on what we call the Civil Military Partnership Board, which I chair. So we're looking at things such as social services, education – the issues which affect people in the community in general."

RAF Odiham began as a grass airstrip in 1925, and was opened as a permanent airfield in 1937 – by General Erhard Milch, Chief of Staff for the Luftwaffe. "There is a story that Milch then spoke to Hitler and said he intended Odiham to be his headquarters after the war and that pilots were not to bomb it," says Councillor Joy. "There may not be any truth in that – but it is a fact that RAF Odiham was never bombed."

Hampshire now has one of the largest Armed Forces communities in Britain and is unique in having all three services located within the county. Hampshire County Council has received the Ministry of Defence's Employer Recognition Scheme Gold Award in recognition of its support for military and ex-service personnel. One of its greatest attributes is its support for reservists. "We are strongly encouraging of those who wish to take on reserve service," says Councillor Joy. "We feel that it's of significant benefit to the county."

Hampshire is part of Forces Connect South East, an effort to raise standards and share best practice across the region in the provision of services to the Armed Forces community. And in 2011 Hampshire County Council was one of the first local authorities to sign the Armed Forces Covenant.

"It has raised council officers' awareness of issues of particular relevance to people involved with the services, particularly families," says Councillor Joy. These include problems related to housing, access to health and social services, benefit support and education.

"Getting children into appropriate schools is sometimes a challenge," he says. "We need to make sure that the schools are aware they are service children. That attracts what's known as the Service Pupil Premium, whereby schools get financial help to provide the additional support that service children sometimes need."

Councillor Joy is proud to report that service children in Hampshire tend to achieve better results than pupils from civilian families – which is not typical of the rest of Britain. "I'd like to think that's because we're getting it right," he says.

As the RAF marks its 100th anniversary, Hampshire's residents have many reminders of the county's historic bond with the Armed Forces. A former RAF base at Calshot Spit is now a recreation centre. And the council provides service families with special camping facilities in the New Forest. "As an ex-military person myself," says Councillor Joy, "I can say that the RAF is very much part of the Hampshire family and warmly embraced by us all."

www.hants.gov.uk

LONDON'S PRIDE

The London Boroughs

As the Royal Air Force celebrates its centenary, London is marking its own contribution to the RAF's history. People from across the capital's diverse communities have played a significant role in the air force's success, and their stories will be remembered in an array of events.

"There are four London boroughs that have very significant RAF links," says Councillor Claire Kober OBE, Chair of London Councils, which represents London's 32 boroughs and the City of London. "Hillingdon, Croydon, Bromley and Barnet have all played an important part in its history and, to this day, there is still a significant amount of pride and community connection with the RAF."

In Hillingdon, RAF Uxbridge provided the headquarters for the No. 11 Group. It was at the nearby Battle of Britain Bunker that Winston Churchill first spoke his famous words, "Never in the field of human conflict was so much owed by so many to so few." Hillingdon Council recently opened a new visitor centre on the bunker site.

The Hendon Aerodrome in Barnet was an important aviation centre from 1908–68, and a place of pioneering experiments. Today it is home to the London branch of the RAF Museum, which has undergone a multi-million-pound transformation in time for the centenary. Croydon Airport was one of London's three main fighter stations during the Second World War, along with Kenley, also in Croydon, and Biggin Hill in Bromley. The RAF Chapel of Remembrance in Bromley is also undergoing conservation for the upcoming Biggin Hill Memorial Museum.

Alongside these landmarks, communities will celebrate the diverse contributions that Londoners from all backgrounds have made to the RAF, from the women who signed up to the Women's Royal Air Force (WRAF), to the pilots from Poland, Czechoslovakia and around the Commonwealth who battled for Britain. "All Londoners had a part to play," says Kober. "Many had very different roles in their civilian life, from postmen to machinery salesman." She uses the picture above as an example, which shows an RAF maintenance crew in 1942. Second from the right is Lilian Hutchings, a seamstress from Lambeth who joined the RAF in 1941 to serve as a maintenance engineer.

Since its inception in 1918, the RAF has been inextricably linked with London. Communities across the capital remain intensely proud of their connections to the air force and will come together to remember the part their own neighbourhood played in the RAF's success.

www.londoncouncils.gov.uk/RAF100

ROCK SOLID SUPPORT

Government of Gibraltar

"Servicemen have always been welcome in Gibraltar," says Stuart Green, a spokesman for Her Majesty's Government of Gibraltar. "The relationship between the government and the British military has always been excellent. Servicemen are part of the fabric of Gibraltar and have been so for more than 300 years."

Gibraltarians retain their enthusiasm for the Royal Air Force – not least because, for many years, the Ministry of Defence was the main employer in this British Overseas Territory. The RAF airfield, originally needed for Operation Torch, the Allied invasion of North Africa, was built from material removed from inside the Rock of Gibraltar during the construction of tunnels for other military purposes.

"There were seaplanes based here before the war," says Green. "But, on the night of 7/8 November 1942, there were no fewer than 650 aircraft parked along the sides of the newly built runway, ready to support the Anglo-American landings in North Africa.

"Until the 1980s, the backbone of Gibraltar's economy was the Royal Naval Dockyard," continues Green. "In those days, RAF Gibraltar was fully manned. Its main role was maritime surveillance but it regularly hosted training squadrons from the UK, who would make use of the sunny weather and clear skies. At that time there were two British Army regiments based here and, with regular visits from Royal Navy ships, the town was just full of servicemen."

The end of the Cold War and successive defence reviews have meant that RAF operations have been reduced enormously. "It's been a much quieter place in the last 15 years or so," says Green.

Today, the airfield's role is that of a "forward mounting base" which means it can quickly become fully operational. "If it were needed," says Green, "everything could be ramped up here in a matter of days to make it a fully functioning station."

And Gibraltar remains a strategically important base for the British military. "We sit where Europe meets Africa and where the Mediterranean meets the Atlantic," says Green. "We are ideally placed to monitor foreign naval shipping, especially that of hostile nations, as it moves into and out of the Mediterranean. And if long-range maritime surveillance of the Mediterranean is ever required again, this is the place from which to do it."

www.raf.mod.uk/rafgibraltar

A MILITARY HERITAGE

Surrey County Council

Carefully tucked away in the archives of Surrey County Council (SCC) are letters, sketches and blueprints by the inventor of the bouncing bomb, Sir Barnes Wallis. These items date from the years when the aviation engineer was working on the now legendary weapon that the RAF used in Operation Chastise, the "Dambusters" raid of May 1943, which struck at Germany's industrial heartland.

A resident of Effingham, Wallis secretly developed the weapon at Burhill Golf Club, making the clubhouse his headquarters, and at Foxwarren Park, while the Germans targeted Brooklands. One of the country's first aerodromes, Brooklands was a major aircraft testing and production site from 1907. In the Second World War, the airfield housed Hawker and Vickers factories making Wellingtons and Hurricanes until it suffered extensive damage in an air raid on 4 September 1940. Also the site of Britain's first Grand Prix race track, Brooklands is now an aviation and motor museum.

These are just a few highlights of Surrey's rich RAF heritage, according to SCC Chairman Peter Martin. "We're very proud of this relationship and the history behind it," he says. "The connection with the RAF continues to this day, with the Air Forces Memorial in Runnymede, which commemorates all air force men and women who lost their lives during the First World War." Also Chairman of the Surrey Civilian Military Partnership Board, Martin works with government agencies, businesses and military partners to foster closer working relationships with the military community.

In 2012, SCC demonstrated its ongoing support for UK servicemen and women by signing the Armed Forces Covenant. This has ensured fairness and equal opportunity for serving and ex-members of the military in Surrey, both in employment and when receiving council services and assistance.

Being in the forces is hugely rewarding but can bring with it a complex set of challenges. "It can mean moving around frequently," says Martin, "so getting your children into the school of your choice can be a problem. Life can be transient, which can raise practical issues such as registering with a GP, or feelings of isolation. But we're trying to lead by example in terms of being military friendly, and sharing best practice with others."

Armed forces charities are linked up with SCC's adult social care team through a referral scheme run by our contact centre to provide practical support. Funding has also just been secured for veterans' drop-in centres across the county. "Many veterans are quite proud," says Martin, "so we're trying to use football clubs and neutral venues as alternatives to council offices or GP services."

To promote a greater understanding of the issues affecting the armed forces and their families, SCC helped establish Forces Connect South East with a Covenant Fund grant. The project's goals include better training for public sector staff in supporting the armed forces community to ensure they are not at a disadvantage. "We recognise that armed forces personnel are not always forward in seeking support," says Martin. "So we're raising awareness of their needs in relation to employment, housing, healthcare and education, for example."

In recognition of its support for the armed forces SCC, in 2016, was one of the first county councils in the country to receive the Employer Recognition Scheme Gold Award from the Ministry of Defence. As a pro-military employer, Surrey employs 25 reservists and many veterans. Initiatives such as work experience placements and raising awareness of vacancies demonstrate SCC's commitment to helping former military personnel into rewarding jobs and careers.

www.surreycc.gov.uk

CARING FOR THE FORCES

Sodexo

After Mark Baker had spent more than 30 years at the sharp end of operations in the RAF – starting on anti-submarine patrols in the North Atlantic and finishing as Deputy Commander of British forces in Afghanistan – he decided it was time to hang up his wings. But that military experience has proved very handy in his new role for Sodexo, where he is Managing Director of Operations, Defence & Government Services in the UK and Ireland. It's a job that sees him working closely with the RAF and other branches of the Armed Forces in the UK.

Sodexo is a French company delivering a variety of facilities for a range of clients. "We provide food, cleaning, accommodation, waste services, logistics and supplies," says Baker. "We work across dozens of messes, as well as hospitals, prisons, airfields and garrisons. We also run shops and bars on bases for personnel, providing leisure facilities as well as selling the things a family might need."

Sodexo is huge – serving 100 million people in more than 80 countries every day – and works with many high-profile clients in the UK, including the Scottish Parliament, the Ministry of Justice and the Department for Work and Pensions. It began operating in Marseille in 1966, serving company restaurants, schools and hospitals. It has since expanded to become the 19th largest employer in the world, but the board is still chaired by the founder's daughter, Sophie Bellon.

Baker believes that this family touch is part of what makes Sodexo unique. "That helps us focus on a variety of areas that others talk about but we actually act upon, such as equality, diversity and inclusion," he says. "We strive to improve the quality of life in whatever way we can in delivering our services. We see ourselves as partners, not sub-contractors, and that pays dividends. Last year we were awarded the MOD's Employee Recognition Scheme Gold Award to acknowledge our support to the UK armed forces community. We also positively recruit ex-service personnel and reservists, and, where we can, support employment for families to help reduce the disruption that regular postings can have on domestic life." Baker explains that this dovetails with the military's "whole force" approach, which reflects a desire to see civil servants, civilian contractors and military personnel as a single integrated team delivering capability.

Sodexo is also a significant partner of SSAFA (Soldiers, Sailors, Airmen and Families Association), the Armed Forces charity. "Through SSAFA, we can reach out across the many countries we operate in and support the many current and ex-servicemen that both deserve and need our help," says Baker. "This is central to our company ethos of delivering 'quality of life'. So we do things such as sponsor events like the SSAFA Young Achiever Award, which recognises young people who have succeeded in the face of adversity." Sodexo funds and co-delivers the awards with its brand ambassador, the England rugby player Matt Dawson. For Baker, this is an example of the value that Sodexo adds to traditional sub-contractor relationships. Sodexo also has a corporate foundation called Stop Hunger, through which an additional £40,000 is donated each year to support SSAFA's homlessness welfare fund.

"We try and knit ourselves into the fabric of our clients' business," says Baker. "This is particularly valued by our military clients as they benefit from our involvement in the military communities where we deliver our services. As a result, we have a very close relationship with our military employers and customers – one we greatly value."

uk.sodexo.com

sodexo

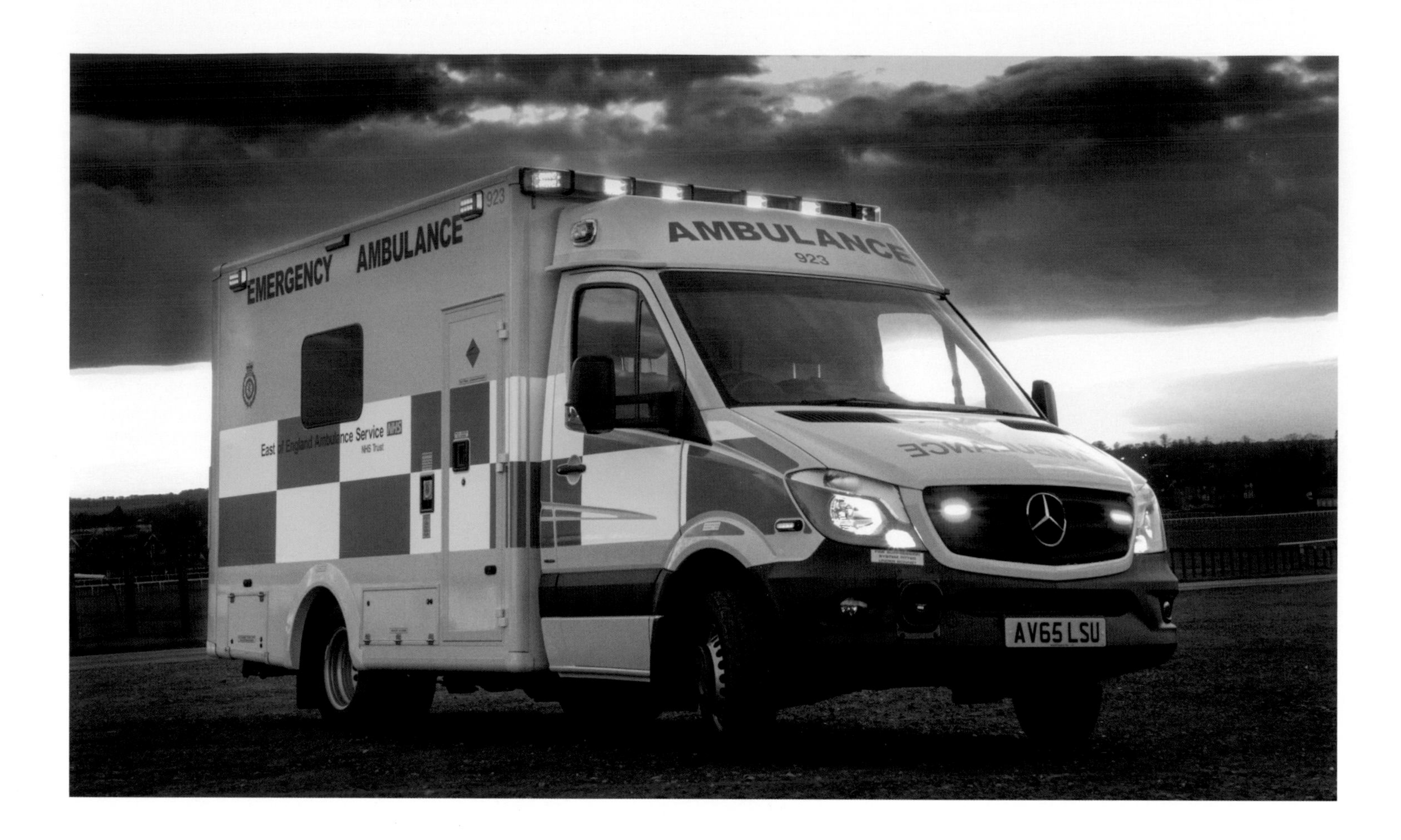

COMMUNITY CHAMPIONS

East of England Ambulance Service NHS Trust

The East of England Ambulance Service NHS Trust (EEAST) provides care and support for up to a million patients across Norfolk, Suffolk, Cambridgeshire, Essex, Hertfordshire and Bedfordshire each year, thanks in part to its dedicated team of 2,600 frontline operational and clinical staff. The sirens, blue lights and ambulance staff responding to 999 emergency calls are all a familiar sight – but, behind the scenes, EEAST also depends on around 2,000 community volunteers, including teams from RAF Marham, RAF Henlow and RAF Honington.

"All our volunteers have a day job, but they go out on behalf of the Ambulance Trust within their community," says Terry Hicks, EEAST's Sector Head for Norfolk and Waveney. "The RAF co-responders are part of that scheme, and they're sponsored by their station commanders to be able to do this."

Before joining EEAST, Hicks spent nine years in the RAF. He's now this NHS Trust's Armed Forces Champion, so he knows just how important the relationship between the two services can be. "A lot of it is about leadership, a can-do attitude and personal resilience, which the Armed Forces instils in you," he explains. "It gives you a very good grounding and aptitude for public service."

EEAST has twice received the silver award for Defence Employer Recognition, and mutual support is very much in line with the trust's values of honesty, care, respect, teamwork and quality. Each team of RAF co-responders attends a blue-light driver training programme and operates as a two-person crew, equipped with a fully marked-up ambulance car, as well as life-saving kit like defibrillators, oxygen and blood-pressure tests.

"The RAF teams are able to do a little bit more than our normal community first responders, so there's a wide range of patient cohorts they will go to," says Hicks. "We try to target those areas that are quite hard to reach – so, for example, in some rural parts of Norfolk, like where the RAF Marham car is, it can be challenging for an ambulance to reach some locations within an allotted time frame."

This means volunteer co-responders are often the first line of defence, attending medical emergencies and administering life-saving treatments, closely followed by backup from a frontline clinical crew. "Time counts when somebody's in a cardiac arrest, or having breathing difficulties, so the quicker we can get someone to a patient's side, the better the outcome," says Hicks. "Our volunteers absolutely do save lives."

www.eastamb.nhs.uk

INDEX

CREDITS

Dedicated to all the men and women who have served.

With thanks to:
Air Chief Marshal Sir Stephen Hillier KCB CBE DFC ADC MA RAF
RAF100 Appeal
RAF100
RAF Media and Communications
Air Historical Branch (RAF)
RAF Museum

And the sponsors who have made this publication possible.

PUBLISHER
St James's House
298 Regents Park Road
London N3 2SZ
Phone: +44 (0)20 8371 4000
publishing@stjamess.org
www.stjamess.org

Richard Freed, Chief Executive
richard.freed@stjamess.org

Stephen van der Merwe, Managing Director
stephen.vdm@stjamess.org

Richard Golbourne, Sales Director
r.golbourne@stjamess.org

Ben Duffy, Communications Director
ben.duffy@stjamess.org

Stephen Mitchell, Head of Editorial
stephen.mitchell@stjamess.org

Aniela Gil, Senior Designer
aniela.gil@stjamess.org

John Lewis, Deputy Editor
john.lewis@stjamess.org

Contributors
Alan Beck, Nina Hadaway

Photography
Daryn Castle (pp172–3), Charles Brown Collection, charlesward.com (pp228–9), Mario Fajit (p171), Getty Images, Imperial War Museum (p124–5), Jan Jasinski (p138), Ministry of Defence (pp150–1), RAF Museum, UK MoD Crown Copyright, Les Wilson (p139)

p128–9 Copyright unknown. Supplied courtesy of Heathrow Airports Ltd.

pp272–3 Contains public sector information licensed under the Open Government Licence v3.0.

p278 Image reproduced by kind permission of London Borough of Lambeth, Archives Department and Lilian Hutchings.

Other images are the copyright of individual organisations.

St James's House, Regal Press Limited
298 Regents Park Road, London N3 2SZ
www.stjamess.org

Printed by CPi Colour on Chorus Silk. This paper has been independently certified according to the standards of the Forest Stewardship Council® (FSC)®.

A catalogue record for this publication is available from the British Library.